A Climber's Guide to the St. Elias Mountains

Volume I

Richard Holmes

*Why do climbers rope themselves together?
To keep the sensible ones from going home!*

Icy Bay Press

Copyright © 2005 Richard Holmes

A Climber's Guide to the St. Elias Mountains, VOL. I

All rights reserved. First Edition. This book or any part thereof may not be reproduced in any form whatsoever, whether by graphic, visual, electronic, or any other means other than for brief passages or reviews without the written permission of the publisher.

ISBN 0-976-39800-1

Published and Distributed By:
Icy Bay Press
775 E. Blithedale Avenue
Suite 400
Mill Valley, California 94941
Email: info@IcyBayPress.com
www.IcyBayPress.com

All photos by Richard Holmes

Front Cover:
Mt. Kaskawulsh and the Kaskawulsh Glacier

Back Cover:
Looking down Hummingbird Ridge with Mt. St. Elias and the Seward Glacier in the background

Acknowledgments

The production of this climbing guide was a long and arduous undertaking. It involved a great deal more work and planning than was originally considered. The completion of this book would not have been possible without the help of several organizations.

First and foremost I would like to thank the pilots and staff of Gulf Air Taxi and Eric Oles of Sifton Air for their tremendous assistance in this project. This project would not have been possible without the patience and skill of the pilots who flew me around the St. Elias Mountains in search of the best photos for this book.

Also, I would like to thank the librarians at the Seattle Mountaineers, the American Alpine Club, the Alpine Club of Canada and the Sierra Club Library in San Francisco for their help and dedication in assisting me with obtaining the articles needed to research this book. This book would not have been possible without access to the tremendous resources available in these libraries which was provided to me by the cooperative staff of these libraries.

I would like to thank Camera Ready Graphics for helping design the book and Buehler Technologies for the CD-ROM.

Contents

Introduction	vi
The Photographs	vii

◆1 **The Boundary Group** — 9
Introduction — 9
Mt. Seattle — 9
Mt. Foresta — 19
Mt. Cook — 30
Mt. Vancouver — 43

◆2 **The Kennedy Group** — 63
Introduction — 63
Mt. Hubbard — 63
Mt. Alverstone — 72
Mt. Kennedy — 76
Weisshorn Mountain — 84
Mt. Poland — 87
Ulu Mountain — 88
Ulu North Peak — 90
Igloo Peak — 93
Pinnacle Peak — 94
Lowell Peak — 98

◆3 **The St. Elias Group** — 103
Introduction — 103
Mt. St. Elias — 103
Mt. St. Elias

Satellite Peaks — 121
Mt. Newton — 121
Mt. Jeannette — 123
Mt. Bering — 125
Mt. Malaspina — 127
Mt. Baird — 127
Mt. Augusta — 129

◆4 **The Logan Group** — 137
Introduction — 137
Mt. Logan — 140
Mt. Teddy — 170
King Peak — 175
Mt. McArthur — 182
Mt. Logbard — 189

◆5 **The Hubbard Group** — 191
Introduction — 191
Mt. King George — 192
Mt. Queen Mary — 197
Gnurdelhorn — 200
Donjek Peak — 200
Mt. Badham — 200

◆6 **The Walsh Group** — 203
Introduction — 203
Mt. Walsh — 203
Mt. Harrison — 209

7	**The Kaskawulsh Group**	**213**		Whitehorse	232
	Introduction	213		Haines Junction	233
	Kaskawulsh Peak	214		Haines	234
	Mt. Maxwell	217		Anchorage	234
	Observation Mountain	218		Yakutat	235
	Mt. Stephen Leacock	218		Glennallen	235
	Mt. St. Jean Baptiste	220	E:	Expedition Equipment	236
	Mt. Wayne Smith	220		Personal Gear	236
	Little Patagonia	220		Group Gear	237
	The Dinosaur Peaks	221		Repair Kit	239
				First Aid Kit	239
8	**The Kluane Group**	**223**	F:	Food List	239
	Introduction	223		Breakfast	239
	Vulcan Mountain	223		Lunch	240
	Mt. Cairnes	225		Dinner	240
	Mt. Archibald	225		Condiment Bag	240
			G:	St. Elias Maps	241
Conclusion		**227**	H:	St. Elias Pilots	241
			I:	St. Elias Weather	243
Appendices		**228**	J:	Geology and Glaciers	243
	A: Expedition Organization	228	K:	Mountain Medicine	246
	B: Ranger Stations	229	L:	The Climbing Rating System	248
	C: Transportation to Kluane Park	230	M:	Objective Hazards	251
	Air Transport	230	N:	Climbing Magazines	252
	Road Travel	231			
	Ferry Service	231	**Volume II**		**252**
	Bus Service	231			
	D: Northern Cities	232	**Index**		**254**

Introduction

This book is the culmination of a large effort to gather photos and relevant information on the mountains and climbing routes in the Wrangell-St. Elias Mountains. The Wrangell-St. Elias Mountains encompass some 25 million square acres of mountains and glaciers. Nearly half of the peaks in this area have no names, let alone any ascents. Those peaks that have names and routes are cataloged as best as possible in the following pages.

The routes that have been done are described and are accompanied by references in the climbing literature when possible. For the routes that have not been done yet the descriptions provided are based on photos available of the route in question.

A large part of the value of this climbing guidebook are the photos that are presented in the book as well as the photos which are on the companion CD-ROM. These photos provide information and insight into the climbs that words alone cannot accomplish.

The St. Elias Mountains are a massive complex of peaks studded with intertwining glaciers. Some of these peaks rise directly out of the sea from tidewater. The contrast of massive snow and ice faces, black rock and sparkling glaciers is a sight that must be seen firsthand to be believed.

The first emotion that captivates a climber venturing into this range is the tremendous size of these peaks. These are huge mountains, in every sense of the word. Standing on a glacier looking up at the peaks surrounding you truly makes you feel small and humble. The mountains have a Himalayan feel to them due to their tremendous size.

Fortunately, the St. Elias Mountain Range offers premiere climbing challenges without the time and expense of organizing a Himalayan expedition. A great expedition of four to eight climbers can be organized to contain less than 1,100 pounds (500 kilograms) of food and gear. The cost of the trip should not exceed $1,500 U.S. per person and the trip can be completed within three weeks.

The challenge and reward of reaching these summits is enormously fulfilling due to the skill and experience necessary to complete these climbs. Climbers who carefully condition and prepare themselves for climbs in the St. Elias Mountains will be rewarded with some of the most exhilarating climbing that they have ever engaged in. These challenges are all experienced within one of North America's greatest wilderness areas. The area is so vast and the possibilities so endless that new routes will be pioneered for generations to come. A trip to the St. Elias Mountains will fill a climber with memories of triumphs and struggles that will last a lifetime.

The St. Elias Mountain Range contains eight of the fifteen highest summits on the North American continent. It is the most glaciated region in the world outside of the polar regions and Greenland. This area is uniquely spectacular. It is a place where humans feel like Lilliputians when gazing at the towering heights and the vast expanses of snow and ice. The area is so unique in fact that it has been designated a United Nations World Heritage Site and is the largest protected wildland area on Earth.

The St. Elias Range is a land of vast expanses and of deceptive distances. It is a land of extremes. At times the midday glare and heat on the glacier are almost unbearable. Storms come and go in a matter of hours or can last for days on end. Snow can fall in amounts measured in feet (meters) and it can rain at lower elevations in copious quantities reminiscent of a tropical monsoon. Winds can be strong and yet some days are cloudless and dead calm. The snow can be as hard as ice one day and the next you will sink up to your armpits in it. It is spectacularly beautiful from all directions. It is the delight and despair of the camera enthusiast. There is the daily temptation to photograph everything in sight only to find out that the next day provides light and texture more beautiful than the one before.

In short, the St. Elias Range is a land of great extremes. It provides the exhilaration and enjoyment sought by the alpine enthusiast and yet can provide challenges that makes one wonder why they left the comfort of their own bed. But the rewards of being in this range and the fulfillment of the unique climbs in these mountains are a reward in itself. It is this contrast of extremes that make climbing in the St. Elias Range one of the great mountaineering experiences in the world.

The Photographs

The photographs in this book were taken over the course of several years by a photographer for Icy Bay Press, while crisscrossing the Wrangell-St. Elias Mountain Range in small airplanes. The patience and cooperation of the pilots in this tedious process was greatly appreciated. There would be no way to produce a comprehensive description of the climbs in this range without a complete photographic record.

The photos in the book are referenced in two ways. Photographs are referred to by a number and are found somewhere within the chapter in which they are referenced. It was impossible to include as many photographs as desired within the space limitations of this book. Therefore, a second set of photographs has been compiled.

This second and more comprehensive set of photographs has been compiled onto a CD-ROM disc. This disc can be accessed by either a PC or Macintosh based platform. This larger collection of photographs provides more complete details of many of the routes on the mountains. These photos are referred to in the book as the digital photos. By looking for the correct mountain and photo number on the companion CD-ROM disc, these photos will provide the reader with greater photographic details of the climbs than could be provided by the book alone.

The photographic collection has been provided to enhance the climber's knowledge of the mountains and their routes. The photos should also aid in the planning stages of the climb to help determine what equipment is needed and where suitable campsites can be found on the routes discussed.

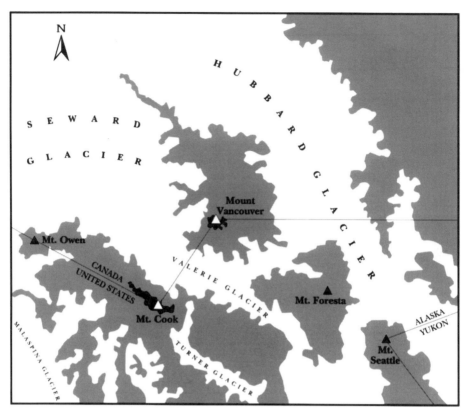

The Boundary Group

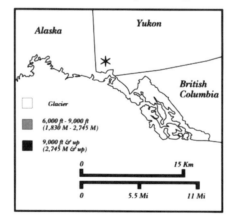

CHAPTER 1

THE BOUNDARY GROUP

Introduction

The Boundary Peaks are a group of mountains that stand astride the boundary that divides the state of Alaska in the United States and the Yukon Territory of Canada. This boundary, as well as the mountains on it, run roughly in an east to west direction. On a clear day these peaks are clearly visible from the nearby Pacific Ocean. They rise dramatically to high elevations while only a short distance inland from the sea. They provide a magnificent view of jagged and glistening snowcapped peaks that dominate the skyline of the St. Elias Mountains.

While these peaks are not really high by St. Elias standards they do provide some of the most challenging climbs that the St. Elias Range has to offer. They are easily accessible by plane or helicopter from either the Alaskan or the Canadian side. The approaches are generally short and uncomplicated with the southern side being the most challenging to approach. Early season climbs in May will provide more snow cover and allow easier glacier travel overall.

This group of peaks is a good area for climbers seeking an introduction to the St. Elias Mountains as the elevations are not extreme. Many enjoyable and straightforward climbs are present here. This area is also a rich source for potential first ascents. Numerous ridges have at this point no recorded ascents. Many other fine climbs have only one ascent. This area provides a wide range of climbs in a wild and beautiful setting.

Mt. Seattle
10,070 feet (3,270 m)

Mt. Seattle is located about ten miles (16 km) from tidewater above Disenchantment Bay. It rises dramatically out of the Hubbard Glacier, which surrounds it on three sides. It can be reached on foot from the sea, as was done by the first ascent party. However, this requires a great deal of effort to haul necessary gear over the highly crevassed Hubbard Glacier. An approach by plane is more logical as there are numerous landing sites within striking distance of the mountain.

The mountain is composed of a dark metamorphic rock and is interspersed with a lighter color sedimentary rock on its southeast side, which is also of a loose and crumbly nature. Nonetheless, Mt. Seattle has many fine ridges to climb which are composed mostly of snow and ice. Most of the routes are easy to reach at their base from a nearby plane drop-off point and the climbs can be done in just a few days.

As of this writing there are only two

Photo 1A   Photo by Richard Holmes

recorded climbs of Mt. Seattle. The first ascent party climbed the direct south ridge and an ascent of the east ridge has been done. Since Mt. Seattle is not one of the higher peaks in the St. Elias Range, climbers appear to choose climbs on the more renowned mountains.

This is unfortunate because Mt. Seattle is a large and complex mountain and is much more challenging and serious than its height would indicate. Due to the proximity of Mt. Seattle to the ocean and the tremendous elevation gain on some of these routes, this mountain provides a true climbing challenge in a wild and unspoiled setting.

Sponsorship from Seattle for the first ascent of this mountain is partly attributable for the name of the peak. However, the name had been accepted by the International Boundary Commission in the 1906-1908 border surveys.

The United States map of this area is USGS Mt. St. Elias Alaska-Canada, scale 1:250,000. The Canadian map is Mt. Seattle 115B/3, scale 1:50,000.

South Face
Direct South Ridge

The south face of Mt. Seattle is dominated by two long ridges which rise out of a feeder glacier called Varigated Glacier, which is an offshoot from Hubbard Glacier. The cirque below the south face can be reached from Upham Col above Varigated Glacier. The unnamed glacier which lies directly below the south face of Mt. Seattle sits in a very deep chasm. This deep chasm is a very wild, isolated and pristine place with the south face of the mountain rising precipitously upwards for nearly 7,000 feet (2,134 m) to the summit. Many hanging glaciers and ice filled couloirs cover this massive face.

The right-hand ridge, which is the direct south ridge, rises out of the cirque directly to reach the summit. See photo 1A and *CD photo (Chapter 1) CD-A01, CD-A02.* This route was the first ascent route of the

Photo 2A *Photo by Richard Holmes*

Photo 3A Photo by Richard Holmes

mountain. This ridge can be reached from any direction at its base. The lower 3,000 feet (914 m) of the mountain is comprised of loose scree and low angle snow slopes. These slopes can be ascended to the base of where the south ridge starts. A safe camp can be placed on flat ground here at about 4,000 feet (1,219 m).

The base of the ridge itself can be ascended through any one of a number of couloirs which bring one onto the narrow crest of the ridge some 800 feet (244 m) higher. *See CD photos (Chapter 1) CD-A03, CD-A04.* A few more rope lengths of climbing bring one to a wider spot where the high camp can be placed at about 7,200 feet (2,195 m). The high camp is about 3,000 feet (914 m) from the summit. The camp is exposed to the full force of the wind that sweeps along the south face. Therefore, the tents should be securely fastened to the rocks.

Above this camp the ridge is narrow for awhile and requires climbing to the left off the ridge on snow and in some steep ice filled couloirs to avoid steeper rock on the right-hand side. The ridge is regained at 8,500 feet (2,591 m) by climbing back onto the main crest of the ridge. One more small rock step must be ascended, which has some tricky fourth class climbing.

The ridge then rises to a corniced knife-edge ridge just below the summit where some 45 degree ice slopes are ascended to reach the summit. See photo 2A. The descent can be made down the same route. A rappel off the summit as well as some fixed rope placed in the steeper sections of the ice filled couloirs will expedite the descent.

The climb can be done within a week and requires the use of some fixed rope to help in the descent. A few rock placements will have to be made to ascend the rock step below the summit and to facilitate the placement of fixed rope in some of the couloirs. The approach will take several more days if the climb is approached on foot from tidewater. This is not a difficult route but does entail a great deal of elevation gain. *First Ascent,* May 1966. Ref. *AAJ* 1967, pp. 265-268.

West Ridge

The other main ridge that projects from the great south face is the west ridge. See photo 1A, 3A. This is a bifurcated ridge with the left-hand ridge line being longer, safer, as well as being the regular route. The right-hand ridge is shorter but is overhung with dangerous cornices. *See CD photo (Chapter 1) CD-A05.*

The base of the ridge can be accessed over easy but loose dark brown rock. The route follows a narrow but well-defined ridge, comprised mostly of rock for about 800 yards (732 m) until the ridge merges into a snow and ice covered face at 8,200 feet (2,499 m). Here on a level patch of snow at the base of the face a secure camp can be dug into the snow.

The route then proceeds straight up this face trending to the right over mixed rock and ice for 500 feet (152 m) until it reaches the broad snow shoulder on the slopes at the base of the northern summit pyramid. Here easy low angle snow slopes are followed to reach the northern summit at 9,500 feet (2,896 m). The climb can be terminated here if desired. However, the southern summit is the true summit and it is 800 feet (244 m) higher and one and one-half miles (2.4 km) away along a sometimes narrow and often windy exposed ridge.

To reach the main southern summit a descent must be made down the north side of the northern summit on easy snow slopes to reach a col at about 8,300 feet (2,530 m). The broad snow covered summit ridge can be followed for about one mile (1.6 km). *See CD photo (Chapter 1) CD-A06.*

The ridge then begins to narrow considerably and as it approaches the true

Photo 4A *Photo by Richard Holmes*

southern summit it rises sharply. It is icy and has an angle of forty degrees in its steepest places. The ridge then ends at the true summit.

As of this writing no known ascent has been made of this route. The descent can be made back along the same lengthy ascent route. Alternatively, a descent down the northeast shoulder of the mountain along easy snow slopes might be easier. The climb can be done in five to seven days.

North Ridge

The north ridge of Mt. Seattle forms the long north-south axis of the mountain. This is not a particularly difficult climb technically as there are only a few pitches on steep icy slopes. However, this is a very long climb as one must first climb up over the northern summit and then down again to reach the long summit ridge leading to the true southern summit. The best approach to this climb is from Hubbard Glacier on the north side of the mountain. The climb can begin from either of two distinct forks at the base of the ridge. See photo 4A and *CD photo (Chapter 1) CD-A07.*

The northernmost or left-hand ridge is the most direct start off Hubbard Glacier. This fork of the north ridge can be gained by climbing easy snow slopes up to the ridge crest. The ridge angles up gently until a few mixed pitches of easy rock and snow are encountered. Here the ridge is very narrow for several pitches until it reaches a cornice. An easy snow ramp on the left side of the ridge leads to a broad and level snow shoulder at 6,000 feet (1,829 m). *See CD photos (Chapter 1) CD-A08, CD-A09.*

The right-hand or southern fork of the north ridge is broader than the north fork. This approach may be technically a little bit easier to climb as it is comprised of broad gentle snow slopes on a wide ridge crest. This fork can be reached by dropping down off Hubbard Glacier and skirting the north fork until the south fork is reached. See photo 5A and *CD photo (Chapter 1) CD-A10.*

Straightforward climbing up mostly broad snow slopes brings one to the snow

Photo 5A *Photo by Richard Holmes*

Photo 6A   *Photo by Richard Holmes*

shoulder at 6,000 feet (1,829 m), which intersects with the north fork. *See CD photo (Chapter 1) CD-A11.* The route continues past the snow shoulder for several hundred yards until the ridge is about 500 feet (152 m) below the northern summit.

The north ridge, past the snow shoulder, begins to steepen noticeably and it becomes much more narrow and corniced. The best approach to climb this section of ridge is to stay on the right-hand or southern face of the ridge just below the ridge crest. This can be followed to the northern summit at 9,500 feet (2,896 m).

The northern summit is the intersection of the west and north ridges. The route from here to the true or southern summit is the same as described for the southwest ridge. *See CD photos (Chapter 1) CD-A12, CD-A13.*

The north ridge is a very long climb. As a result of its length a descent down the easy northeast ridge from the southern summit might be the easiest descent if one has continued to the true southern summit. As of this writing no recorded ascents of the north ridge have taken place.

East Ridge

Rising out of the broad expanse of Hubbard Glacier is the northeast face of Mt. Seattle. This is an expansive rock and ice face which faces northeast towards the rising sun and has an average angle of 65 degrees. There is only one ridge which splits this face and this is the east ridge.

The east ridge is a fairly short climb compared with those on the south side of the mountain. The climb begins at 4,000 feet (1,219 m) on the Hubbard Glacier. The best approach to obtain this ridge is to work a route through a small icefall on the right side of the ridge. See photo 6A. Good solid snow bridges should be present early in the season. This brings one to the base of a steep face.

A bergschrund must be crossed at this point to begin the climb, then ascend up moderate slopes on a triangular shaped patch of snow to reach the ridge. *See CD photo*

16   *The Boundary Group*

(Chapter 1) CD-A14. The ridge at this point is very narrow. The best approach is to stay to the left or east side of the ridge, which is less corniced. The ridge crest is followed for about two rope lengths and the ridge then merges with broad smooth low angle slopes of the north face itself. *See CD photo (Chapter 1) CD-A14.*

At the top of the snow slope a camp can be placed just below a bergschrund at 8,500 feet (2,591 m). *See CD photo (Chapter 1) CD-A15.* The slope steepens noticeably above the bergschrund for about three rope lengths. At this point the crux of the climb is encountered. A large nearly vertical serac barrier spills off the summit plateau. This serac barrier guards the exit off the east ridge onto the summit ridge. The route goes for about two rope lengths around these seracs on loose rock and hard ice to reach the summit ridge.

The climb through the serac barrier may provide the most interesting and challenging climbing moves on the entire mountain. Some long ice screws and a few pieces for rock placements will be helpful in this section.

Once upon the summit ridge the route goes left about one mile (1.6 km) to reach the true southern summit. This follows the same route described for the north ridge. Alternatively, the northern summit is just 100 yards (91 m) to the right of the top of the east ridge. The northern summit is only about 100 feet (30 m) lower than the true southern summit and provides wonderful views back into the St. Elias Range as well as beautiful views of Disenchantment Bay to the south.

The east ridge has one recorded ascent and the climbers reached the northern summit. This was the first ascent of the east ridge and the second ascent of the mountain overall. Ref. *AAJ* 2000, p. 221.

Northeast Ridge

The northeast ridge of Mt. Seattle is comprised of two forks which ultimately intersect just below the summit. These two forks are the right and left forks of the northeast ridge. See photo 7A.

Northeast Ridge
Right Fork

The northeast ridge can be accessed

Photo 7A *Photo by Richard Holmes*

Photo 8A *Photo by Richard Holmes*

from a large flat snow plateau that sits directly between the left and right forks of the northeast ridges. *See CD photo (Chapter 1) CD-A16.* This plateau is easily reached off Hubbard Glacier.

From this plateau an easy snow slope of 100 feet (30 m) brings one to the crest of the right fork. The ridge is narrow and corniced in several places. The ridge is followed for about three rope lengths and begins to broaden the further you ascend. Some wind slab slopes are crossed to reach a serac barrier. This serac barrier is not as steep and broken as the one found at the top of the east ridge.

Nonetheless, steep climbing for one rope length trending up and right brings one to another large flat snow plateau at the base of the summit pyramid. A good safe camp can be placed here at 9,000 feet (2,743 m). From this second plateau a snow chute directly above camp can be followed to reach the summit ridge. Then traversing left for several rope lengths brings one to the true southern summit.

Northeast Ridge
Left Fork

The left fork of the northeast ridge can be accessed from the same plateau that the right fork is accessed from. The route can ascend either rocky slopes or an easy snow ramp to reach the crest of the ridge. *See CD photo (Chapter 1) CD-A17.* Once the ridge crest is reached easy climbing along the ridge brings one to the large second plateau. The route from here to the summit is the same as for the right fork route.

Both forks of this ridge are fairly easy. The left fork is much easier as no serac barrier is encountered. The northeast ridge is probably the easiest and most direct ascent of Mt. Seattle. The ascent route of the northeast ridge can be used for the descent. This climb can be done in two to four days.

Southeast Ridge

The southeast ridge is one of the large south face climbs. It has a tremendous elevation gain, nearly 8,000 feet (2,438 m), as the direct south ridge route. This climb can be accessed from the same isolated cirque that is used to begin the direct south ridge route.

The route follows an obvious path up easy low angle rock outcrops for nearly 3,000 feet (914 m) until a sharp pronounced apex is reached on the ridge. A good camp can be place here. See photo 8A.

From this camp a horizontal traverse across a very narrow ridge crest is followed for about five rope lengths. After the horizontal traverse the ridge then steepens onto a broad shoulder.

The route then begins to go up a dark and crumbly metamorphic type rock. The route follows the broad outline of the ridge and is not very steep. Easy scrambling is encountered in this section and not much protection needs to be placed. The shoulder proceeds for about 2,500 feet (762 m) and then the ridge begins to narrow a little.

The narrow section of ridge is climbed straight up for about 1,500 feet (457 m). The upper part of the ridge follows icy but moderate slopes. The ridge tops out directly at the true southern summit. There are no recorded ascents of this ridge and the ascent route can be used for the descent.

Mt. Foresta
11,960 feet (3,645 m) N.E. Summit
11,040 feet (3,365 m) S.W. Summit

Mt. Foresta is really two mountains with two separate summits. The northeast summit is roughly 900 feet (274 m) higher than the southwest summit. Interestingly, during the first ascent of the northeast summit by the east ridge route the climbers made an interesting observation about the altitude. Although the climber did agree that by visual observation the northeast summit of Mt. Foresta is slightly higher than the southwest summit, their own altitude observations are different than those recorded on the maps. Utilizing both GPS equipment and an altimeter, the climbers recorded the height of the northeast summit of Mt. Foresta to be exactly 1,000 feet (305 m) below that of the height recorded on the map. Consequently, the same error probably exists for the southwest summit as well. Perhaps future mapmakers will be able to rectify this discrepancy and clarify the difference.

Mt. Foresta is a triangular complex of a mountain and it rises out of the juncture between the Hubbard and Valerie Glaciers. The southern side of Mt. Foresta sits no more than four miles (6.4 km) from the ocean at the inlet of Disenchantment Bay.

The mountain sits entirely in the United States in Alaskan territory. Mt. Foresta is located at nearly the exact geometric center of the Boundary Peaks which comprise the southeast portion of the St. Elias Mountains. The mountain is characterized by long steep ridges rising sharply out of the glacier with many beautiful snow mushrooms. Mt. Foresta provides several challenging unclimbed ridges. At this writing there has been only one documented ascent of the mountain.

The northeast peak is a long wedge-shaped mountain running along an axis almost due east and west. Several long and moderately steep ridges descend along the north face of this peak. There are no recorded ascents of any of these ridges. Consequently, there is ample opportunity for many first ascents along the north side of the northeast peak of Mt. Foresta.

There is a central col that sits between the southwest and the northwest summits. The top of the col is about 500 feet (152 m) below the surrounding summits. This col can provide an easy descent from the summits or perhaps be utilized for an easy glacier type route to reach the summits. The eastern entrance to this col is long, broad and has a very gentle incline. It has one

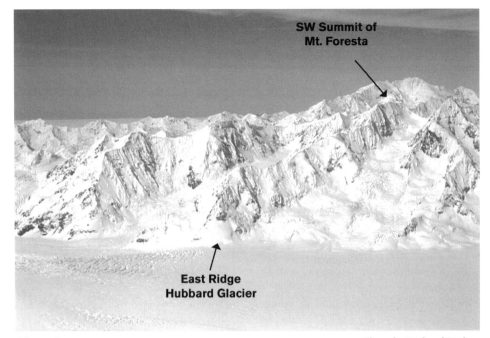

Photo 1B *Photo by Richard Holmes*

icefall about halfway up the col which can be circumvented on the right side. The west entrance to the col is much shorter and is much steeper. Very steep ice slopes lead up the last few rope lengths of the west side of the col. The col is also more heavily crevassed on the west side; therefore, the approach on the eastern side is better for ascents and descents.

Mt. Foresta is not one of the higher peaks in the St. Elias Mountains; however, it provides a number of very exciting climbs along beautiful ridges. Many of these ridges have never had any ascents. It would be best to do this mountain in the month of May before the temperature begins to warm up and while the snow is still consolidated.

The base of some of the ridges are guarded by heavily crevassed glacier approaches which will be easy to cross early in the season but will be more difficult later in the year. Some of the south-facing slopes are prone to slushy soft snow avalanches due to the mountain's proximity to the ocean. Therefore early season climbing of this mountain is recommended.

Mt. Foresta is entirely in Alaskan territory; therefore, the map for this peak is USGS Mt. St. Elias Alaska-Canada, scale 1:250,000.

Southwest Peak
11,040 feet (3,365 m)

East Ridge

The east ridge of the southwest summit can be easily accessed from its base directly off the level and broad expanse of Hubbard Glacier. The base of the ridge is split into a right and left fork; however, the left fork is the easier and safer option. See photo 1B.

The left fork rises up out of Hubbard Glacier for 500 feet (152 m) to reach the main crest of the east ridge. The ridge narrows initially as it proceeds and then

Photo 2B   Photo by Richard Holmes

widens further along. The ridge can be followed for about one mile (1.6 km) until a broad and level platform is reached. This platform is about halfway along the length of the route to the summit. To this point the ridge has barely gained 800 feet (244 m) above Hubbard Glacier.

The ridge then narrows considerably as it begins a nearly horizontal traverse over the course of about 0.5 miles (0.8 km). *See CD photo (Chapter 1) CD-B01.* The ridge, which continues to be narrow, then steepens noticeably as it rises to a forty degree angle. This steeper portion of the ridge climbs over some mixed rock and ice; therefore, some rock protection can be used here. This steeper section of the route continues another 0.5 miles (0.8 km) and is climbed until it reaches a false summit about 300 feet (91 m) below the southwest summit. This false summit is directly above the col which connects the southwest and northeast summits. *See CD photo (Chapter 1) CD-B02.*

The east ridge then proceeds over a narrow section which ultimately becomes broad as it approaches the true southwest summit. From the false summit to the true southwest summit is about 0.75 miles (1.2 km).

The route can be descended utilizing the ascent route. Another alternative would be to drop down from the false summit directly into the col as this is a descent of only about 500 feet (152 m).

As of this writing no recorded ascents have been made of this route. The route is easy to approach from Hubbard Glacier and is long but not unusually so. It offers good places to camp as well as some very interesting climbing. This route would be a very interesting and challenging ascent. It could be done from base camp in eight to ten days. Some rock placements might be needed in addition to the usual ice protection gear.

South Ridge

The south ridge of the south peak is split into two separate forks. The right fork rises out of Hubbard Glacier and moves up and curls left towards the southwest summit. This ridge can be accessed easily at its base from Hubbard Glacier. It is very narrow at first but not too steep and gains and loses elevation several times as the ridge proceeds towards the summit.

The ridge generally gets wider the further it goes. It curves sharply to the left as it rises to a sub-peak at roughly 9,000 feet (2,743 m). At this point it connects with the left fork of the south ridge. This is a very long ridge with little interesting climbing. It rises over the course of nearly three miles (4.8 km) before reaching the sub-peak at 9,000 feet (2,743 m). See photo 2B and *CD photo (Chapter 1) CD-B03.*

The left fork of the south ridge also rises out of Hubbard Glacier only about 800 yards (732 m) left, or due west of the right-hand fork. The left fork of the south ridge can be gained easily directly off the glacier by easy snow slopes.

The left fork offers slightly more interesting climbing than the right-hand fork, and this route is considerably shorter. The ridge does not wander back and forth at all but rises in nearly a straight line to reach the sub-peak at 9,000 feet (2,743 m). The ridge is very narrow and corniced in places and it is still a relatively long route. *CD photo (Chapter 1) CD-B04.*

Between the two ridges is a broad cirque with a gentle snow slope running the entire length of the cirque. This gentle snow slope rises out of the cirque to meet at the intersection of the right and left fork of the south ridge. The slope out of the cirque ends about 300 feet (91 m) below the 9,000 foot (2,743 m) sub-peak that marks the intersection of the forks of the south ridge. *CD photo (Chapter 1) CD-B05.*

Due to the very long, sinuous and corniced nature of both forks of the south ridge, it appears that the central cirque might

Photo 3B   *Photo by Richard Holmes*

offer the best approach to the south side of the mountain. The central cirque is direct and avoids the monotonous climbing that will be encountered on either the right or left fork routes. The central cirque also offers greater protection from the strong winds that blow in off nearby Disenchantment Bay.

A good high camp can be placed on the north side of the sub-peak. A level platform will have to be dug out of the snow but this spot offers ample room for tents as well as protection from the wind. *See CD photo (Chapter 1) CD-B06.*

From the 9,000 foot (2,743 m) sub-peak the ridge drops down slightly and proceeds across a nearly horizontal traverse. The traverse is wide at first but becomes very narrow and corniced. The traverse proceeds for about six rope lengths before it reaches another prominent false summit at 9,300 feet (2,835 m). *See CD photo (Chapter 1) CD-B07.*

The route then proceeds slightly downhill from the false summit over a rounded shoulder. The ridge becomes horizontal for a short stretch and once again becomes very narrow. The ridge then rises to about a forty degree angle and broadens as it rises. This ridge ends directly at the southwest summit. The route can be descended, however a descent down the east col route might be easier.

West Ridge

The west ridge runs along the main east-west axis of the mountain and leads directly to the southwest summit. The west ridge has the only recorded ascent of the entire Mt. Foresta complex.

The best approach to the west ridge is from the long east-west col that divides the mountain into its northern and southern halves. The west ridge can be approached from Hubbard Glacier down an unnamed subsidiary glacier to reach the main east-west col. The climb begins near the north end of the base of the west ridge, at the entrance to the col. See photo 3B.

The best approach to begin the climb appears to be up an ill defined ridge on the left side of the ridge crest. This avoids a large crevasse field on the right side. The climb proceeds up this narrow ridge crest for about three rope lengths over mixed ice and rocks.

The ridge then broadens as it approaches a large rounded snow capped feature dubbed the "Helmet." Several rope lengths of climbing up broad, smooth avalanche prone slopes brings one to the top of the Helmet. The Helmet provides an excellent spot for an advanced base camp. *See CD photo (Chapter 1) CD-B08.*

The route then proceeds from the Helmet toward the summit. The route is narrow and corniced at first but rises at a very subtle angle. The route steepens after several rope lengths but the ridge also becomes very broad and smooth for the remainder of the distance to the summit. The ridge should be traversed on its southern side which will avoid the corniced north face of the ridge. *See CD photo (Chapter 1) CD-B09.*

The climb is not technically difficult and it can be done in three to five days. The route can be descended along the ascent route. The first ascent of the route was done in July of 1979. Ref. *AAJ* 1980, pp. 487-489.

Southwest Spur

A much more interesting approach to the main west ridge of the southwest peak is the southwest spur. In fact this route may provide some of the most interesting climbing on the entire Mt. Foresta complex. This route gains about 1,000 feet (305 m) before intersecting the west ridge route. The southwest ridge is also relatively free of avalanche danger.

This ridge can be accessed from a small unnamed glacier which is an offshoot of the long glacier that parallels the west side of Mt. Foresta. These glaciers are smooth with small crevasses and good snow bridges early in the season. However, by the middle of June the approach to the climbs on the western and southern sides of Mt. Foresta become more complicated as the snow melts and large crevasse fields open up.

The southwest spur can be accessed on its left-hand side. The climb proceeds up one rope length over smooth snow slopes to reach the ridge crest. The climb follows the narrow and sometimes corniced ridge crest for 1,000 feet (305 m) to meet the main west ridge. *See CD photo (Chapter 1) CD-B10.*

The southwest spur intersects the main west ridge at the feature dubbed the Helmet, where a good camp can be placed. The remainder of the climb to the summit is the same as that described for the west ridge.

The southwest spur is very narrow and has no good places for camps. The north facing side of this climb is somewhat corniced. The cornices can generally be avoided by staying on the right-hand side/south side of the ridge crest. As of this writing there are no recorded ascents of this ridge.

The West Col

The west col route follows the obvious glacier that divides the southwest from the northeast peaks. This col can be reached by dropping down off Hubbard Glacier onto the unnamed glacier that runs along the entire length of the west side of Mt. Foresta.

The glacier that leads into the col is followed up smooth gentle snow slopes. Approximately halfway up this glacier sits a small icefall with very wide crevasses. This icefall can be passed easily and safely on its left-hand side on a smooth unbroken snow ramp. The left side is relatively free from avalanches from the slopes above.

Once the small icefall is passed, then the upper glacier is unbroken until one reaches the foot of the col itself. The upper portion of this glacier is directly below the heavily snow laden north face of the southwest summit.

Consequently, this is a very avalanche prone area and climbing time in this area should be minimized. Additionally, it might be safer to do this part of the route in the early hours of the morning.

The climb from the foot of the col starts up smooth low angle slopes for about three rope lengths. At this point the first bergschrund is reached and can be passed easily on its right-hand side. The route then steepens to about forty degrees for one rope length until the second bergschrund is reached. The second bergschrund is bigger than the first, but it can be passed easily on its far left-hand side. One steep snow and ice pitch of 45 degrees takes one from the top of the second bergschrund to the top of the col. *See CD photo (Chapter 1) CD-B11.*

The crest of the col sits directly below the northeast and the southwest summits. The col is fairly broad and safe from avalanche danger. From the top of the col a low angle summit ridge proceeds up for about 500 feet (152 m) until it intersects the east ridge of the southwest peak. A good camp can be placed here. The climb then proceeds the remaining one mile (1.6 km) along the narrow east ridge to reach the southwest summit. *See CD photo (Chapter 1) CD-B11.*

Also from the top of the col a rocky ridge ascends up the other side of the col at an angle of about 45 degrees. This ridge is a combination of mixed rock and snow and is followed for about four rope lengths until it ends directly at the summit of the northeast peak. *See CD photo (Chapter 1) CD-B12.*

A descent down the eastern arm of the long east-west corridor between the southwest and the northeast peaks is probably the safest and easiest descent. The west side of the col is an enjoyable climb but the avalanche potential on the west side precludes this from being an easy descent route. The long and gentle nature of the eastern side of the col in addition to lower avalanche danger makes the eastern branch of this corridor the safer,

Photo 4B   Photo by Richard Holmes

easier and much more recommended descent route. As of this writing the col separating the southwest and northeast peaks of Mt. Foresta has never been reached and there are no recorded ascents up to the col.

Northeast Peak
11,960 feet (3,645 m)

West Ridge

The west ridge of the northeast summit runs along the main east-west axis of the mountain and leads directly to the northeast summit. The west ridge can be reached from an unnamed glacier which is an offshoot of the massive Hubbard Glacier. The unnamed glacier flows south off Hubbard Glacier and flows along the entire west side of Mt. Foresta.

Utilizing this unnamed glacier as an approach, the base of the west ridge is easily reached. The climb proceeds up smooth but avalanche prone slopes in the direct center of the ridge. At this point two alternatives exist to reach the ridge crest. The climb along the right side of the ridge proceeds over smooth, moderately angled snow slopes. However, the approach up the right side is very prone to slab avalanches and should be considered the more dangerous route.

Alternatively, the left side of the ridge follows a narrow ridge crest as it curves elegantly in a broad, right sweeping arc until it reaches the main crest of the west ridge. The left side approach is much safer but is technically more difficult. The ridge is very narrow in places and fixed line would be recommended to facilitate carrying heavy loads up the mountain.

Both the right and the left approaches of the west ridge eventually meet about 800 feet (244 m) above the starting point on the glacier. A few more rope lengths of climbing over easy snow will bring one to a wide spot on the ridge. A good camp can be placed at this point. *See CD photo (Chapter 1) CD-B13.*

From this camp the west ridge is climbed along it's very crest. The route rises gently along a very narrow and sometimes corniced ridge for about 1.5 miles (2.4 km). The final quarter of a mile (0.4 km) rises about 500 feet (152 m) on a broad shoulder to reach a false summit about 200 feet (61 m) below the true northeast summit. The southwest side of this false summit provides sufficient space to place tents in a good camp. The area is wide but not level, so that tent platforms will have to be dug out. *See CD photo (Chapter 1) CD-B14.*

The route then proceeds along the crest of the west ridge. Initially, the route starts down the false summit along a narrow ridge crest. The crest is followed to a col between the false summit and the true summit. This col is about 500 feet (152 m) below the main summit. The ridge crest is very corniced in this area. The cornices can be avoided by staying to the right, south side, of the ridge. The distance from the false summit to the true summit is about 0.75 miles (1.2 km). *See CD photo (Chapter 1) CD-B15.*

The route can be retraced and the ascent route can be descended. A shorter alternative is to drop down from the northeast summit into the central col that sits in the long east-west corridor between the two peaks. This descent can be made by descending about 700 feet (213 m) down the rocky ridge that descends the south side of the northeast summit. This brings one to the top of the col in the long east-west corridor. The descent can then be followed down the long smooth two mile (3.2 km) glacier that flows down the eastern side of Mt. Foresta. As of this writing no recorded ascents have been made of the west ridge of the northeast peak of Mt. Foresta. Additionally, no recorded ascents have been made of the northeast peak along any of its routes. Since the northeast summit is the higher of the two peaks, this summit is still awaiting a first ascent.

North Face of the Northeast Peak

The large sweeping north face of Mt. Foresta rises nearly 8,000 feet (2,438 m) out of Hubbard Glacier. The face is blanketed in a variety of wild undulating snowcaps and cornices. Two significant ridges rise out of the north face. Looking directly at the north face one sees the north ridge on the right-hand side of the face. This ridge rises majestically in a long left sweeping curve toward the summit.

To the left of the north ridge is the northeast ridge. This ridge splits the north face directly into two halves and rises immediately out of the Hubbard Glacier and directly to the true summit. The northeast ridge might be the most aesthetically pleasing line on the entire mountain. See photo 4B and *CD photo (Chapter 1) CD-B16.*

The North Ridge

The north ridge anchors the northern and western corner of the mountain. The north ridge rises in a long left sweeping arc to meet the west ridge at the false summit, which was described in the west ridge route. The north ridge can be approached over the level Hubbard Glacier directly to the foot of the ridge. The ridge is split at its base into a right and left fork.

The right-hand fork is itself split into two forks. The right-hand side is easy to approach. The climb proceeds directly onto the ridge up a forty degree snow face to reach the ridge crest. The ridge crest is razor thin at this point. There follows another three rope lengths of climbing to reach a point where the right and left sides of the right-hand fork of the northeast ridge intersect. *See CD photo (Chapter 1) CD-B17.*

The left side is also approached from an offshoot of Hubbard Glacier. The climb proceeds up at an average angle of forty degrees over mixed ice and rock on a buttress that is sometimes wide in places and occasionally very thin. The route proceeds for about five rope lengths until it reaches the intersection with the right side. *See CD* photo (Chapter 1) CD-B18.

The intersection of the right and left sides of the right fork of the north ridge then proceeds along the crest of a very thin ridge which is nearly horizontal. The route proceeds for about three rope lengths until the ridge widens into a broad snow shoulder.

At this point the right side proceeds up the broad snow shoulder. However, this route is blocked higher up by loose overhanging seracs. Consequently, it might be easier at this point to traverse left across the broad snow shoulder to intersect the left fork of the north ridge. *See CD photo (Chapter 1) CD-B19.*

The left fork of the north ridge can also be easily approached from the level confines of Hubbard Glacier. The route begins at the base of the ridge on its far left side just to the right of an obvious icefall. The climb proceeds up a moderate angle mixed snow and rock face to reach a fluted ridge crest. This ridge crest can be climbed easily on its left face for about three rope lengths to reach a broad snow shoulder at a level spot on the ridge. This level spot is the intersection of the left and right-hand forks of the north ridge. *See CD photo (Chapter 1) CD-B19.*

The route proceeds up moderate angle snow slopes staying left of the overhanging serac barrier. There is an easy but key exit pitch that follows easy snow slopes past the uppermost part of the serac barrier. The route proceeds over a broad snow shoulder to once again meet the narrow ridge crest of the north ridge. *See CD photo (Chapter 1) CD-B19.*

The narrow ridge crest is followed up gentle slopes until it reaches the false summit described in the west ridge route. A camp can be dug into the false summit on its south side if desired. The route then proceeds down into a shallow col and back up again to meet the true summit. *See CD photo (Chapter 1) CD-B20.*

The north ridge involves some interesting climbing over varied rock and ice. The climb can be done in three to five days. The ascent route can also be descended. As of this writing there is no recorded ascent of the north ridge.

Northeast Ridge

Directly in the center of the great north face of Mt. Foresta sits the elegant northeast ridge. This ridge rises directly out of the Hubbard Glacier and proceeds in a direct line to the true summit of the northeast peak. This may be one of the most aesthetically attractive climbs on the entire Mt. Foresta complex.

The base of the ridge can be approached off Hubbard Glacier. The best approach is to stay left of the open crevasse field that sits directly below the ridge. The climb begins directly off the glacier up and onto the crest of the northeast ridge. *See CD photo (Chapter 1) CD-B21.*

The crest of the ridge is followed for several rope lengths along its narrow apex. Some mixed rock and snow is encountered further along. The ridge then steepens for about two rope lengths as the climb proceeds up a 45 degree snow face. The face ends on a broad and heavily crevassed snow shoulder.

The crevasses on this shoulder can be passed easily on the right and then higher up on the left across a good snow ramp. The broad snow shoulder is climbed for another 800 feet (244 m) until it reaches the base of the narrow summit ridge. Here on the broad snow buttress at the base of the summit ridge a good camp can be placed at about 10,000 feet (3,048 m). *See CD photo (Chapter 1) CD-B22.*

The final part of the ascent climbs the exhilarating forty degree summit ridge. The ridge, which is fairly narrow along its entire length, rises from the top of the snow buttress about 1,000 feet (305 m) along a direct line to end directly on top of the true summit

Photo 5B *Photo by Richard Holmes*

of the northeast peak. The ascent route can also be used as the descent route. As of this writing there are no recorded ascents of the northeast ridge. *See CD photo (Chapter 1) CD-B23.*

East Ridge

The east ridge of the northeast peak of Mt. Foresta dominates the eastern skyline. This route runs directly along the east-west axis of the northeast peak. This route can be accessed directly off Hubbard Glacier. The route proceeds up a snow basin over very easy low angle snow slopes. At the top of the basin a small rock pyramid is encountered. There is an easy snow chute up the left side of this pyramid which brings one to the top of the pyramid. See photo 5B.

The route from the pyramid drops down just a bit and follows the nearly level ridge crest. The ridge is nearly horizontal for many rope lengths and is also quite narrow and corniced. The crest is mixed snow and rock. The best approach to climb the narrow sections of this ridge is to stay to its left at the interface of rock and snow.

The route proceeds across the ridge until some exposed rock is encountered further along. It is still best to stay on the left, south side of the narrow portions of the ridge. Some of the narrow sections are corniced on the right-hand/north side of the ridge.

After about three-quarters of a mile (1.2 km), the ridge broadens into a broad snow shoulder. The route proceeds up this increasingly steeper and broadening snow shoulder until it reaches a level section. A good camp can be placed on this broad level section at about 10,500 feet (3,200 m). *See CD photo (Chapter 1) CD-B24.*

The route then proceeds another three-quarters of a mile (1.2 km) over a very level and broad section of the ridge. It is best to stay to the far left, south side of the ridge as the right-hand/north side of the ridge is heavily corniced. This broad shoulder is followed to the base of the summit pyramid.

The summit ridge can be followed to

the top of the summit pyramid. The summit ridge is narrow, curving elegantly and gently up and to the right over the final 800 feet (244 m) of the climb. The summit ridge ends directly on the true summit of the northeast peak. The ascent route can also be used for the descent. The first ascent of this route was done in the summer of 2003. *See CD photo (Chapter 1) CD-B24.* Ref. *AAJ* 2004, p.218.

East Col

Encompassing the entire eastern side of the Mt. Foresta complex is the east col route. This is a glaciated basin which rises gently out of the Hubbard Glacier and proceeds gradually uphill over a distance of about 2.5 miles (4 km). This basin is the eastern side of the great east-west corridor that divides the two summits and it ends at the col that separates the southwest summit from the northeast summit. *See CD photo (Chapter 1) CD-B25.*

The route begins directly in the center of the basin, up smooth and obvious snow ramps with large crevasse fields on either side. The route then proceeds up and right toward the largest crevasse field in the basin. Here, at the midway point of the climb, this large crevasse field can be passed on its farthest right extremity, skirting the edge of the cliffs below the east ridge. A good camp can be placed here that is free from the avalanche danger from the seracs that overhang much of the basin. *See CD photo (Chapter 1) CD-B25.*

The route then continues up the basin trending mostly up and to the right-hand side and passes two more smaller crevasse fields. The route continues up gentle snow slopes until it reaches the top of the col that separates the southwest peak from the northeast peak. From the top of the col either of the two peaks can be climbed from ridges accessed from the col itself. The nature of these ridges was discussed in the west col route.

Despite the fact that this is the easiest approach up the mountain there is no recorded ascent of this route. This route also affords the possibilities of surmounting both summits fairly easily. The east col route can also be used as a descent route for many of the climbs on Mt. Foresta.

Mt. Cook
13,760 feet (4,194 m)

In the midst of the boundary peaks, sitting astride the U.S. and Canadian border, is Mt. Cook. This mountain is named after the great English navigator, Captain James Cook, who was the first European to sight and describe the peaks of the St. Elias Mountains during his eighteenth century "Voyage of Discovery."

Mt. Cook is bound by Seward Glacier on its north and western approaches, Valerie Glacier on its east and several smaller glaciers on its southern flanks. Mt. Cook is not high in altitude but is large in circumference at its base. It is a massive and complex peak with many challenging ridges. It has a spectacular steep north face with a large hanging glacier giving it the appearance of a half eaten heavily frosted wedding cake.

Despite Mt. Cook's moderate altitude, easy approach and obvious visibility from many vantage points, there are very few recorded ascents of this peak. Considering the numerous complex ridge systems on Mt. Cook and the previous lack of commitment to this mountain there currently exists the possibility for many first ascents. There are numerous challenging and rewarding ridges to be climbed on Mt. Cook that have yet to experience the boot of a single climber.

The United States map of this area is USGS Mt. St. Elias Alaska-Canada, scale 1:250,000. The Canadian map is the Corwin Cliffs 115C/8 & 115C/1, scale 1:50,000. In addition the other Canadian map of this area

Photo 1C   *Photo by Richard Holmes*

is Mt. Vancouver 115B/5 & 115 B/4, scale 1:50,000.

East Ridge

The east ridge is a long straight ridge that rises out of Turner Glacier and proceeds directly to the true summit of Mt. Cook. There are numerous aretes that spill down off the south side of the east ridge providing ample opportunity for excellent climbing in an isolated and pristine area. There are currently no recorded ascents of the east ridge or its subsidiary aretes. Therefore, this area is rich in potential first ascents.

The climb of the east ridge begins at the foot of the east ridge directly off Turner Glacier. See photo 1C. The base of the ridge is funneled outward into a broad base and the ridge can be ascended by either one of two low angle snow ridges. The left one is probably a little bit easier but neither one is technically very difficult.

These two ridges converge about 800 feet (244 m) above the glacier. The route continues up a very low angle ridge another 500 feet (152 m) until it levels out onto a large rounded snow dome. *See CD photo (Chapter 1) CD-C01.*

The ridge winds left then straight up and becomes considerably narrower at this point. This narrow section is followed until the route intersects the main crest of the east ridge at a very sharp and pronounced promontory. A good camp can be placed here. *See CD photo (Chapter 1) CD-C01.*

The route proceeds up from this promontory along a broad low angle snow ramp. *See CD photo (Chapter 1) CD-C02.* The ridge then narrows but remains rounded and wide enough to facilitate relatively easy progress.

This part of the ridge undulates up and down a little as the ridge drops down into small notches only to rise again on the other side. The ridge is followed for about a mile and one half (2.4 km) until the ridge intersects with the central spur of the east ridge. *See CD photo (Chapter 1) CD-C03.* The ridge then broadens significantly into a rounded snow shoulder. The route proceeds another half-mile (0.8 km) until it reaches a false summit at roughly 13,000 ft. (3,962 m) where a good camp can be placed.

The route then proceeds along the ridge towards the summit over generally broad slopes. At a point about a half mile (0.8 km) from the summit the route drops down into a sharp notch. The 300 feet (91 m) of climbing that is required to get back out of the notch involves some tricky rock moves. So a few pieces of rock protection might be useful here. *See CD photo (Chapter 1) CD-C04.* The route then continues over broad snow slopes to the summit.

The ascent route can be used as the descent route. This is a long but rewarding route. The climb can be done in five to seven days. As of this writing there are no recorded ascents of the east ridge of Mt. Cook.

Southeast Spur

The southeast spur of the east ridge is a prominent ridge that rises to meet the main crest of the east ridge. This spur starts about a half mile (0.8 km) to the left, due west, of the start of the regular route of the east ridge.

The route begins on easy snow slopes on the right side of the base of the spur. The crest of the spur is reached a few rope lengths above the glacier. The narrow ridge crest is then climbed as it ascends upward. About halfway along its length is a wide level section where a good camp can be placed. *See CD photo (Chapter 1) CD-C05.*

The route then continues up the spur, which becomes increasingly narrow and ultimately merges into a broad buttress, which is climbed for several rope lengths. The buttress then merges into a 45 degree snow face. The final three rope lengths continue up this increasingly steeper snow face until the main crest of the east ridge is joined. The climb then proceeds along the same route as the regular east ridge route. As of this writing there are no recorded ascents of the southeast spur.

Central Spur

The central spur of the east ridge of Mt. Cook is a large prominent ridge that splits the south face of the east ridge almost directly in half. This route begins one mile (1.6 km) left, due west of the starting point of the southeast spur.

The route begins off the unnamed glacier in the cirque below the south face of the east ridge. This cirque can be reached from the head of Turner Glacier.

The climb begins on the right side at the base of the spur. The route starts up an obvious snow crest and climbs up and to the right for several rope lengths. The crest is followed until it merges with a rocky buttress. Two rope lengths of climbing are needed to overcome this buttress.

The route then proceeds about 500 feet (152 m) up a broad snow face until the route reaches a large rounded snow dome. To the left of the snow dome is a large level amphitheater. A good camp can be placed in this amphitheater. *See CD photo (Chapter 1) CD-C06.*

The route then proceeds up a narrow snow crest for a few rope lengths. The climb then widens onto a broad snow shoulder and the final 500 feet (152 m) of climbing proceed up this shoulder. The central spur meets with the main crest of the east ridge about a half mile (0.8 km) from the false summit. The climb then proceeds along the same route as described for the regular east ridge climb. As of this writing there are no recorded ascents of the central spur of the east ridge.

South Buttress

The south buttress of Mt. Cook is the last of the three aretes that drop down off the south face of the east ridge of Mt. Cook. *See CD photo (Chapter 1) CD-C07.* The south buttress ultimately intersects with the direct

Photo 2C   *Photo by Richard Holmes*

south ridge near the top of the south ridge.

The south buttress can be accessed from the head of the Turner Glacier. The route begins about a half mile (0.8 km) to the left, due west of the beginning of the central spur. *See CD photo (Chapter 1) CD-C08.* The route begins from the head of Turner Glacier up a broad and rounded shoulder on easy snow slopes. *See CD photo (Chapter 1) CD-C08.* The climb proceeds up the snow slopes until the route narrows onto the crest of the buttress, which winds up and left. A very pronounced and sharp promontory is ultimately reached at about 6,000 feet (1,829 m).

The route then follows the apex of the ridge for approximately three-quarters of a mile (1.2 km). The apex of the ridge at this point is very narrow but the ridge is nearly level across this section.

The climb opens up onto a broad and heavily crevassed shoulder. This snow shoulder is ascended by winding through the crevasse fields for about 2,000 feet (610 m) until the south buttress intersects with the direct south ridge. A good camp can be placed at the intersection with the south ridge on fairly level ground.

The route proceeds up past this camp for several rope lengths until it intersects with the main crest of the east ridge. The climb to the summit is the same as for the regular route of the east ridge.

As of this writing there are no ascents of the south buttress of the east ridge of Mt. Cook. The ascent route can be descended and the climb is not very technical and can be done in three to five days.

The South Face

The South Face of Mt. Cook is a massive complex of ridges and icefalls spilling their way down from the summit to nearly sea level. The massive nature of this structure therefore presents many spectacular climbing opportunities. There has been very little climbing activity in the south face area; consequently, there is ample opportunity for

33

great climbs and numerous first ascents in a wild and pristine setting.

South Ridge

The great south ridge rises directly up the south face to meet the summit of Mt. Cook. This massive ridge is the largest feature in the south face complex. There are a number of ways to approach the beginning of this climb.

The direct route begins at the foot of the ridge directly off Lucia Glacier. The climb begins on a large triangular shaped feature that looks like a massive snow covered pyramid. See photo 2C and *CD photo (Chapter 1) CD-C09*.

The climbing proceeds up a low angle but narrow snow covered ridge for about 500 feet (152 m) to reach a large level area. The route then proceeds up the narrow and occasionally corniced ridge of the pyramid that comprises the lower third of the climb. This section of the climb rises about 1,000 feet (305 m) off the glacier. The top of the pyramid is a narrow pointed structure. However, on its backside, which is the north facing slope, a good camp can be dug in on relatively level ground. This is a good site for Camp I.

An alternative approach to climb this pyramid structure is to follow a ridge on its left side, which is the west face. This ridge begins off Hayden Glacier and ends at the same point on the top of the pyramid and gains the same amount of elevation. However, this west side ridge is a bit steeper and traverses over some snow slopes that are prone to slab avalanches.

From Camp I the route drops down into a col about 200 feet (61 m) below Camp I and then proceeds up a forty degree rocky buttress. This buttress is followed for about 600 feet (183 m). *See CD photo (Chapter 1) CD-C10*. The ridge then broadens into a wide snow covered shoulder. The route proceeds to a large level plateau where Camp II can be placed.

The route proceeds up from Camp II on a broad low angle snow face to meet the east ridge about 600 feet (183 m) above Camp II. *See CD photo (Chapter 1) CD-C09*. The route at this point intersects the east ridge route and the remainder is the same as described for the east ridge route from the false summit to the true summit.

There is one other alternative route on the south ridge. This is a ridge which rises out of Turner Glacier and begins to the right of the direct start of the south ridge. *See CD photo (Chapter 1) CD-C11*. This route begins about a half mile (0.8 km) left, due west, of the beginning of the south buttress route. This right-hand alternative begins up a broad pyramid structure rising about 1,000 feet (305 m) off Turner Glacier. From a narrow and pointed promontory at the top of this pyramid the route proceeds along a very narrow ridge. This section is not only narrow but occasionally corniced. It is nearly horizontal and proceeds for about one-half mile (0.8 km).

After the horizontal traverse the route broadens into a large low angle snow buttress that is heavily crevassed. The route proceeds up this buttress through the crevasse fields for about 1,000 feet (305 m) to reach the main south ridge. This intersection occurs at a point just below Camp II on the direct south ridge. From this point onward, the climbing is the same as for the direct south ridge route.

As of this writing there are no recorded ascents of the south ridge or any of its alternate approaches. The south ridge is not a difficult climb and has good campsites and the base of the ridge is easily accessed. The route can be done in about four to six days and the ascent route can also be used for the descent.

South Amphitheater

One of the best unexploited treasures

Photo 3C *Photo by Richard Holmes*

on the south side of Mt. Cook is the great southern amphitheater. This is a large southern exposed basin bounded on the east by the direct south ridge and on the west by the long and sinuous west ridge. See photo 3C.

This high level basin has at least three routes that have not yet been done or even attempted. The routes in this basin are interesting in that they are characterized by being relatively short, since the basin itself sits at about 8,000 feet (2,438 m). The routes are mixed rock and ice and are relatively steep. The climbing angle can range from 45 to 65 degrees. The climbs are very interesting and challenging but are never severe.

An excellent and safe camp can be placed on either the far right side or the far left side of the basin. This will minimize exposure to avalanches. Additionally, these campsites, particularly on the left side, are well sheltered from the wind. The basin sits above the confluence of the Hayden and Lucia Glaciers. The direct approach into the basin is guarded by long, exposed and highly active icefalls. There are, however, two reasonable approaches into the basin.

The first of these approaches starts at the head of the confluence of the Lucia and Hayden Glaciers. *See CD photo (Chapter 1) CD-C12.* This is the beginning of the south ridge route. A large 1,000 foot (305 m) high pyramidal shaped buttress can be ascended from either its far right or left-hand ridge. (See description for the south ridge route). After reaching the top of the pyramidal structure the route drops down into a shallow col. In this col one can climb down the west side of the ridge on easy snow slopes to get into the basin. *See CD photo (Chapter 1) CD-C13.* It does involve some route finding as one small icefall is encountered and can be passed on its far left side. *See CD photo (Chapter 1) CD-C13.* Then one can climb up into the main basin within the amphitheater by passing through one more icefall which can be passed on its far right side. After passing the second icefall, easy snow slopes can be followed into the main amphitheater.

The other approach into the south amphitheater begins again at the head of the Lucia and Hayden Glaciers. This approach begins at the left side of this confluence and goes up an easy low angle snow ridge. *See CD photo (Chapter 1) CD-C14.* The route drops down into a small col and then back up easy snow ridge to the base of a buttress blocking the entrance into the basin. A narrow ridge can be climbed up this buttress to gain access into the amphitheater. The ridge up this buttress is low angle at first but becomes steeper near the top. *See CD photo (Chapter 1) CD-C15.*

An alternative to the ridge that ascends the buttress is to drop down to the left onto a snow slope below the buttress. A difficult icefall can be passed easily by staying far to the right. Another ridge is then encountered. This is an easier and more low angle ridge than that found on the buttress itself. This ridge can be climbed into the basin. *See CD photo (Chapter 1) CD-C15.*

Once into the basin the real fun begins. Several interesting climbs can be done from a single base camp. All the routes are enjoyably steep but not severe, and all lead to the summit. These exciting ridges can all be climbed within the confines of a magnificent and secluded high mountain amphitheater.

South Amphitheater Right Pillar

The first route in the South Amphitheater is the right-hand pillar. On the broad curving face of the amphitheater on its right side is the very distinct right-hand pillar. This route is characterized by a thin rocky rib which ascends up and to the left.

The route can be accessed at its base along easy snow slopes. *See CD photo (Chapter 1) CD-C16.* The snow gives way quickly to a thin rocky ridge. The ridge can be climbed at the interface of snow on the left side and rock on the right side. This rib can be ascended for about 800 feet (244 m). The pillar then turns left and becomes a narrow snow and ice ridge for about 500 feet (152 m).

The snow ridge then intersects a rock buttress which can be climbed over mixed ice and rock following natural ledges. The buttress starts out at a relatively steep angle of about sixty degrees but reclines to a more gentle slope of about forty degrees some distance higher. The buttress is followed for about 800 feet (244 m) and gives way to a low angle narrow snow and rock ridge. This route ends on the summit ridge about 300 feet (91 m) below the true summit. This summit is about 400 yards (366 m) up and to the left. The climb is challenging but not severe. It is a very interesting variation from the other climbs on Mt. Cook. The route can be done in a day from a base camp high in the South Amphitheater. The route can be descended but the easiest descent is down the left rib.

South Amphitheater
Central Pillar

The central rib is a large rounded pillar that rises to end at the true summit. The central pillar can be accessed easily from a base camp in the amphitheater. *See CD photo (Chapter 1) CD-C17.* The foot of the pillar can be gained on its right side on easy snow slopes. The base is subject to some avalanche danger so the climb should be started early in the day.

The route proceeds over the snow slopes and moves up and to the right to a gully. An overhanging rock face in the center of the pillar can be passed on its right side in this gully. Easy snow climbing in this gully allows one to move up and left, which brings one to the top of the rock face after about 900 feet (274 m) of climbing. The gully is subjected to avalanches from loose seracs above so it should only be climbed in the early morning hours.

Above the rock face the climb proceeds up a rounded snow ridge on easy angle snow slopes. The route proceeds over a small snow cornice. This is most easily passed on its far left-hand side. Above the cornice the route proceeds over very easy angled snow slopes to the true summit about 1,000 feet (305 m) higher.

The route can be easily accessed from a base camp in the amphitheater. The best descent from this route is down the left-hand rib. The route is not long but is very interesting. There is some objective danger from slab avalanches high on the route so the climb should be done early in the day.

South Amphitheater
Left Rib

The left-hand perimeter of the South Amphitheater is demarcated by a long right-hand curving snow ridge. This route is probably the easiest route of the three climbs in the South Amphitheater. The climb can be ascended from high in the South Amphitheater on the left side. *See CD photo (Chapter 1) CD-C17.*

The climb proceeds up over fairly easy snow slopes staying to the right side of an obvious ridge. The route ascends the easy low angle snow slopes for about 1,000 feet (305 m) until reaching a level spot on top of a rounded snow pyramid. The route then goes up and right on the obvious ridge. The ridge is narrow and slightly corniced for a short distance until it broadens again.

The route curves up and right over easy snow slopes until the true summit is reached about 1,000 yards (914 m) further. The left rib can be climbed easily in one day and has very little objective hazard. The route can be descended and used as the descent route for all the climbs in the South Amphitheater. As of this writing there are no recorded ascents of any of the climbs described in the South Amphitheater.

Photo 4C *Photo by Richard Holmes*

Photo 5C
Photo by Richard Holmes

Southwest Ridge

The western corner of Mt. Cook is anchored by the long and sinuous southwest ridge. This ridge starts just left of the southern amphitheater and runs up and to the right to reach the main summit of Mt. Cook.

The southwest ridge can be reached from the head of the Marvine Glacier which flows downhill to intersect with the great Malaspina Glacier and ultimately out to the Gulf of Alaska. See photo 4C.

The base of the southwest ridge can be accessed up a small fluted ridge and up an unstable snow face to gain a nice campsite in a saddle on the ridge crest. The climb begins immediately out of camp by climbing up a snow face. The snow gives way to a narrow bit of climbing on an icy ridge. This yields to the top of a pyramidal feature about 800 feet (244 m) above the first camp.

The climb continues above this pyramid along a very narrow ridge crest which is mostly snow covered for another half mile (0.8 km) gaining another 900 feet (274 m) of elevation. At this point one reaches the top of a very pronounced sharp gendarme.

The climb proceeds past the sharp gendarme over a very narrow ridge crest to reach a snow covered rounded gendarme about a half mile (0.8 km), further on. The climb drops down from the snow covered gendarme and down into a saddle. The ridge along this section is narrow but fairly rounded and snow covered which makes it easy to traverse.

Above the saddle the snow ridge rises to reach the summit of Northwest Cook. A good camp can be placed on the south face of Northwest Cook near its summit. The area is not very level but a good platform can be dug in here. This area is out of the wind and receives a lot of sun.

From the camp on Northwest Cook the route swings to the right along a narrow ridge crest which is nearly horizontal. The ridge then proceeds until you reach the crux of the climb. This is a rock notch which can be climbed with low fifth class climbing on loose rock. The climb then proceeds along the ridge towards the summit. *See CD photo*

(Chapter 1) CD-C18.

Shortly after the rock notch the ridge blends into the face of the main bulk of the mountain. The climbing becomes low angle snow slogging from this point to the summit about three-quarters of a mile (1.2 km) away.

The ascent route can be descended. If you wish to carry all your gear with you in an alpine type ascent a very short easy descent can be made down the north face. The route is long and interesting. It is fairly easy snow walking and ridge climbing except for a few hundred feet in the rock notch between Northwest Cook and the main summit. As of this writing the lower portion of the climb up to Northwest Cook has not been climbed. The route from Northwest Cook to the main summit has been done once.

Southwest Ridge
North Buttress

An interesting alternative to climbing the southwest ridge from its base is to climb the steep and exhilarating north buttress of the southwest ridge. *See CD photo (Chapter 1) CD-C19.* This buttress intersects the ridge at the rounded snow gendarme on the main crest of the southwest ridge.

The north buttress can be accessed from a branch of Seward Glacier above its intersection with Malaspina Glacier. This side branch of Seward Glacier enters a wild, beautiful and seldom visited cirque. From the head of the cirque the base of the north buttress of the southwest ridge can be reached through a small icefall.

The route proceeds up over broken lightly crevassed snow slopes. The climb proceeds up a steep snow face to reach a level portion of the ridge about 800 feet (244 m) higher. The route then proceeds over a narrow icy section which gives way to a narrow rock crest. The ridge broadens for awhile until about 200 feet (61 m) below the ridge crest.

Here a narrow and steep rocky outcrop is climbed to reach the main crest of the southwest ridge. The north buttress intersects the main southwest ridge at a point where the large rounded snow gendarme sits on top of the southwest ridge. The climb to the main summit from this point is the same as described for the southwest ridge route. As of this writing this variation of the southwest ridge has not been climbed.

Northwest Cook

Mt. Cook has twin summits. Just as the name implies, Northwest Cook is the northwest twin summit of Mt. Cook. The summit of Northwest Cook is 11,100 feet (3,383 m), which is about 2,600 feet (792 m) below the true summit of Mt. Cook at 13,760 feet (4,194 m). See photo 5C.

A very interesting route has been established on the north side of Northwest Cook. A good base camp can be established on Seward Glacier directly below the north face of Northwest Cook at 5,412 feet (1,650 m). The route ascends the thin but obvious north ridge which rises precisely in the middle of the north face. See photo 5C. The climb consists of ridge climbing over soft snow and some rotten ice with the ice pitches going as steep as 75 degrees. There are two good bivouac sites on large rounded natural snow platforms at 6,888 feet (2,099 m) and 8,856 feet (2,699 m) as the route rises to reach the summit of Northwest Cook.

The route from the summit of Northwest Cook to the true summit of Mt. Cook follows the route described for the southwest ridge route. The ridge connecting Northwest Cook to Mt. Cook drops down into a saddle and goes through the crux of the climb which is a steep rock notch. The connecting ridge blends into the main massif of Mt. Cook and easy snow slopes are followed to the summit. *See CD photo (Chapter 1) CD-C20.*

The descent down the mountain from

Photo 6C *Photo by Richard Holmes*

the true summit goes down easy snow slopes on the northeast face to the north buttress. A good snow ramp can be followed down the north buttress to reach Seward Glacier. This is the route of the first ascent of the mountain and is the easiest and most direct non-technical route on the mountain.

This is a very interesting and enjoyable route following an excellent line up a prominent ridge on Northwest Cook. The route can be climbed in about a week from base camp. Some rock protection should be included for the crux pitch in the rock notch. Ref. *AAJ* 2000, pp. 219-220.

North Ridge

The north ridge of Mt. Cook is one of the most spectacular looking geologic features in the entire St. Elias Mountain Range. This is a very narrow serrated snow and rock rib that rises directly out of Seward Glacier to rise directly to the summit. See photo 6C.

The climb begins directly from the base of the north ridge up easy snow slopes. The route proceeds up a low angle triangular shaped face to reach a point where the ridge begins to narrow. The narrow ridge is followed to a crest about 1,500 feet (457 m) above the glacier.

The route proceeds directly along the spine of the narrow and sometimes serrated north ridge. The ridge is very narrow along this section and anchor points for belays may be difficult to find. The ridge rises gently after about three-quarters of a mile (1.2 km) to ascend a small rocky outcrop.

From the peak of this small outcrop the route descends about 200 feet (61 m) into a small saddle. The ridge begins to broaden slightly starting in the saddle. A secure, although highly exposed camp can be dug into this saddle. The route then rises at an angle of about 65 degrees as it follows the now slightly broader ridge.

The route then intersects the cornices which guard the upper plateau of the mountain. The climb through this corniced section is on relatively unstable air-filled ice for about two pitches. Long ice screws or one-half length snow pickets can be used to protect this section of the climb. The route proceeds through the cornices and then onto the easy low angle snow slopes of the upper portion of the north face. The route follows these easy low angle snow slopes the remaining 3,000 feet (914 m) to the summit.

The easiest descent is down the northeast face and down the easy snow ramps of the north buttress. *See CD photo (Chapter 1) CD-C20.* This is a spectacular ridge which as of this writing has not been climbed.

North Buttress

The north buttress of Mt. Cook was the first ascent route of this mountain. From a secure base camp on Seward Glacier the north buttress can be ascended. *See CD photo (Chapter 1) CD-C21.*

There are two possible ascent lines on the lower north buttress. The line on the left follows the largest and most pronounced buttress. This is very broad and rounded at its base. About halfway up, the buttress blends into the face and follows an indistinct rib up a snow face to the top of the north buttress.

The right-hand of the two ascent lines follows a less distinct buttress which climbs over easy snow slopes to meet at the top of the north buttress. The right-hand buttress has some very unstable avalanche prone snow slabs along the upper portion of the route. Consequently, the left line may be somewhat safer. *See CD photo (Chapter 1) CD-C21.*

Both buttress routes meet at the top of the north buttress. The route proceeds into a broad and gentle snow saddle. A safe secure advanced base camp can be placed here. The remainder of the route to the summit follows easy low angle snow slopes up the remaining 3,500 feet (1,067 m). The summit can be reached in a long day from the advanced base camp up this low angle face.

The ascent route can also be descended and this climb was the route used for the first ascent of Mt. Cook. Although this is not a difficult climb it is an enjoyable experience in a beautiful setting. Ref. *AAJ* 1954, pp. 32-38. *CAJ* 1954 (37), pp. 35-39.

Northeast Buttress

An interesting alternative to the north buttress is the northeast buttress. This route follows an easy low angle snow face up the central face of the northeast ridge. *See CD photo (Chapter 1) CD-C22.* The snow ramp is followed up 1,500 feet (457 m) to reach a prominent point on the northeast ridge. The broad and curving snow slopes of the northeast ridge are followed until one intersects the saddle near the top of the north buttress. The route to the summit is the same from here as it is for the north buttress route. There are no recorded ascents of this route.

Turner Glacier

A long and physically challenging way to climb Mt. Cook is via Turner Glacier. It can be ascended where it begins to flow off Mt. Cook on its southeast side. *See CD photo (Chapter 1) CD-C23.* This broad and gentle glacier can be ascended on skis for its eleven mile (17.7 km) length. Turner Glacier ultimately reaches the head of the cirque from which it originates. From the head of the cirque one can climb the easy snow slopes to meet the same saddle as described for the northeast buttress and the north buttress routes. *See CD photo (Chapter 1) CD-C21.* The easy snow slopes of the north face are followed to the summit.

This is an extremely long route over a heavily broken and crevassed glacier. The greatest difficulty that would be encountered on this climb is the route finding through the maze of open crevasse fields. The north buttress is the easiest and shortest descent route after completing the Turner Glacier climb. As of this writing there are no recorded ascents of Turner Glacier.

Mt. Vancouver
True North Summit
15,850 feet (4,831 m)

South Summit
(Good Neighbor Peak)
15,683 feet (4,780 m)

Mt. Vancouver is typical of many mountains in the St. Elias Range in that it is a large and complex massif. Mt. Vancouver is bound on the north and east by the extensive Hubbard Glacier. Hubbard Glacier is 75 miles (120.7 km) long and as such this makes it the longest valley glacier in the world. The initial twenty miles (32 km) of the Hubbard Glacier may be the most heavily crevassed area of any glacier anywhere in the world. Its western and southern flanks rise out of the wide and smooth expanse of Seward Glacier.

Mt. Vancouver is characterized by steep corniced ridges and large blocky rock faces. Vancouver appears to look like a well-iced wedding cake from its north side. Conversely, Vancouver looks more like the Matterhorn of Switzerland when viewed from the south. There are definitely many interesting and challenging climbs that can be done from all sides on Mt. Vancouver.

The Vancouver massif and its ridges run in a generally north-south direction. Mt. Vancouver forms the eastern edge of the deep and massive Seward Glacier basin. The accumulation of snow which falls in this one basin alone is staggering. As the snow is compressed to ice to ultimately form the Seward Glacier, it flows down a narrow three-mile wide gap between Mt. Augusta and the adjacent Mt. Cook. Millions of tons of ice flow down this slot to feed the Malaspina Glacier, which is the world's largest Piedmont type glacier.

In 1874 W.H. Dall and Marcus Baker of the U.S. Coast Survey named Mt. Cook and Mt. Vancouver after having viewed them from the sea. The peak was originally named Boundary Peak 181 after the work of the twentieth century Boundary Commission Survey.

The names Cook and Vancouver, as well as their elevations, were inadvertently reversed on the first maps published for this area. It is fairly certain that the Coast Guard Survey team had originally intended the higher mountain to display the name of Cook. After all, Captain James Cook was the more famous of the two eighteenth century British navigators. Nonetheless, the names stuck as they were originally coined although the correct elevations were eventually applied to the peaks.

Mt. Vancouver has two main summits, north and south, which are connected by a horizontal ridge. The north or true summit is slightly higher and is entirely in Canadian territory. The south peak is only 150 feet (46 m) lower and sits astride the boundary between Alaska and Canada. Thus it has adopted the name Good Neighbor Peak.

Mt. Vancouver is a striking mountain in a beautiful setting within full view of the Gulf of Alaska some twenty miles distant. Vancouver has climbs that will satisfy both inexperienced climbers and those seeking great challenges. The United States map for Mt. Vancouver is Mt. St. Elias Alaska-Canada 1959, scale 1:250,000. The Canadian map for Mt. Vancouver is 115 B/5 and 115 B/4, scale 1:50,000.

Northwest Ridge

The northwest ridge of Mt. Vancouver was the route of the first ascent of the mountain. This route was climbed in the summer of 1949. The climb was noteworthy for several reasons beyond the fact that it was

Photo 1D *Photo by Richard Holmes*

the first ascent of the mountain. This was one of the first times that crampons were used by climbers in North America. The fixed nail boot, better know as the hobnail boot, had been in favor previously.

The use of double boots and double sleeping bags were introduced here as well. The move to dehydrated food was another addition replacing the old style of bringing heavy canned goods. This party did, however, use parachute drops of supplies at higher elevations. This must have been a wonderful way to bring supplies to the higher camps, although it might prove to be somewhat unethical today.

The climb begins in a basin below the southwest side of the north ridge. Base camp can be placed in a very commanding position on the wide expanse of Institute Glacier at about 6,000 feet (1,829 m) near a rock nunatak. See photo 1D. The route then proceeds up Institute Glacier to the head of the cirque below the northwest ridge. A small icefall is negotiated here on the left-hand side. Just above this icefall and just below the ridge is a good place to establish Camp I. *See CD photos (Chapter 1) CD-D01, CD-D02.* The climb to Camp I should be made in the early morning hours as large cornices avalanche off the massive west face of Mt. Vancouver on the opposite side of Institute Glacier.

The climb moves left up a rocky and snow covered couloir for about 800 feet (244 m) until the crest of the northwest ridge is reached. The ridge crest is followed until it begins to rise slightly. At an obvious wide spot on the ridge, Camp II can be placed at about 10,000 feet (3,048 m). *See CD photos (Chapter 1) CD-D03, CD-D04.* The last 500 feet (152 m) leading up to Camp II are very icy and steep. The angle of the climbing on this one short, steep section reaches 45 degrees.

The climb past Camp II follows the ridge crest. The route winds around seracs and cornices. The ridge begins to broaden as it approaches the obvious rounded summit of Institute Peak at 13,150 feet (4,008 m). The climb stays to the left (east) of the summit

Photo 2D *Photo by Richard Holmes*

of Institute Peak. Camp III, a good camp, can be dug into the slopes on the northeast face of Institute Peak at about 12,600 feet (3,840 m). *See CD photos (Chapter 1) CD-D03, CD-D05.*

The climb then proceeds up and right over wind slab snow slopes. The climb proceeds to an obvious col high on the mountain at 13,500 feet (4,115 m). *See CD photo (Chapter 1) CD-D06.* This col sits directly below the true northwest ridge. This is a windy area and most of the snow is usually blown away from the col leaving exposed rock.

The climb proceeds up the now obvious northwest ridge for about 1,000 feet (305 m). At this height an obvious and unavoidable ice face is encountered. *See CD photo (Chapter 1) CD-D07.* This face can be climbed with easy front pointing techniques as the slope leans out to be about sixty degrees in angle in its steepest spots. It may be a good idea to leave a fixed line on this 500 foot (152 m) section to facilitate the descent.

The climbing encountered after the ice face is lower angle and easier and follows the obvious notch to the true northern summit. The summit of Vancouver is a narrow wedge-shaped snow crest running north and south. It provides magnificent views of the Seward and Hubbard Glaciers as well as many of the peaks in the interior part of the St. Elias Range. See photo 2D.

The descent can be done by the ascent route. The route is non-technical and has little route finding difficulty. The short 500 foot (152 m) section below Camp II and the short section above the high col should be fixed with rope for ease on the descent. The climb can be done in about a week. Ref. *AAJ* 1950, Vol. 7, No. 4, pp. 367-378. *CAJ* 1950, Vol. 33, pp. 1-18.

Northwest Ridge
North Rib Variation

An interesting and labor saving alternative to the northwest ridge is the north rib of the northwest ridge. This climb begins off Hubbard Glacier on the north side of Mt. Vancouver. This variation can be approached

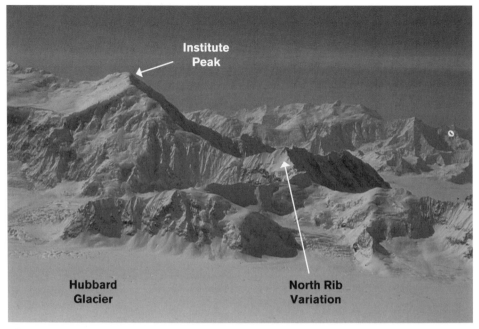

Photo 3D   *Photo by Richard Holmes*

in one of two ways. The first is an obvious small glacier, which flows off the north rib. See photo 3D. This small glacier is guarded by a heavily crevassed icefall. This small but heavily broken icefall can be passed on its far right side. Once above this icefall the route proceeds over the smooth glacier and up a snow shoulder on the right side. The route wanders back left under a pyramidal face and up to a large flat platform. A good campsite can be placed here.

The other approach to the north rib is from the far left or east side. Directly off Hubbard Glacier is a large rounded buttress. The center of this buttress can be climbed up a snow face to its ridge crest. This rounded but corniced ridge can be followed along its length to the level campsite reached by the icefall route. See photo 3D.

The route from the platform camp proceeds over a narrow and corniced ridge crest. The ridge is snow at first and then becomes rocky further along. This crest gives way to a narrow snow ridge which rises up to meet the northwest ridge route. From this point on the route is the same as that described for the northwest ridge.

North Buttress

The most direct route to the true north summit of Mt. Vancouver is via the north buttress route. This rounded and sometimes corniced route starts on Hubbard Glacier and rises 10,000 feet (3,048 m) directly to the true summit of Mt. Vancouver. See photo 4D. The first ascent of this route was done in the summer of 1975 by a Japanese climbing party. The details of their ascent are somewhat sketchy but there is sufficient data to provide an adequate route description.

The north buttress is generally a very rounded buttress with many cornices and large crevasses. The only narrow part of the ridge is at the very bottom of the route which has a short, steep knife-edge section. The remainder of the route is comprised of snow slopes and seracs. This route is very prone to wind slab avalanches that sometimes blanket

Photo 4D *Photo by Richard Holmes*

the entire north face. Consequently, it is best to do this route early in the season in May when the snow is well consolidated and the snow bridges are still intact.

A good base camp can be placed at 5,400 feet (1,646 m) on Hubbard Glacier a safe distance from the mountain to avoid avalanches. There are two alternatives to begin this ridge. The one that was chosen by the first ascent party was the ascent of a very narrow but obvious ridge on the far right side of the north buttress. *See CD photo (Chapter 1) CD-D08.*

This ridge can be ascended from its left side up a steep snow face. *See CD photo (Chapter 1) CD-D09.* This will then allow one to gain the crest of the knife-edge ridge. The knife-edge must be followed for 600 feet (183 m) until a small platform is reached below a large bergschrund. See photo 8D.

The other alternative is around the corner from the base of this ridge. It is not quite as steep and does not force one to traverse the knife-edge section of the ridge. However, this alternative does force one to climb on unstable snow slopes as well as climb directly below some cornices which have the potential to avalanche down the route.

Nonetheless, this second alternative starts up the right side of a small icefall. The route continues up a snow face below some cornices. The climb goes up and to the right around the cornices then back up a steep snow face to reach the same platform obtained using the first route.

Directly above the small platform is a steep face and a fifteen foot (4.6 m) wide bergschrund. The bergschrund can be crossed on a delicate snow bridge. The small ice face can be climbed directly using front points for half a rope length or it can be by passed on its left if the snow conditions provide a path.

Above the bergschrund the angle eases back and an easy snow slope is followed another 800 feet (244 m) to reach a small level spot on the ridge at about 9,300 feet

Photo 5D *Photo by Richard Holmes*

(2,835 m) where Camp I can be placed. *See CD photo (Chapter 1) CD-D08.*

The climb from Camp I to the summit involves more route finding problems than technical difficulties. Immediately past Camp I a small snow bridge is climbed to reach another low angle plateau. *See CD photo (Chapter 1) CD-D10.* This snow plateau is climbed until another bergschrund is reached at the head of the plateau and is easily crossed at its left side across good snow bridges. The route proceeds up and to the right along the easy snow ridge until another small crevasse field is reached. These crevasses can easily be passed on their left side and a large broad plateau on the upper face of the mountain is reached at about 11,500 feet (3,505 m). Camp II can be placed on this large plateau. A careful selection of campsites on the left side of the plateau will put the camp outside of most avalanche danger and it will also be out of the wind.

From Camp II there are two alternative routes to the summit. The route chosen by the first ascent party was up the left side. *See CD photo (Chapter 1) CD-D10.* The left side has some steep but not serious ice pitches as it winds up towards the summit. The steep pitches can be avoided on the right-hand alternative. However, the right side alternative is prone to more avalanches. The entire face on the right-hand route is a large wind slab slope with some menacing cornices near its top. The route up the remaining 4,300 feet (1,311 m) to the summit from Camp II can be achieved in a single day using either one of the right or left alternative routes.

In either case the north buttress can be climbed in about a week. The climb has moderate technical difficulty and a great deal of route finding objectives. The first 1,000 feet (305 m) of the climb is the only place that would necessitate the use of fixed rope both on the ascent and the descent. Ref. *AAJ* 1977, pp. 199-200. *CAJ* 1977, p. 67.

Northeast Ridge

The north side of Mt. Vancouver does not have a lot of good climbing routes. The one exception to this fact is the northeast ridge. The northeast ridge rises out of the great expanse of Hubbard Glacier on the far left corner of the north side of Mt. Vancouver. This ridge is a long, moderately steep route that rises gracefully up and to the left, ending at the true northern summit of Mt. Vancouver.

In the summer of 1975 a climbing party made the first ascent of this beautiful ridge. The first ascent team placed a good base camp at 4,800 feet (1,463 m) on Hubbard Glacier near the base of the northeast ridge. See photo 5D. From base camp the route to get onto the ridge goes through the obvious and active icefall that guards a large amphitheater on the south side of the northeast ridge. It is necessary to do some rather complicated route finding to get through this icefall, although the far left side of the icefall is the least broken portion of this area. Above the icefall a good level space on the glacier can be found at 7,100 feet (2,164 m) where a good site exists for Camp I.

The ridge is most easily accessed up 1,100 feet (335 m) of snow gullies found in a rocky buttress on the south side of the northeast ridge. Fixed line could be used here to facilitate carrying loads up this face as well as for the descent. Finally, a large level snow plateau is reached at 8,200 feet (2,499 m) on the ridge where Camp II can be placed.

Directly above Camp II and the large snow plateau is a moderately angled triangular rock face. The climbing on this face represents the crux of the technical climbing on the northeast ridge. *See CD photo (Chapter 1) CD-D11.* The best approach to climbing this triangular rock face is along its right-hand side. Some rock climbing is involved and some of the climbing is in snow gullies. It is useful to have some rock protection here such as medium-sized angle pitons or camming devices. The first ascent team ultimately fixed a line up the central gully of this 1,600 foot (488 m) rock face.

Above the triangular rock face the ridge becomes nearly level but narrows to a knife-edge. The knife-edge section is followed for about four rope lengths until the second step in the ridge is reached. *See CD photo (Chapter 1) CD-D11.* Placing fixed line on the knife-edge section will facilitate climbing on its left or south side.

The second step, which is directly above the knife-edge section, is the last steep section of climbing on this route. The best line through the second step is up the central snow gully of this face. This leads to easier climbing on a low angle and broad snow ridge. This ultimately reaches a prominent peak on the ridge at 10,600 feet (3,231 m). A good site for a camp can be found just beyond the peak at 10,600 and Camp III can be placed here.

The climbing above Camp III to the summit is on relatively easy terrain. The first ascent team encountered only one difficult ice pitch between Camp III and the summit. They made an early start and reached the summit from Camp III taking only bivouac equipment. This is a long day and entails 4,500 feet (1,372 m) of elevation gain. The climbing is fairly straightforward, however, and the summit can be reached fairly easily from Camp III.

This climb is of moderate technical difficulty. The crux of the climb is found in the triangular rock face immediately above Camp II. Fixed lines might be useful leading up to Camp II and on the triangular rock face as well as on the second step. The climb can be done in ten days and can be descended by the ascent route. Ref. *AAJ* 1976, pp. 462-463.

East Ridge

The eastern side of Mt. Vancouver is dominated by a large heavily sculpted amphitheater. A large active icefall leads out of Hubbard Glacier into this amphitheater. At the head of this voluminous amphitheater is the east ridge of Mt. Vancouver. This ridge is comprised of two parts. The lower section of the ridge is thin and steep. At mid-height

Photo 6D   Photo by Richard Holmes

on the east ridge the terrain broadens out to a wide, low angle slope that glides easily to the true northern summit of Mt. Vancouver.

A good base camp can be placed at 4,800 feet (1,463 m) on Hubbard Glacier. An active and glacier-wide icefall must be surmounted in order to enter the amphitheater. The icefall is less broken on its far left side. See photo 6D. Above the icefall the broad level plateau of the amphitheater is reached. A good camp can be placed at 7,300 feet (2,225 m) just below and to the right of the base of the east ridge. This area is out of the wind and is safe from avalanches.

The climb begins at the center of the base of the east ridge. The bergschrund must be crossed on a snow bridge on the right side. Low angle easy snow slopes lead up and left past a rock face and then back to the right. The snow face then leads up onto the crest of the east ridge at 8,000 feet (2,438 m). *See CD photo (Chapter 1) CD-D11.*

The crest of the ridge is very narrow and corniced in places. The knife-edge is followed for about four rope lengths until the ridge begins to steepen noticeably. The knife-edge section can be fixed with rope to secure transit along this section. Above the knife-edge section is the crux of the climbing. The ridge is still narrow and begins to rise to about 45 degrees in angle. The ridge then blends into a rock band which is mixed with snow. Fixed line can be secured along the left-hand side of the rock band to facilitate passage through this section.

Above the rock band the ridge broadens into a wide snow face and the angle relaxes dramatically. Further along the low angle snow face is a good level place to secure Camp II at about 10,000 feet (3,048 m). *See CD photo (Chapter 1) CD-D11.* The route above Camp II is also on a low angle snow face. The climbing is easy for several rope lengths until a large bergschrund is encountered. This bergschrund is most easily passed on a good snow bridge at its far left-hand side. The climb proceeds past the bergschrund up low angle snow slopes. A good level site in a basin is encountered at 11,500 feet (3,505 m). This is a good place to secure Camp III. See photo 6D.

The true summit of Mt. Vancouver can be reached in one day from Camp III. The ascent route is the easiest route of descent. Fixed line through the small rock band and up the knife-edge section of ridge will facilitate an easier descent. The climb is of moderate technical difficulty. As of this writing there are no published ascents of this climb.

Southeast Ridge
Clone Ridge

The most dominant feature on the east side of Mt. Vancouver is the long and gracefully curving mass of the southeast ridge. This is a long ridge rising out of the Hubbard Glacier and ending at Mt. Vancouver's south summit, Good Neighbor Peak. There are many steep and fluted aretes that fall away from the main southeast ridge. The first ascent party chose to climb the most direct of these aretes, the large headwall arete on the south face of the southeast ridge, to gain access to the ridge crest.

The southeast ridge is a long and challenging climb. It has significant elevation gain from base camp to the summit and is exposed to fairly constant wind from the south. There are narrow sections of ridge to be climbed as well as heavily corniced sections. The route is never extremely steep, not exceeding 45 degrees in angle in many places. Overall the southeast ridge is a good climbing challenge in an aesthetically pleasing location.

It is not clear how this ridge obtained its nickname, "Clone Ridge." It is uncertain whether this is in reference to the biochemical process of cloning or whether it has some other ephemeral meaning. However, since the name Clone Ridge does appear in the climbing literature its name will be cloned here as well.

The climb starts on a small crevassed feeder glacier off Hubbard Glacier. The beginning of the climb is accessed from the left-hand or south side of the southeast ridge. Base camp, at 7,000 feet (2,134 m), is made at the foot of the large and obvious headwall leading to the southeast ridge crest. *See CD photo (Chapter 1) CD-D13.*

The climb proceeds up the obvious rib, splitting the headwall buttress directly off the glacier above base camp. The headwall gradually leans back to more gentle snow covered slopes ending at the top of a small rounded snow dome. Camp I can be placed at 10,168 feet (3,099 m) and is set back from the crest of the ridge directly behind the snow dome. This location will protect the camp from the wind.

The route past Camp I traverses along a relatively level section of ridge. This section is heavily corniced and some of the climbing must be done on the steep slopes on the south side of the ridge. Fixed line along this section will not only facilitate the climbing but also the load carrying. Camp II is placed past the end of this corniced portion of the ridge beneath a large headwall. The section of ridge that is traversed to get to Camp II is a very difficult portion of the ridge; however, the ridge does not gain much altitude across this area. Camp II is placed at 10,000 feet (3,048 m) nestled into the snowbank at the base of the headwall that looms above it. See photo 7D.

The route above Camp II goes up a moderately steep headwall. The route stays on the ridge crest and to the right bypassing a small rock buttress on the left. The route continues up past seracs on a 45 degree snow and ice slope. The ridge finally becomes broader. Camp III is placed at 12,300 feet (3,749 m) on a broad section of ridge about 2,000 feet (610 m) below the top of the southeast buttress.

The route above Camp III is a long trudge through snow to reach a high camp

Photo 7D *Photo by Richard Holmes*

in a col at 15,000 feet (4,572 m), where Camp IV is placed. This high camp is in good striking distance to make a summit bid. *See CD photo (Chapter 1) CD-D14.* The route to the summit traverses up snow and ice slopes directly to the south summit of Mt. Vancouver's Good Neighbor Peak. From here one can descend or traverse the two miles (3.2 km) of nearly level snow slopes to reach the north summit which is only about 150 feet (46 m) higher than the south summit.

The ascent route can also be used for the descent. Fixed line will facilitate the descent down the headwall and back across the corniced section of ridge. The climb can be done in ten days. Some rock protection is useful on this route; however, one will need mostly snow and ice protection. Long snow pickets and half-length snow pickets are useful. Deadmen and deadboys are also very useful for securing fixed line. Ref. *AAJ* 1980, p. 532. *CAJ* 1980, pp. 85-85.

Southeast Ridge
North Rib Variation

The first ascent party selected the very obvious headwall buttress on the south face of the southeast ridge to gain access to the ridge crest. However, another significant rib joins the southeast ridge at the crest of the southeast buttress from the north. This is the north rib variation. This rib can be accessed off Hubbard Glacier on a small side glacier. Access is blocked by an active icefall which is just to the left/south of the icefall, which blocks the entrance into the amphitheater containing the east ridge.

Fortunately, there is a nice smooth snow ramp that glides gently between these two icefalls. A nice route can be followed up this ramp which goes up and left to the base of the north rib of the southeast ridge. At the head of this small side glacier there is an obvious low angle snow ridge which rises up to join the crest of the north rib. The climb begins on this low angle snow ridge. *See CD photo (Chapter 1) CD-D15.*

A good base camp can be placed at the head of the icefall. It should not be placed any higher in the cirque due to danger from avalanches from cornices that overhang the cirque. The low angle snow slope can be climbed to reach the crest of the north rib at 8,000 feet (2,438 m). There is a good rounded platform at this altitude with sufficient space to place a camp. Camp I can be placed at 8,000 feet (2,438 m) and all the supplies for the remainder of the climb can be brought up from base camp and stored here.

The route above Camp I starts out at a low angle. However, the ridge is very narrow here as well as being corniced. This narrow and corniced section is fairly short and rather quickly joins the main bulk of the mountain where the ridge begins to broaden. The angle also becomes steeper on the first two pitches. Above the first two steep pitches the rib broadens and averages 55 degrees in angle. The further the rib goes the more it broadens out into a rounded snow shoulder. Camp II can be placed at an obvious level spot on the rib at 10,000 feet (3,048 m).

The route above Camp II follows the rounded snow shoulder over constant 45 degree slopes. The route eventually reaches the crest of the southeast buttress at 14,300 feet (4,359 m). At this point the north rib variation joins the original first ascent route at the crest of the southeast buttress. The route to the summit of Good Neighbor Peak is the same as the first ascent party. As of this writing there are no recorded ascents of this rib.

Southeast Ridge
East Rib Variation

Further down the southeast ridge from the north rib is another variation to begin climbing the long and complex southeast ridge. This variation is the east rib route. This route can be reached from Hubbard Glacier where a good secure base camp can be placed. *See CD photo (Chapter 1) CD-D16.* Access to the start of this rib is also guarded by a small but heavily broken icefall. Fortunately, this icefall can be bypassed on its left side fairly easily.

The route past the icefall continues up easy snow slopes and eventually up an increasingly steep snow face. The route continues until it reaches the crest of the east rib at 8,000 feet (2,438 m). Here on a level spot is a good site for Camp I.

The route above Camp I ascends through a very broken snow face. Several seracs and two bergschrunds must be negotiated here to gain access to the upper slopes. The face is not very steep but somewhat unstable and climbing in the cold hours of the early morning will make ascending this slope easier.

Another set of bergschrunds must be bypassed higher up. Finally the slope eases back in angle and reaches the top of the headwall buttress that was climbed by the first ascent party from the opposite side. Camp II can be placed near the crest of this headwall at 10,168 feet (3,099 m). The remainder of the route to the summit of Good Neighbor Peak is the same as that described for the first ascent climb of the southeast ridge.

The Centennial Route

On the east-facing slopes of the south face of Mt. Vancouver is a large tongue of ice and snow. This ice face has one enjoyable, technically straightforward climb, the Centennial Route. This route was done in 1967 by a group of Americans and Canadians to celebrate the joint Centennial of the date of purchase of Alaska and the confederation of Canada. The Centennial Route is not technically difficult but it is a nice line up the otherwise difficult south face.

The Centennial Route can be reached from the head of the Valerie Glacier. See photo 8D. A good base camp can be placed on a level spot on the glacier. The approach

Photo 8D *Photo by Richard Holmes*

to the route winds up to the right around an icefall and reaches a shallow col at the base of the ridge at 9,200 feet (2,804 m). This is a convenient place to generate a supply dump for carrying loads higher on the ridge.

The route above the col leads over a shattered rock ridge. The ridge starts out horizontally but rises to be a little steeper near the end of the rock. This section is very narrow and becomes a knife-edge in some sections. It is not difficult and no fixed rope is really required here but it does take a little time to surmount this section. A good level spot for Camp I can eventually be found just beyond the rock ridge on top of a rounded snow dome at 10,300 feet (3,139 m). *See CD photo (Chapter 1) CD-D17.*

The route above Camp I is the steepest part of the climb. The route proceeds up a broad face initially but becomes narrower. An obvious ramp of snow and ice leads through the narrow section. This is a wild spot where the ridge falls off on both sides for several hundred feet. At the top of the narrow section a small bergschrund must be surmounted. This bergschrund can be passed most easily on the left side. The route then broadens out onto a wide snow shoulder. A good site can be found on a level spot for Camp II at 11,800 feet (3,597 m). *See CD photo (Chapter 1) CD-D18.*

Above Camp II the route consists of fairly easy climbing. The climb proceeds up an easy low angle snow and ice apron. A good spot for a camp can be found in a level place on the snow apron just below the crest of the southeast buttress at 14,000 feet (4,267 m) where Camp III is placed.

The route above Camp III follows the remaining 300 feet (91 m) to the crest of the southeast buttress. At this point the Centennial Route intersects the southeast ridge route. The remaining 1,400 feet (427 m) to the summit of Good Neighbor Peak follows the crest of the southeast ridge. Although this ridge is steep in places it is wide enough that difficult sections can be passed on one side or the other.

Photo 9D *Photo by Richard Holmes*

The ascent route can be descended and some fixed line should be placed lower on the climb in order to facilitate the passage over the bergschrunds. The route is not technically difficult but is very enjoyable and provides spectacular sweeping views of the great south face of Mt. Vancouver. This route provided the first ascent of Good Neighbor Peak and the second ascent of the true summit of Mt. Vancouver. Ref. *AAJ* 1968, pp. 36-42. *CAJ* 1968, pp. 34-41.

Centennial Route
Left Side

An interesting alternative to the Centennial Route is to begin the climb further to the left of the regular route. See photo 9D. To the left of the regular route is a small rounded rocky buttress that starts out fairly steep but has lower angle snow and ice climbing higher on the buttress.

The climb begins in a small indistinct couloir on the right-hand side at the base of the buttress. *See CD photo (Chapter 1) CD-D19.* This start will avoid the deep and wide bergschrund on the left side of the buttress. The route works up to the base of a snow face and this is climbed for several rope lengths until a very narrow snow bridge is encountered.

The snow bridge is climbed directly at its center. This bridge is surrounded on both sides by steep ice faces that fall away to the glacier below. Despite the fact that this snow bridge is narrow it is not too steep. Above this snow bridge the climbing becomes easier as the route opens onto a broad snow shoulder. A good site for Camp I can be placed on this level snow shoulder at about 11,000 feet (3,353 m). *See CD photo (Chapter 1) CD-D19.* The route above Camp I is then identical to the regular Centennial Route.

Centennial Route
Right Side

Another interesting and longer alternative to the start of the Centennial Route begins further to the right of the

Photo 10D   Photo by Richard Holmes

regular route. *See CD photo (Chapter 1) CD-D20*. This route begins above base camp in a small cirque below an icy face. The easiest approach to this route is to climb up a very obvious snow ramp directly at the head of the cirque. *See CD photo (Chapter 1) CD-D21*. This snow ramp will involve a little route finding and some small crevasses but the climbing is not difficult.

Above the snow ramp the climb widens onto a very gentle snow plateau. One bergschrund must be crossed on this plateau; however, there are numerous snow bridges that make passage across the bergschrund quite easy. The route continues past this bergschrund up the gentle broad snow slopes of this rounded shoulder until the route once again reaches a narrow point. A very easy snow ramp leads through this narrow point to reach easier snow slopes above. Just above the narrow passage is a good level spot to place Camp I at 10,500 feet (3,200 m).

Above Camp I the route traverses very easy low angle broad snow slopes for many rope lengths. Some crevasses are encountered along this stretch but they are easy to pass on one side or the other. The route eventually intersects the regular Centennial Route at Camp II at 11,800 feet (3,597 m). The route above Camp II is the same as for the regular Centennial Route.

The South Spur

The south side of Good Neighbor Peak is dominated by a massive triangular shaped rock face that rises 7,000 feet (2,134 m) out of the cirque at the head of the Valerie Glacier. There are three prominent ridges that split this face with the right-hand ridge being the south spur. See photo 10D.

The south spur is a long classic St. Elias Range climbing route. This route encompasses a sharp ridge, significant elevation gain, loose rock, snow and ice pitches coupled with a magnificent view in a beautiful and wild setting. This route is frequently done alpine style in two to four days. However, an expedition style approach will work just as well although some of the camp platforms are a little small.

The route begins in a snow gully on the left (west side) of the base of the spur. *See CD photo (Chapter 1) CD-D22.* This snow gully is climbed to reach the crest of the ridge. The route follows loose rock and snow over easy fourth and low fifth class climbing. A good camp can be placed at 10,500 feet (3,200 m) where the route becomes noticeably steeper. *See CD photo (Chapter 1) CD-D22.*

Above Camp I an easy snow gully is climbed on the right side of the ridge for many rope lengths until it re-emerges back onto the crest of the ridge just to the right of an obvious and massive hanging glacier. *See CD photo (Chapter 1) CD-D23.* From the top of the snow gully the route proceeds up a low angle face of snow and rock until it comes to the base of a steep rock step.

The best approach to avoid this steep section, which is comprised of loose rock, is to descend left onto snow slopes. These slopes lead to an obvious couloir that splits the arete. This couloir is climbed up onto easier snow slopes which end at the base of a knife-edge section of ridge. Here a good camp can be placed at 12,500 feet (3,810 m) to make Camp II.

Above Camp II the knife-edge ridge must be climbed directly. The typical approach to climbing any knife-edge ridge in the St. Elias Mountains is to climb below the cornice on the soft snow slopes. The anchors are usually poor with half-length snow pickets being the best anchors to use. Above the knife-edged section of ridge a few pitches of ice climbing lead onto the hanging glacier at the top of the spur. *See CD photo (Chapter 1) CD-D24.* A good camp can be placed at 14,300 feet (4,359 m) on the south spur itself.

Above Camp II the crest of the south spur can be followed to an obvious notch that leads through the "Rime Rolls" on the crest of the southeast ridge. From the crest of the southeast ridge a very short walk of 150 yards (137 m) leads to the summit of Good Neighbor Peak.

From the summit of Good Neighbor Peak the long traverse over to the true north summit can be made. From there a descent down the northwest ridge can be followed. Alternately, from the summit of Good Neighbor Peak, a descent down the snow slopes of the Centennial Route can be made very easily. The south spur involves a moderate degree of technical climbing difficulty. The route can be done in two to four days in an alpine style ascent. The climb can be done with an expedition style ascent in about one week. The climb requires rock protection and snow anchors as well as ice screws. Ref. *AAJ* 1994, pp.87-89.

Southwest Ridge

The second of the three prominent ridges that split the great south face of Mt. Vancouver is the southwest ridge. This is the prominent ridge that rises just left of the south spur route. See photo 11D. This is an exciting and moderately difficult route on a rock and ice ridge that ends directly at the summit of Good Neighbor Peak.

This ridge can be approached from two angles. The first and most direct approach is to ascend a col on the east face of the southwest ridge. *See CD photo (Chapter 1) CD-D25.* The path of this approach lies directly beneath a set of massive overhanging cornices. These cornices avalanche on occasion and they will bury anything below them. Therefore, it is important to spend as little time as possible on the approach to the col as well as doing this section in the coldest hours of the early morning.

The climb up the col is straightforward climbing on easy snow slopes. However, the snow in the col can be loose, so fixed line should be placed here. There is ample opportunity to obtain good rock placements for the fixed line. The approach from the east, just below the south spur route, is

Photo 11D *Photo by Richard Holmes*

the preferred approach. This col can be approached from the opposite side on its west face as well. However, this approach requires climbing on very unstable snow over loose and overhanging seracs. The first ascent team suffered a fatality on this section of the climb just below the col on the western approach. Therefore, the eastern approach is the preferred route and this approach leads to an obvious saddle where Camp I can be placed on a wide section of the ridge. The first ascent team placed a camp here at 10,175 feet (3,101 m).

The second approach to attain the southwest ridge is safer but longer. This approach climbs the buttress on the extreme southern end of the southwest ridge to reach the col at 10,175 feet (3,101 m). *See CD photo (Chapter 1) CD-D26.* This buttress can be climbed up an obvious snow face to reach a rocky outcrop. This blocky rock outcrop is climbed to reach the crest of the southwest ridge. A short section of narrow and horizontal ridge must then be traversed to reach the saddle where Camp I is placed.

The route above Camp I becomes fairly steep and ascends over mixed rock and snow. It is easiest to ascend by following the rock and ice interface on the left side of the ridge crest. The placement of some fixed rope along this section will make the ascent more secure. This ridge crest is climbed to a spot just beneath where a rocky buttress juts out. The first ascent team placed a camp here in a snow cave on the snow slopes on the left side of the ridge at 12,200 feet (3,719 m). A good snow cave at this spot is probably the best way to make a camp which is secure from avalanches and free from the wind and this is where Camp II is located. *See CD photo (Chapter 1) CD-D27.*

The route above Camp II climbs over the rocky protruding buttress. A small triangular snow face is climbed until it levels out at an obvious flat space where the next camp can be placed. The first ascent team placed Camp III here in a snow cave at 13,000 feet (3,962 m), which is only 800 feet (244 m) above Camp II.

The route above Camp III climbs over an interesting section of ridge that is knife-edged over most of its length. This section will require some fixed line to make it secure. The knife-edge section ends at the foot of a rock step. Below the rock step the ridge broadens a little and a good camp can be placed here at 14,000 feet (4,267 m) creating Camp IV.

The route from Camp IV first ascends the rocky buttress directly above the camp. The rock buttress gives way to a low angle snow face. The snow face is ascended until the ridge narrows again to a knife-edged section of snow and ice. This knife-edged section is followed until a prominent snow and ice face is encountered which leads through the "Rime Rolls" at the ridge crest. The southwest ridge ends almost directly at the summit of Good Neighbor Peak.

This route follows a beautiful ascent line directly to the summit of Good Neighbor Peak. The climb can be done alpine style in about three days. The first ascent team did an expedition style climb and used twelve days for the ascent. If fixed line is left in place the ascent route can then be descended. If the climb is done alpine style then the best descent route is down the Centennial Route. Ref. *AAJ* 1969, p. 382.

Southwest Buttress

The third and final prominent feature on the great south face of Mt. Vancouver is the southwest buttress. The lower half of this route involves climbing on a rock face and the gullies that split the face. Meanwhile the upper part of the route climbs a buttress and sharp ridge crest. *See CD photo (Chapter 1) CD-D28.*

The lower half of this climb is subject to extreme avalanche danger. Consequently, this climb cannot be done in an expedition style ascent which would subject the climber to prolonged periods in areas too prone to avalanches. Although this is a challenging route the only safe opportunity for success is to do a rapid alpine style ascent.

The climb begins at the base of the southwest buttress in a snow gully directly below the center of the face. *See CD photo (Chapter 1) CD-D29.* The route ascends this gully for several rope lengths and moves left onto a snow face. The snow face is climbed up and to the right to the base of a rocky buttress. A shallow indistinct gully leads up the left side of this rock buttress and emerges at the top of the buttress.

From the top of the buttress a snow face is climbed to reach a knife-edge ridge. This section can be climbed on its left side at the interface of snow and rock. This knife-edge section leads to the base of a rocky buttress where a bivouac can be found at 13,000 feet (3,962 m). This is the first safe place to bivouac on the lower part of the route. From this point on the avalanche danger is greatly diminished.

The climb from the bivouac leads directly up a snow gully that splits the rock buttress. *See CD photo (Chapter 1) CD-D30.* Near the top of the buttress the gully ends and some rock climbing must be done over a blocky face to reach a snow face. The snow face is climbed adjacent to the crest of the southwest buttress until it reaches the top of the southwest buttress. The climb ends only a short distance from the summit of Good Neighbor Peak.

This route has never been ascended. It has above-average objective danger due to avalanches. The best descent from the top of this climb is down the Centennial Route.

West Face

Directly below the true northern summit of Mt. Vancouver on the south side of the mountain is a long curving amphitheater of hanging glaciers, buttresses and seracs. In the middle of this amphitheater is a triangular buttress upon which the west face climbing route begins. *See CD photo (Chapter 1) CD-D31.*

A good base camp can be placed on Seward Glacier at a safe distance from the mountain. There are a lot of hanging glaciers on the west face of Mt. Vancouver that avalanche on occasion. These avalanches are large and cascade down the mountain and well out onto the glacier. Therefore, it is important to place base camp at a safe distance from the mountain.

The climb begins in the system of snow gullies on the right side at the base of the west face. *See CD photo (Chapter 1) CD-D32.* The gullies are generally filled with snow and have an average angle of 55 degrees. The first ascent party used 1,600 feet (488 m) of polypropylene fixed line and did a "rolling siege tactic" method of climbing. The rope was fixed up the snow gullies, loads were then carried up the ropes and the process was then repeated. Three stages of this method were used to ascend and exit out of the gullies onto a smooth snow face. A tent platform can be chopped out of the snow here to create Camp I at 11,500 feet (3,505 m).

The smooth snow face can be easily ascended. The angle of the climb begins to ease considerably at this point. A large rounded dome is encountered at the top of the snow face. This dome provides a good site to place a camp and Camp II can be established here at 12,300 feet (3,749 m).

The ridge above Camp II is narrow but not too steep. The ridge is corniced on the left and sits above slab avalanche slopes on the right. The climb treads carefully between these two sections just a little below the crest of the ridge. A small ice step is encountered at 13,000 feet (3,962 m). Some fixed rope will facilitate the ascent and the descent of this section.

Above the ice step the route opens onto a broad low angle snow face. This face is ascended for about 2,000 feet (610 m) until a short but steep ice wall is encountered at 15,000 feet (4,572 m). Below the base of the ice wall in a serac field is a large flat area where Camp III can be established.

The most difficult pitch of the climb is encountered on this ice wall. A fifty foot (15 m) section of overhanging rotten ice must be ascended to surmount the ice cliff. It is feasible to use direct aid with the shafts of ice axes and to use deadboys as anchors on this pitch. Once the ice wall is surmounted a few more rope lengths of moderately steep snow climbing up a snow headwall are required to reach the crest of the west face route. The climb to the true northern summit then follows the ridge crest from the top of the snow head wall to the summit.

The first ascent team climbed this route in an expedition style climb. The technique of rolling siege tactic climbing was very useful in the lower steeper gullies. A few other steep but short ice pitches needed to be fixed as well. The first ascent team needed twelve days for the ascent. The route is subject to some avalanche danger and is probably best climbed early in the season in the month of May. Ref. *AAJ* 1978, pp. 544-545. *CAJ* 1978, pp. 45-46.

West Buttress

The south side of Institute Peak protrudes out in a large complex rocky buttress. This buttress has several ridges leading up onto it and has many rock ramparts decorating its features. The complex multi-faceted face of the buttress gives it the appearance of a large cathedral. The west buttress is an enjoyable ascent that is not technically very difficult and it encompasses both rock and snow climbing. *See CD photo (Chapter 1) CD-D33.*

A secure base camp for this climb can be placed near the base of the buttress on Seward Glacier. *See CD photo (Chapter 1) CD-D34.* Towards the right side of the base of the buttress is a low angle rocky rib where the climb begins. This rib is ascended over easy fourth class rock climbing to reach a large flat platform where Camp I can be placed at 10,100 feet (3,078 m).

Rising above Camp I is a large smooth snow face leading to a rock tower. This rock tower is passed on its left side by traversing snow slopes which rise up and left of the tower. A narrow rocky ridge must first be ascended on the left side of the tower. This ridge is ascended directly upwards towards the top of the rock tower. However, just before reaching the top of the tower the route turns left onto easy low angle snow slopes, which bypass the summit of the rock tower. *See CD photo (Chapter 1) CD-D35.* Above the rock tower easy snow slopes are climbed to reach a large level shelf below a bergschrund where Camp II is placed at 12,100 feet (3,688 m).

The bergschrund can be passed on its right side over good snow bridges. *See CD photo (Chapter 1) CD-D36.* An easy snow ramp is followed to the top of Institute Peak at 13,150 feet (4,008 m) where Camp III can be placed. The route from Camp III to the true northern summit follows the same route as described for the northwest ridge route. The west buttress route and the northwest ridge route merge at the summit of Institute Peak. The west buttress route can be descended easily.

The west buttress has no recorded ascents. The climb is fairly straight forward involving fourth class climbing and easy snow ramps. Some of the sections of ridge traversing the rock tower above Camp I are fairly exposed to a large drop off on either side of the ridge. This yields some very enjoyable scenic climbing in an exposed and beautiful setting.

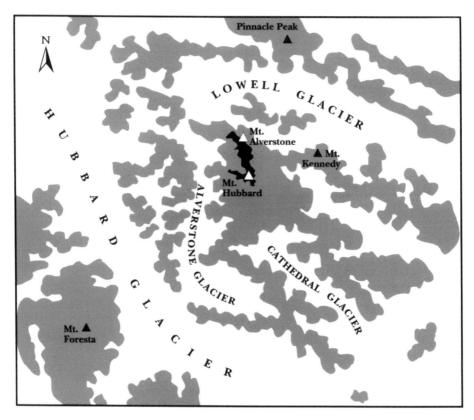

The Kennedy Group

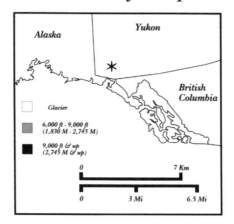

CHAPTER 2

THE KENNEDY GROUP

Introduction

The Kennedy Massif is a group of beautiful mountains which straddle the Canadian-Alaska border on the eastern corner of the St. Elias Mountains. These mountains are part of a rectangular plateau which measures roughly 15 miles (24 km) long and 12 miles (19 km) wide. This entire plateau is glaciated with the upper end of the plateau containing the summits of the main peaks in this range: Mt. Kennedy, Mt. Hubbard and Mt. Alverstone. The plateau slopes downwards from north to south with the foot of the Cathedral Glacier being at the southern terminus.

This massif provides enormous opportunities for climbs covering all conceivable technical possibilities. There are long, serrated rock ridges and easy snow faces. Some of the most difficult ice climbing in the entire St. Elias Range can be found here in the Kennedy Group. However, there are also routes involving easy glacier travel. Consequently, climbers of all skill levels will find something to match their interest in the Kennedy Group. There is also the very unique glacier system comprised of the Cathedral Glacier. This ten mile (16 km) long glacier provides easy access to the foot of the summit pyramids of the three largest peaks in this range. Consequently, from one high camp, all three summits can easily be ascended.

The peaks are not very high by St. Elias standards but the elevation gain is significant. The western escarpment of Mt. Hubbard and Mt. Alverstone rises 7,500 feet (2,286 m) out of Alverstone Glacier. The uniquely spectacular north ridge of Mt. Kennedy also ascends a beautiful and highly aesthetic 7,000 feet (2,134 m) out of Lowell Glacier to reach its pyramidal snowcapped summit. As a result the north ridge of Mt. Kennedy is one of the most challenging and rewarding climbs in the entire St. Elias Mountain Range.

Considering all of the parameters that are displayed by the Kennedy Massif, including moderate elevation and variety in routes, this group displays one of the richest places to climb in the Wrangell-St. Elias Mountain Range.

Mt. Hubbard
15,015 feet (4,577 m)

Mt. Hubbard was named after the Catholic priest, Father Bernard Hubbard, the Indiana Jones of Alaska. He led annual expeditions to Alaska and the Yukon from the late 1920's through the early 1950's. He ultimately developed the nickname, "the Glacier Priest" as a result of his exploits.

Photo 1E *Photo by Richard Holmes*

Bernard Hubbard would ultimately shoot over 700,000 feet of motion pictures as well as several thousand still photos. He would begin each day with prayer and mass and then proceed to shoulder his one hundred-pound load for the day's adventure. He helped introduce the world to the splendor of the far north.

Mt. Hubbard anchors the southwest corner of the Kennedy Massif. Mt. Hubbard is a mountain which displays two types of climbing options. The east side of the mountain can be approached by the Cathedral Glacier and as such the routes are generally low angle snow climbs. Many interesting snow ridges can be ascended on the east side and the climbing is never too severe.

The west side of Mt. Hubbard is characterized by the massive western escarpment that comprises the west face of both Mt. Hubbard and Mt. Alverstone. This 7,500 foot (2,286 m) rock and ice face is split by several long sinuous ridges which rise to the summit plateau. The western escarpment provides some of the most magnificent and challenging climbing routes found anywhere in the St. Elias Mountain Range.

The United States map to this region is USGS Mt. St. Elias Alaska-Canada, scale 1:250,000. The Canadian maps are: Mt. Alverstone 115 B/6, scale 1:50,000, Mt. Kennedy 115 B/7, scale 1:50,000, Mt. Seattle 115 B/3, scale 1:50,000 and Ulu Mountain 115 B/2, scale 1:50,000.

Cathedral Glacier

The first ascent of Mt. Hubbard was done in the summer of 1951 with an expedition led by the ubiquitous Colonel Walter Wood. This expedition was funded by the Arctic Institute of North America. The expedition performed glaciological studies in the St. Elias Mountains as well as undertaking climbing objectives in the Mt. Kennedy Group. The mountain of prime interest to this expedition was the previously unclimbed Mt. Hubbard.

Mt. Hubbard is the tallest mountain in the Kennedy Massif and has many potentially interesting climbing routes. See photo 1E. The expedition led by Colonel Walter Wood endeavored to climb Mt. Hubbard by way of the Cathedral Glacier route. The Cathedral Glacier is a true alpine glacier measuring up to the extreme standards of the St. Elias Range. Cathedral Glacier is nearly ten miles (16 km) long and becomes as wide as 2.5 miles (4 km). *See CD photo (Chapter 2) CD-E01.*

Cathedral Glacier conveniently runs from its intersection at the South Lowell Glacier some ten miles into a high basin that sits in a spectacular col centered beneath the three main peaks of the Kennedy Massif: Mt. Hubbard, Mt. Alverstone and Mt. Kennedy. Therefore the Cathedral Glacier route provides the easiest means to reach the summit of all three main peaks in the Kennedy Massif. It was this glacier route that attracted the 1951 expedition to pioneer the first ascent of Mt. Hubbard.

The Cathedral Glacier route is easily reached from its intersection with the South Lowell Glacier at 4,500 feet (1,372 m). *See CD photo (Chapter 2) CD-E02.* This base camp can be easily reached by ski plane or helicopter. The route proceeds up the smooth surface of the glacier, passing one low angle icefall to reach Camp I at 8,500 feet (2,591 m). *See CD photo (Chapter 2) CD-E03.*

The route immediately above Camp I encounters the crux of the climb which is a heavily broken icefall. The icefall can be surmounted with some route finding. Bamboo wands should be placed throughout the icefall to facilitate the ascent and the descent particularly if the weather turns bad during the descent. *See CD photo (Chapter 2) CD-E04.*

The route continues up the smooth glacier until a second icefall is encountered at 12,500 feet (3,810 m). This second icefall is not as heavily broken as the first and can be easily surmounted on its left side. The route above the second icefall reaches the high col below the summit pyramids of all of the main peaks in the Kennedy Massif. A site can be found on this high plateau to establish Camp II at 13,100 feet (3,993 m), from which the summit attempts can be launched. *See CD photo (Chapter 2) CD-E05.*

The first ascent party climbed the obvious snow face of the northeast side of Mt. Hubbard. A few rope lengths below the true summit is reached, the route levels out onto a ridge. The ridge can be climbed to the left to reach the summit of East Hubbard which rises to 14,450 feet (4,404 m). The ridge can be climbed to its conclusion by climbing along the right side of the ridge to reach the true summit of Mt. Hubbard. *See CD photo (Chapter 2) CD-E06.*

This is an easy glacier ascent route. However, it is long and significant elevation gain is encountered. Snow shovels should be brought along for use in digging snow platforms and building snow walls at the high camp. The climb will require the use of many bamboo wands with good visible flags to wand routes through the icefalls. Wands will facilitate the descent through the icefalls as well as down the otherwise featureless glacier in bad weather. This was the route climbed by the first ascent party of 1951. Ref. *AAJ* 1952, pp. 227-236. *CAJ* 1952, pp. 5-11.

South Face

A very interesting alternative to the classical Cathedral Glacier route is the south face of Mt. Hubbard. See photo 2E. The start to the south face of Mt. Hubbard begins in an identical fashion as the normal Cathedral Glacier route. Cathedral Glacier is followed until the climb bypasses the first small icefall on its left side. Camp I can be placed on a level part of the glacier above the icefall at 7,100 feet (2,164 m).

The route from Camp I proceeds to

Photo 2E *Photo by Richard Holmes*

Photo 3E   *Photo by Richard Holmes*

the left on an obvious small feeder glacier. The route at this point goes through a small icefall with very wide crevasses. The route goes through the crevasse field starting out on the right side and then goes diagonally back to the left, which will avoid the largest crevasses. Above the crevasse field is a small level plateau. A good site can be found on this plateau for Camp II, which can be placed at 10,500 feet (3,200 m). *See CD photo (Chapter 2) CD-E07.*

Above Camp II there exist two possible alternatives to reach the upper plateau at the base of the summit pyramid. The first alternative is to climb a very narrow rock and snow covered ridge. The route follows the crest of this very narrow ridge which falls away sharply on both sides. *See CD photo (Chapter 2) CD-E08.*

The second alternative is technically easier but more precarious. This alternative follows the obvious snow face leading to the upper plateau. This snow face is an active avalanche zone and should only be climbed during the cold hours of the early morning. A very easy route can be climbed up the left side of this snow face. Both alternatives lead to the upper plateau where a good site can be found for Camp III at 13,000 feet (3,962 m). *See CD photo (Chapter 2) CD-E09.*

From Camp III the route follows the obvious ridge up the southwest corner of the summit pyramid of Mt. Hubbard. The ridge begins at an angle of 45 degrees and is usually comprised of snow over a layer of hard ice. The angle of the ridge decreases as it ascends until it finally terminates at the summit of Mt. Hubbard. *See CD photos (Chapter 2) CD-E09 and CD-E10.* The ascent route can be used for the descent. As of this writing there are no recorded ascents of this route.

South Buttress

There exists another interesting and unclimbed route on the south face of Mt. Hubbard. This route is the south buttress. This large rock buttress has a well-defined rib running down the center of it which provides an excellent route for climbing. *See CD photo (Chapter 2) CD-E11.* This route begins in the same location as does the standard Cathedral Glacier route. The route passes the first icefall on its left and Camp I can be placed at 7,100 feet (2,164 m). The route then proceeds up to the small feeder glacier as described for the south face route and Camp II is established on a small platform at 10,000 feet (3,048 m).

The route from Camp II then drops down a small snow shoulder to a level plateau below the base of the rock rib that splits the face of the south buttress. *See CD photo (Chapter 2) CD-E12.* The route then ascends this rock rib over its length to reach the high plateau at the base of the summit pyramid. The rib is narrow at its base but eventually widens to a more blocky rib at mid-height. The upper part of the rib widens onto a rocky face, which is split by a snow couloir. This couloir can be climbed to the top of the face and over the ice cap which rings the top of this buttress. The high plateau at the base of the summit pyramid is a good spot for Camp III at 13,000 feet (3,962 m). The climbing to the summit follows the same summit ridge as that described for the south face route.

This route is of moderate technical difficulty. However, the technical difficulties are encountered only on the rib splitting the face of the south buttress. Fixed rope can be used on the rock rib to facilitate the descent. The ascent route can be descended if fixed rope is used. Alternatively, the south face route can be descended. As of this writing there are no recorded ascents of the south buttress route. This would make an excellent alpine style ascent.

Southwest Ridge

The great western escarpment of the Hubbard-Alverstone Massif rises some 7,500 feet (2,286 m) out of the Alverstone Glacier. The extreme southwest corner of this great escarpment is punctuated by a rocky leftward curving ridge, which is known as the southwest ridge. This route was first climbed in the summer of 1973 along its ridge crest. This is a challenging climb over rock and ice over a ridge that becomes precariously narrow in several places. See photo 3E.

The route begins directly off the Alverstone Glacier on the north side of the ridge. The route proceeds up easy snow slopes to reach the crest of the col on the ridge crest. *See CD photo (Chapter 2) CD-E13.* The route then continues up a moderate angle rock and snow ridge which levels out into another col at 8,300 feet (2,530 m). A good spot can be found here to establish Camp I. *See CD photo (Chapter 2) CD-E14.*

The route proceeds up the crest of the southwest ridge above Camp I generally staying to the left, north side of the ridge. The north side of the ridge facilitates climbing on firm snow and avoids the jagged rocks on the south side of the ridge. The route proceeds until it reaches the top of a small rounded snow dome at 10,000 feet (3,048 m). A good site can be found to establish Camp II here. *See CD photo (Chapter 2) CD-E14.*

The route proceeds beyond Camp II over a snow covered ridge and follows the ridge crest on its left side. The ridge is not very steep along this section and does not gain much altitude. This section of the ridge proceeds until it comes to the base of the steepest part of the ridge, which rises sharply. A good place can be found at the base of the steep section of the ridge at 11,000 feet (3,353 m) to establish Camp III. *See CD photo (Chapter 2) CD-E14.*

The next 2,000 feet (610 m) above Camp III is the crux of the climb. The climb above Camp III follows a narrow section of ridge for a few rope lengths. The ridge then rises sharply and the ridge is followed along its crest.

At the halfway point on this steep section a snow gully can be followed on the right

Photo 4E *Photo by Richard Holmes*

side of the ridge. This bypasses a steep rotten pillar of rock. The snow couloir is followed until it intersects a wide snow face near the top of the steep part of the ridge. *See CD photo (Chapter 2) CD-E15.* The ridge then becomes narrow again for a few rope lengths until it reaches the high plateau at 13,000 feet (3,962 m). A good site for Camp IV can be established here.

The route up the summit pyramid is the same as that for the south buttress and the south face routes. The obvious ridge in the middle of the south face of the summit pyramid is followed to reach the summit. The southwest ridge was first climbed in the summer of 1973. This climb is a moderately difficult route technically. The steepest part of the ridge can be secured with fixed line to facilitate the ease of the descent. Rock protection will be needed on this route including medium and large angle pitons. The use of camming devices will also be helpful for protection. The snow protection will require full and half-length pickets as well as deadmen and deadboys. Ref. *AAJ* 1974, p. 139. *Climbing Magazine* Sept/Oct, 1973, pp. 20-27.

West Ridge
Central Pillar, Left Side

The great western escarpment of Mt. Hubbard-Alverstone is one of the great geologic features of the St. Elias Mountains. This spectacular wall of rock and ice has two long and challenging ridges which rise out of the Alverstone Glacier to reach the summit of Mt. Hubbard. See photo 4E.

The west ridge central pillar route was first ascended in the summer of 1973. There are two prongs at the base of the central pillar which rise up to meet at 10,000 feet (3,048 m). The first ascent team chose to climb the left prong of the central pillar to begin their climb. The left prong can be ascended at its base through an easy snow gully. *See CD photo (Chapter 2) CD-E16.*

The climb up the snow gully leads to the ridge crest several rope lengths higher.

The ridge crest is followed over snow and some exposed rock until a good platform is found at the base of a rock face. Here on this platform at 9,700 feet (2,957 m), is a good site to establish Camp I. *See CD photo (Chapter 2) CD-E16.* This location is exposed to the winds from the south. A strong, well equipped Italian climbing party had their tent and supplies blown off the ridge at this point in 1970. A good tent platform with snow walls should be able to prevent this difficulty from happening to future expeditions.

The climb from Camp I becomes very steep and ascends a lot of rock pillars. The next 1,500 feet (457 m) is the crux of the climb. The climb above Camp I begins on a pillar's steep face. The climb ascends the snow and ice which covers the broken rock. This section will require ice as well as rock protection. Fixed line should be used on this section to facilitate the descent. *See CD photo (Chapter 2) CD-E17.*

The route proceeds over and around some very distinctive black diorite pillars, which are clearly visible from base camp on Alverstone Glacier. Above the black pillars the route encounters some blue ice with a sixty degree angle. After this short section of ice the route proceeds into a small and rounded snow bowl at the base of a vertical pink orthoclase rock face at 10,000 feet (3,048 m). This vertical rock face is where the rock begins to change composition. At this point, the crumbly black diorite rock gives way to more solid granite, which is also found on the north side of the Kennedy Massif.

The vertical rock face, which is now encountered on the route, is the technical crux of the entire ridge. This section can be free climbed for most of its length with a small section of aid required to surmount some difficult moves. The first ascent team rated this crux section 5.6, A1.

The climb above the vertical face reaches the top of a well-defined rock pinnacle on the crest of the ridge. The route drops down from this pinnacle into a col where a good campsite can be found. In this level col at 11,100 feet (3,383 m) is a good place to establish Camp II. *See CD photo (Chapter 2) CD-E18.*

From Camp II the climb switches back to mostly snow and ice climbing. A short rock buttress is ascended to reach a snow and ice ridge. This narrow ice ridge is ascended to a point just below where the crevasse fields of the upper face begin. The first ascent party made a summit bid from Camp II. However, this required an open bivouac. A safer alternative would be to place a camp at a good spot at the end of the exposed rock, just below the beginning of the crevasse field. This spot at 13,000 feet (3,962 m) would be a good spot to establish Camp III and would be a perfect location from which to make a summit bid. *See CD photo (Chapter 2) CD-E19.*

Above the exposed rock section, the climb enters hanging serac and crevasse fields on the upper west face. The route winds through this morass of ice and crevasses to reach the summit plateau about 500 feet (152 m) below the summit pyramid of Mt. Hubbard. The climb to the summit ascends the snow covered north face of the summit pyramid.

The ascent route can be descended if fixed rope is left in place. This route is a moderately difficult technical route on a large and beautiful rock and ice escarpment. The climbing is rated 5.6, A1. The route will require about fifty pitons ranging in size from small knife-blades to large four-inch angles. An assortment of nuts and camming devices will also be useful here. The usual snow and ice protection of full-length as well as half-length snow pickets are also required. Deadmen and deadboys should also be available for use. Ref. *AAJ* 1974, pp. 28-30. *CAJ* 1974, pp. 15-17.

Photo 5E
Photo by Richard Holmes

West Ridge
Central Pillar Right Side

An interesting alternative to the left prong of the west ridge central pillar is to initiate the climb on the right-hand prong. *See CD photo (Chapter 2) CD-E20.* This alternative is more of a rock climb than the left prong. The two routes meet near the crux of the entire ridge at the base of the vertical pink orthoclase rock face at 10,000 feet (3,048 m). The lower portion of the right prong is somewhat steeper than the left prong and involves more rock climbing.

The right prong can be ascended from its base on the right side through some easy snow gullies. The snow slopes are followed until they intersect with the ridge crest. The narrow ridge crest is followed over rock and ice until it begins to level out. This level section of ridge at 8,300 feet (2,530 m) is a good spot to locate Camp I. *See CD photo (Chapter 2) CD-E20.*

The route above Camp I becomes really interesting. The climb ascends a rock face for several rope lengths until a level bench is reached. Above this bench a long series of moderately steep ice gullies and rock faces are ascended. The route then proceeds up a wide but very steep rock face which is generally free of snow until another bench is reached.

The next section above the bench follows the ridge crest, which still averages 55 degrees in angle and is also quite narrow. The narrow section of ridge ends in a deep couloir at the base of the prominent pinnacle, which is on the main ridge crest. This area at the base of the couloir may be the only place on this section of ridge in which to secure a good camp. Camp II can be located at 9,800 feet (2,987 m) back in the depths of this well-shaded couloir. *See CD photo (Chapter 2) CD-E21.*

The route above Camp II follows steep ice pitches in the back of the deep couloir until the couloir intersects with the black diorite pillars which are encountered on the main ridge crest. Once the black pillars have been surmounted the crux of the climb is encountered on the 500 foot (152 m) vertical rock face. Above the vertical rock face the level col is encountered at 11,000 feet (3,353 m) where a good camp can be located. The remainder of the climb is the same as described for the west ridge central pillar left side route.

As of this writing there have been no recorded ascents of the right-hand prong to the west ridge central pillar route. This approach is probably more difficult than the left prong approach as it involves more rock climbing over difficult gendarmes and more steep ice pitches. The protection that is needed for fixing rope is the same as that described for the left prong approach.

West Ridge Left Pillar

On the great western escarpment of the west face of Mt. Hubbard-Alverstone are two spectacular ridges which split the face. The first is the west face central pillar, which was first climbed in the summer of 1973 and the second is the more northerly of the two, the west ridge left pillar. The left pillar was first climbed in the summer of 1977. The first ascent team made an alpine ascent of this route with one bivouac. See photo 5E.

The climb begins off the Alverstone Glacier at the foot of the ridge on its right, south side. The ridge crest can be reached by climbing easy snow slopes. *See CD photo (Chapter 2) CD-E22.* The route proceeds along the narrow and sometimes corniced ice covered ridge. The ridge does not gain much altitude at the beginning as it proceeds over and around a few rock gendarmes.

Eventually, the rock ends and the ridge blends into the west face. The route becomes progressively steeper and involves snow and ice climbing. At the base of the steep snow face at 11,000 feet (3,353 m) the ridge is broad enough to dig out a tent platform This site is a good location for Camp I.

Above Camp I the route goes up the steep snow face, which is relatively free of crevasses. The climbing in this section can be done fairly quickly. The route proceeds to the right side of the face and goes directly up towards an obvious couloir at the top of the snow face. *See CD photo (Chapter 2) CD-E23.* The face starts out at an angle of 35 degrees and ends at 55 degrees. The steepest part of the exit couloir is sixty degrees.

The route then proceeds across the level summit plateau to the base of the summit pyramid of Mt. Hubbard. The summit pyramid is climbed via the easy north ridge.

If this route is done in an alpine ascent it is most easily descended by the Cathedral Glacier route. If fixed ropes are left in place it can easily be descended on a rappel. Some rock protection is needed for the lower section. An assortment of 25 ice screws, snow pickets and deadmen will be needed for the upper section of snow and ice. Ref. *AAJ* 1997, p. 200.

Mt. Alverstone
14,565 feet (4,439 m)

Mt. Alverstone anchors the northwest corner of the Kennedy Massif. Mt. Alverstone was named after the British Lord Chief Justice, Viscount Alverstone, who helped fix Alaska's boundaries in 1903. Mt. Alverstone can be approached from three sides and as such offers a wide variety of climbing opportunities. The east side can be approached via the Cathedral Glacier. The routes on the east side are therefore relatively straightforward glacier routes.

The west face of Mt. Alverstone is comprised of the great western escarpment of Mt. Alverstone-Hubbard. The west face of Mt. Alverstone is split by one ridge, the west ridge. This 7,500 foot (2,286 m) high ridge offers excellent and technically demanding climbing opportunities. Additionally, there is an outcrop of beautiful granite below and to the north of the great west face of Mt. Alverstone at Point Blanchard. This outcrop is a very unique formation. There is not only excellent granite for rock climbing here but because of the deeply shaded couloirs on Point Blanchard, some of the best ice climbing in the St. Elias Range can be found here as well.

The north side of Mt. Alverstone is composed of snow faces and ice ridges. There are several routes on the north side of moderate technical difficulty. Consequently, there are interesting and challenging routes found on all sides of this beautiful and splendid mountain.

The United States map to this region is USGS Mt. St. Elias Alaska-Canada, scale 1:250,000. The Canadian maps are: Mt. Alverstone 115 B/6, scale 1:50,000, Mt. Kennedy 115 B/7, scale 1:50,000, Mt. Seattle 115 B/3 1:50,000 and Ulu Mountain 115 B/2, scale 1:50,000.

Cathedral Glacier

The first ascent of Mt. Alverstone was done in the summer of 1951 by the expedition led by Colonel Walter Wood. This expedition used the Cathedral Glacier route to establish a high camp in the basin at the foot of the summit pyramids of Mt. Hubbard and Mt. Alverstone. The climbers proceeded to climb Mt. Alverstone from their high camp on the plateau just below the summit.

The expedition entered the Cathedral Glacier at its junction with the South Lowell Glacier. *See CD photo (Chapter 2) CD-F01.* The route passes one small crevasse field on its left. The route proceeds to 8,500 feet (2,591 m) on the glacier where Camp I was established. The crux of the climb is directly above Camp I where an icefall with wide crevasses must be negotiated. *See CD photo (Chapter 2) CD-F02.*

The route above the crux icefall follows the glacier until a second icefall is encountered at 12,500 feet (3,810 m). This icefall is not as large or as heavily crevassed as the first icefall and is easily surmounted. The route above the second icefall leads to the high plateau just below the summit pyramids of Mt. Hubbard and Mt. Alverstone. A good site can be found here to establish Camp II at 13,100 feet (3,993 m) from which the summit attempt can be initiated. *See CD photo (Chapter 2) CD-F03.*

There are two ridges, the south and the northeast summit ridges, that extend down from the summit of Mt. Alverstone to the high plateau. Both of these ridges are about the same in terms of technical difficulty. The first ascent team chose to climb the northeast summit ridge. This approach is somewhat less steep than the south summit ridge and avoids a tricky section of rock climbing found at the base of the south summit ridge.

The northeast summit ridge begins on some low angle rocks. After ascending the rocks a short section of ice is encountered which reaches an angle of forty degrees. After the ice is surmounted the remainder of the distance to the summit is over a broad low angle snow shoulder. The ascent route up Cathedral Glacier can be used for the descent. This is not a technically difficult climb but elevation gain and weather conditions make it a serious yet enjoyable undertaking. Ref. *AAJ* 1952, pp. 227-236. *CAJ* 1952, pp. 5-11.

West Ridge

The west face of Mt. Alverstone is split by one long imposing 7,500 foot (2,286 m) rock and ice covered ridge. This ridge is similar to the west ridges of Mt. Hubbard in that it involves a great deal of rock climbing as well as snow and ice climbing over snow covered rock bands. This spectacular ridge was first climbed in an alpine style ascent in the summer of 1995.

The west ridge of Mt. Alverstone can be accessed through a snow couloir, which is found some distance up the small feeder glacier at the base of the west face, on the right-hand side of the west ridge. *See CD photo (Chapter 2) CD-F04*. This couloir is climbed to its head at the base of a rock face. A good sheltered spot can be found here at 9,500 feet (2,896 m) to establish Camp I. The route above Camp I proceeds up and to the right through a second rock couloir. *See CD photo (Chapter 2) CD-F05*. This second couloir is considerably more narrow than the first couloir and is comprised of ice and rock. This couloir is ascended until it reaches a snow covered rock band that is most easily ascended in a right facing dihedral on the left side of the rock face. *See CD photo (Chapter 2) CD-F05*.

The rock band can be ascended through a dihedral which leads to a low angle snow face. The upper part of the snow face has a good spot at 12,500 feet (3,810 m) where Camp II can be located. The summit can be reached in a single day from Camp II. The route above Camp II follows a narrow snow covered rock ridge for several rope lengths. The top of the west ridge ultimately blends into the north ridge of Mt. Alverstone. This broad snow covered north ridge can be followed the remainder of the distance up the summit pyramid of Mt. Alverstone to reach the top.

The route can be descended if fixed rope is left in place. If the climb is done in an alpine style ascent the Cathedral Glacier can be used as the descent route. The first ascent team descended the northeast face route to reach the head of the Lowell Glacier. An expedition will need an assortment of fifty pitons and camming devices to fix ropes. Full-length and half-length pickets are useful for snow and ice protection as well as ice screws, deadmen and deadboys. Ref. *AAJ* 1996, p. 188. *Rock and Ice* Vol. 69 Sept/Oct, 1995, p. 28.

Northwest Ridge

A very enjoyable route with only moderate technical difficulty is the northwest ridge. *See CD photo (Chapter 2) CD-F06*. This route begins at the head of Alverstone Glacier. The route proceeds up easy snow slopes onto a snow dome. *See CD photo (Chapter 2) CD-F07*. The route proceeds across the northern side of the snow dome over easy snow slopes until a level spot for Camp I can be established at 12,500 feet (3,810 m).

The route beyond Camp I proceeds over a snow crested ridge which becomes progressively more narrow as it proceeds. *See CD photo (Chapter 2) CD-F08*. The ridge proceeds over a small sub-peak and continues towards the north face of Mt. Alverstone. *See CD photo (Chapter 2) CD-F09*. The ridge eventually becomes broader as it approaches the north face of Mt. Alverstone. A good spot for Camp II can be established at 13,000 feet (3,962 m) at the base of the summit pyramid of Mt. Alverstone. *See CD photo (Chapter 2) CD-10F*.

The route from Camp II to the summit ascends the smooth snow face on the right-hand side of the summit pyramid. *See CD photo (Chapter 2) CD-F10*. Eventually this face ends directly at the summit of Mt. Alverstone. As of this writing there are no recorded ascents of this route. The ascent route can be used as the descent route. A good selection of snow pickets and deadmen can be used to fix rope along the crested ridge between Camp I and Camp II.

North Ridge

An interesting and easier alternative to the northwest ridge route is to climb the north ridge. These two routes intersect at mid-height on the mountain and the north ridge route presents very few technical difficulties. The north ridge can be accessed from the head of Lowell Glacier on the north side of Mt. Alverstone. *See CD photo (Chapter 2) CD-F11*. This route proceeds up a low angle snow slope to gain the crest of the northwest ridge where the north ridge and northwest ridge routes intersect.

The narrow and sometimes corniced ridge is followed until the route reaches the base of the summit pyramid. A good camp can be established at the base of the summit pyramid. The route to the summit follows the right-hand side of the snow face of the summit pyramid to reach the summit of Mt. Alverstone. As of this writing there are no recorded ascents of this route.

Northeast Ridge

The second ascent of Mt. Alverstone was done via the northeast face. This route is a variation of the north ridge route. The northeast face route can be ascended from a side branch of the Lowell Glacier below the north face of Mt. Kennedy. *See CD photo (Chapter 2) CD-F12.* The route climbs a steep buttress on its right-hand side up a face of blue ice for about four rope lengths. This buttress reaches a shelf below Mt. Alverstone. This shelf is overhung by many hanging seracs and ice cliffs. Consequently, it is wise to climb across this shelf during the coldest hours of the early morning and to make this traverse as rapidly as possible. The shelf ends at the base of the summit pyramid of Mt. Alverstone where a good camp can be placed. *See CD photo (Chapter 2) CD-F13.* The route above the camp ascends to the summit of Mt. Alverstone by climbing the right-hand side of the summit pyramid. Ref. *AAJ* 1967, pp. 363-364. *CAJ* 1967, pp. 57-58.

Point Blanchard

Located at the head of the Alverstone Glacier, below the western escarpment of Mt. Alverstone, is a granite outcrop known as Point Blanchard. This area provides quite a variation from the usual climbs of the St. Elias Mountain Range. Point Blanchard contains an outcrop of good solid granite perforated by deep couloirs. The couloirs contain solid sheets of steep ice. Consequently, some of the best technical rock climbing and steep ice climbing can be found at Point Blanchard. *See CD photo (Chapter 2) CD-F14.*

Point Blanchard Central Pillar Pugilist at Rest

In the exact center of the granite outcropping of Point Blanchard is the central pillar route. This long beautiful granite buttress was first climbed in the summer of 1998. The route follows the crest of the longest ridge in the center of Point Blanchard. *See CD photo (Chapter 2) CD-15F.* The route is 3,000 feet (914 m) long and ascends mixed rock and ice. The route can be descended by rappel or via the northwest ridge, which provides easy down climbing. The first ascent team rated this climb 5.10, A3, M5. Climbing protection should contain a large assortment of camming devices and some small angle pitons, which fit nicely into the frost shattered rock. Ref. *AAJ* 1999, pp. 265-267. *Climbing Magazine* Nov. 1998, p. 27.

Wilford Couloir

Just to the left of the Pugilist at Rest route is a deep and permanently shaded couloir. Inside this couloir is solid and very steep ice. This couloir was also first ascended in the summer of 1998. The route involves a lot of ice climbing with some rock climbing. The route can be descended from the top of the couloir, which is 2,700 feet (823 m) long. Alternatively, the remainder of the face can be climbed by joining the Pugilist at Rest route by climbing a short snow face to gain the ridge crest. *See CD photo (Chapter 2) CD-F16.* The first ascent team rated the climb 5.9, M4, WI5. The climbing protection should contain a large rack of ice screws and some camming devices as well as some small pitons for rock protection. Ref. *AAJ* 1999, pp. 265-267.

Point Blanchard Left Pillar

Another granite outcropping of significant size and value exists about 500 feet (152 m) to the left of the Pugilist at Rest route. This is the Point Blanchard Left Pillar climbing route. *See CD photo (Chapter 2) CD-F17*. There is a rock pillar, which ascends the center of this large granite outcrop. This 3,000 feet (914 m) pillar is similar in size and content to the Pugilist at Rest route. Consequently, it can be expected that a route can be done on this pillar which is similar in length and difficulty to the Pugilist at Rest route. The main difference is that 800 feet (244 m) below the top of this route the ridge turns from mostly rock climbing to mostly snow and ice climbing.

Just to the left of this pillar is another deep and permanently shaded couloir similar to the Wilford Couloir. This couloir undoubtedly contains steep solid ice as does the Wilford Couloir. The northwest ridge route can be used as a descent route for either of these two climbs. As of this writing there are no recorded ascents for either the left pillar route or the couloir beside it. The climbing protection used will be similar to that for the central pillar and Wilford climbing routes.

Point Blanchard Right Pillar

Another excellent climbing opportunity exists about 500 feet (152 m) to the right of the Pugilist at Rest climbing route. This area is the Point Blanchard Right Pillar climbing route. This pillar is at a lower angle than the Pugilist at Rest route and the upper half of the climb follows a snow ridge to the top. *See CD photo (Chapter 2) CD-F18*. The snow face to the right of this route can be descended with easy rappels. As of this writing there are no recorded ascents of this route.

Mt. Kennedy
13,905 feet (4,238 m)

Mt. Kennedy was named by the Canadian Government in January of 1965, in honor of the late American President John F. Kennedy. Mt. Kennedy anchors the northeast corner of the Kennedy Massif. The 6,000 foot (1,829 m) north face of Mt. Kennedy is one of the great rock and ice climbs in all of Canada. When viewed from the north it is easy to appreciate that this spectacular mountain, composed of granite and ice, is in fact a mountain truly worthy of a President's name. Mt. Kennedy sits at the northeast corner of the Kennedy Massif plateau, and the routes that rise to reach this plateau, and ultimately to the summit of Mt. Kennedy, all provide interesting and spectacular climbing routes. Mt. Kennedy has several of the most spectacular climbing routes in the entire St. Elias Range, some of which have still not been climbed.

The United States map to this region is USGS Mt. St. Elias Alaska-Canada, scale 1:250,000. The Canadian maps are: Mt. Alverstone 115 B/6, scale 1:50,000, Mt. Kennedy 115 B/7, scale 1:50,000, Mt. Seattle 115 B/3, scale 1:50,000 and Ulu Mountain 115 B/2, scale 1:50,000.

Cathedral Glacier

The expedition to make the first ascent of Mt. Kennedy embarked on its voyage in the early spring of 1965. This expedition was organized and financed in part by the National Geographic Society of the United States. Included in this expedition was Senator Robert F. Kennedy, the brother of the late President John F. Kennedy, for whom the mountain was named.

The climbing party, including Senator Robert Kennedy, were flown by the Royal Canadian Air Force in a heavy lift Boeing-Vertol helicopter to their base camp at 8,750

Photo 1G   Photo by Richard Holmes

feet (2,667 m) on the Cathedral Glacier. *See CD photo (Chapter 2) CD-G01.* The team then ascended the first icefall on Cathedral Glacier. The route proceeds up Cathedral Glacier and then through the second icefall to where a high camp was placed in the upper basin at 11,700 feet (3,567 m). *See CD photo (Chapter 2) CD-G01.*

From the high camp at 11,700 feet (3,566 m), the team ascended what really is the west ridge of Mt. Kennedy to reach the base of the summit pyramid. The route proceeds up the west ridge and the south face of the summit pyramid of Mt. Kennedy. A difficult vertical step about a third of the way up the summit pyramid can be avoided by traversing to the right around it on steep ice. The remainder of the distance to the summit follows the west ridge, which is very narrow as it approaches the summit. *See CD photo (Chapter 2) CD-G01.* Senator Robert Kennedy was allowed to be the first to set foot on the summit of Mt. Kennedy and to unfurl the flag bearing the family coat of arms. This accomplishment was made all the more remarkable in as much as Robert Kennedy made the round-trip to the summit of Mt. Kennedy and back to Washington, D.C. in barely five days. This is truly an amazing feat considering that Senator Kennedy had never climbed anything before in his life.

The Cathedral Glacier route on Mt. Kennedy is an enjoyable and challenging mountaineering route. Some of the most spectacular views in the Yukon Territory of Canada can be found at the summit of Mt. Kennedy. Ref. *AAJ* 1966, pp. 93-97. *CAJ* 1966, pp. 56-62. *National Geographic Magazine* July, 1965, pp. 1-33.

North Ridge

When looking at the uniquely spectacular knife-edge features that comprise the long, steep, serpentine nature of the north ridge of Mt. Kennedy, one can only stare in amazement. It is easy to understand why Bradford Washburn, one of North America's most prolific climbers and premiere mountain photographers, called the 6,000 foot (1,829 m) long north ridge of Mt. Kennedy one of the great climbing challenges in all of Canada. See photo 1G.

The first ascent of this magnificent ridge took place in the summer of 1968. The team used siege tactics to place fixed rope and camps along the ridge as they proceeded. The first ascent team used nearly 8,000 feet (2,438 m) of fixed rope. The second ascent team used just over 2,000 feet (610 m) of fixed rope. The climbers during their descent removed most of the fixed rope. The route has been done in an alpine style ascent with the descent going down Cathedral Glacier.

The entrance to this climb generally begins to the right of the foot of the ridge on a broad ice face. *See CD photo (Chapter 2) CD-G02.* The climb ascends the steep ice and proceeds through a small rock band. The route climbs the steep ice above the rock band traversing to the left to rejoin the crest of the ridge above a rock outcrop.

At a point just above the rock outcrop, the ridge is somewhat rounded and provides the only spot on this part of the ridge for a campsite. Even though Camp I can be located on this rounded shoulder it will still take some effort to chop out enough snow and ice to create a platform large enough for tents. The north ridge is continuously steep, which requires that climbers be tied to their ropes at all times. The route should be treated like a big wall climb with climbers roped up constantly, even while sleeping.

The route above Camp I stays mostly to the right of the ridge crest. The climb follows the indistinct snow couloir to the right of the ridge for several rope lengths until it intersects with the ridge crest. *See CD photo (Chapter 2) CD-G03.* The ridge crest is followed for about two rope lengths until the ridge reaches the bottom of the rock face. Below this rock face is one of the only naturally occurring wide spots on the entire ridge. This wide spot can be used to establish Camp II. *See CD photo (Chapter 2) CD-G03.*

The next 2,000 feet (610 m) of climbing above Camp II is where the route really becomes steep. The route proceeds out onto the ice face to the right of the steep rock face. The climbing proceeds up the ridge on snow and ice. A small rock band is passed on the left side and the route proceeds onto a broad ice face. The climb proceeds up this broad ice face to the base of a large vertical rock band. *See CD photo (Chapter 2) CD-G04.*

This vertical rock face, which is just over halfway up the climb, represents the technical crux of the climb. This rock face is about four rope lengths of steep rock climbing over mostly solid, although frost shattered, granite. The first ascent team rated this section of climbing 5.8, A3. The only known alpine ascent of this ridge climbed the right-hand margin of this rock band. These climbers were able to surmount this rock face by piecing together several pitches in iced up chimneys to the right of the rock face and were therefore able to circumvent most of the rock climbing altogether.

Above the crux rock face the climb proceeds on snow and ice pitches once again. The route stays to the left of the ridge crest on the snow face until it reaches the base of a rock face. At the base of this rock face a good safe spot can be found to chop out tent platforms for Camp III. *See CD photo (Chapter 2) CD-G04.*

The route above Camp III climbs this rock buttress directly. The rock buttress looks steep from below but it never exceeds fifty degrees in angle. The difficulty on this buttress is that is ascends mostly loose diorite rock which is featureless and provides very little opportunity for protection. This section of rock climbing is exhilarating but is never very severe at any point. *See CD photo (Chapter 2) CD-G05.*

The ridge above the diorite rock band is narrow but becomes lower angle. The ridge crest is followed for several rope lengths until the ridge broadens out into the summit snowfield. The summit snowfield is followed to the summit of Mt. Kennedy. This is a very challenging and enjoyable climb. The route is reasonably safe from major avalanche hazards. There may be occasional spindrift avalanches coming down from the summit snowfield following snowstorms, but they provide more of an inconvenience than any real hazard.

It is good climbing etiquette to remove as much of the fixed line that is used as possible to allow future climbers the opportunity to enjoy the pristine nature of this route. The first ascent team rated the climb Alaskan Grade VI, 5.8, A3. They used several thousand feet of fixed line to facilitate the ascent and the descent. The protection used was a wide selection of one hundred pitons and the same number of ice screws and deadmen.

The route has been done in an alpine style ascent and this team used the Cathedral Glacier as their descent route. Another team attempting an alpine style ascent was forced off the climb due to bad weather. Remarkably, they were able to traverse to the left, off the face high on the mountain, onto the massive hanging glacier that sits directly in the middle of the northeast face. They then traversed onto the east ridge of Mt. Kennedy which they were able to down climb. Ref. *AAJ* 1969, pp.404-405. *AAJ* 1997, pp.72-79.

North Face

The north face of Mt. Kennedy presents a 6,000 foot (1,829 m) monolith of steep ice and rock. One of the most technically difficult climbs that has been done to date in the St. Elias Mountain Range goes directly up the middle of the north face. *See CD photo (Chapter 2) CD-G06.*

The route begins on the Alverstone ice shelf at the base of the north face. The route proceeds directly up into the rock band in the middle of the north face of Mt. Kennedy. This section entails many pitches of very steep and very difficult mixed rock and ice climbing.

The route emerges above the rock face onto a large ice face which is ascended until the next rock band is reached. This smaller rock band is ascended on its left side and the route then merges with the north ridge route about 1,500 feet (457 m) below the summit. The route follows the remainder of the north ridge route along the diorite rock ridge to reach the summit of Mt. Kennedy. The north ridge route can be descended on a rappel or the Cathedral Glacier route can be down climbed for the descent.

There is only one recorded ascent of this beautiful and difficult face. This is a very serious undertaking in a wild and isolated location. The route requires the use of a haulbag and a portaledge. This route is not entirely safe from objective hazards as much of the north face is overhung by a large band of hanging seracs. The first ascent team rated this climb Alaskan Grade VI, M6, WI5+. There are at least fifty difficult pitches of climbing on this route. Ref. *AAJ* 1997, pp. 80-91.

East Ridge

Adjacent to the great northern escarpment of Mt. Kennedy is the east ridge. The east ridge of Mt. Kennedy is a marvelous climb because it combines the best features of an alpine climb. The route is on a beautiful mountain in a remote location and the climb encompasses both moderate rock and ice climbing. See photo 2G. The approach to the climb is fairly easy and the rock climbing, which is encountered higher on the ridge, is challenging but never severe.

This route has seen several ascents. The first ascent team approached the route on

Photo 2G *Photo by Richard Holmes*

the South Lowell Glacier. Unfortunately, this approach forces one to address the ridge underneath a series of massive and unstable overhanging ice cliffs. These ice cliffs are so unstable and dangerous that an approach from this side is both unwise and unnecessary.

A much safer and easier approach to this climb is directly off the main branch of the Lowell Glacier. *See CD photo (Chapter 2) CD-G07*. This approach allows for an easy walk up a snow couloir onto the lower part of the east ridge. The route proceeds onto a rounded snow dome where a good campsite can be established for Camp I. *See CD photo (Chapter 2) CD-G08*.

From Camp I, the route descends down the snow dome into an obvious col. The ridge is narrow but horizontal in the col. The route proceeds out of the col and up onto the upper part of the east ridge which becomes steep fairly quickly. The east ridge is comprised of loose diorite rock exposed on a narrow ridge crest. The climb is low fifth class rock climbing as it proceeds over this loose diorite. *See CD photo (Chapter 2) CD-G09*.

Near the top of the diorite rock section the climb moves onto a narrow ice ridge that is followed the remaining rope lengths to reach the summit of Mt. Kennedy. The ascent route can be easily descended. The summit has been reached and a return trip made back to the col in a single twenty-four hour push. Fixed ropes are generally not needed on this route. A small selection of pitons and camming devices are useful for belays on the rock section. A small selection of ice screws and deadmen will prove useful to protect the ice ridge near the summit. This is an enjoyable route with moderate technical challenges. The climbing is interesting but never severe. Ref. *AAJ* 1984, p. 189. *CAJ* 1984, pp. 43-44.

Southeast Buttress

A very interesting climb of only moderate technical difficulty is the southeast buttress of Mt. Kennedy. This blocky stairstep style rock and ice buttress is tucked away deep in a canyon near the head of the South Lowell Glacier. *See CD photo (Chapter 2) CD-G10*. This rocky buttress is comprised mostly of black diorite rock. The route ascends over mixed rock and ice climbing on the diorite buttress.

Southeast Buttress Right Side

There are two approaches to begin this climb. The right-hand approach begins at the left side of the foot of the far right-hand buttress. *See CD photo (Chapter 2) CD-G11*. The route ascends a small snow face between two rock pillars and climbs up and to the right. In the middle of the buttress the route then follows an obvious couloir directly up the face of the buttress. *See CD photo (Chapter 2) CD-G11*.

The route climbs out of the couloir and onto the spine of the crest of the buttress. The spine of the buttress is very narrow and comprised of snow and ice. The spine is ascended to a good-sized level platform at 10,500 feet (3,200 m). This platform is a good place to establish Camp I. This beautiful little platform is naturally level and resembles an eagle's nest. The platform is large enough to accommodate a couple of tents. This campsite collects sunlight from both the early morning sun and the afternoon light as well.

The route above Camp I climbs a small and narrow diorite ridge to the very small summit of a sub-peak on the southeast ridge. The route then traverses the broad snow covered southeast ridge towards the summit of Mt. Kennedy. The route along the southeast ridge drops down into a very large, broad and flat saddle where a good spot can be found to place Camp II at 11,000 feet (3,353 m).

Photo 3G *Photo by Richard Holmes*

The route from Camp II ascends a low angle snow and rock ridge along the eastern flank of South Kennedy 11,992 feet (3,655 m) and the summit of South Kennedy can easily be reached from here. The climb to the summit of South Kennedy is an enjoyable and inspirational ascent in itself. The best approach to the summit is along the easy snow covered north ridge. The summit of South Kennedy is a small point sticking straight up into the sky and is so small in fact that only one person can stand on it at a time. Even then it is still a tight squeeze. The route from South Kennedy to the true summit of Mt. Kennedy follows the broad plateau that sits below the summits of Mt. Hubbard, Mt. Alverstone and Mt. Kennedy. The route up the summit pyramid of Mt. Kennedy is the same as that for the Cathedral Glacier route.

Southeast Buttress
Left Side

The other alternative start to the southeast buttress is to begin the climb on the left rib of the buttress. *See CD photo (Chapter 2) CD-G12.* This is a more direct start than the right side and is probably a more enjoyable climb than the right-hand start as well. The route begins by ascending a very narrow and obvious rib on the left-hand buttress. The climb then moves onto the black diorite face of the southeast buttress. The climb follows very enjoyable climbing over this blocky rock buttress.

The route then becomes much steeper at the base of a rock tower. This tower can be passed on its left through an obvious but narrow couloir. This couloir leads directly to the level eagle's nest platform at 10,500 feet (3,200 m) where Camp I can be established. This left side approach now intersects the main route of the southeast buttress and the route to the summit is the same as that described for the right-hand approach of the southeast buttress route.

The ascent route can be followed for the descent route. A small collection of pitons and camming devices can be used for protection on this climb. A small set of ice screws will be useful in the steep couloirs. There is probably no need to fix any rope on this climb. The route will involve some occasional low fifth class climbing. As of this writing there are no recorded ascents of the southeast buttress.

South Buttress

One of the true hidden gems of the St. Elias Range is the south buttress of Mt. Kennedy. See photo 3G. This 2,000 foot (610 m) solid granite buttress sits in the deep recesses of South Lowell Glacier. It is mainly because of the hidden location of this buttress that it has never received any attention. This buttress is, however, quite easy to approach up the gentle South Lowell Glacier.

The climb begins at the foot of this buttress. The route starts out on the loose black diorite rock, which is also found on the southeast buttress. Fortunately, the rock quickly changes to solid pink orthoclase granite, which is more common on the north ridge of Mt. Kennedy. There are several routes that can be established on this buttress. *See CD photo (Chapter 2) CD-G13.* The far right and the far left sides of the buttress have a protruding flying buttress style appearance. Good routes can be established on the steep faces of either of these flying buttresses.

Between these flying buttresses is a couloir reminiscent of the super couloir on Fitzroy in Patagonia in the South American Andes. Any of these approaches will yield beautiful climbing up 2,000 feet (610 m) of steep solid granite in a magnificent and isolated setting.

The buttress ends 2,000 feet (610 m) above the glacier on the crest of the southeast ridge. The key to success on this climb is to use a careful approach to the base of the south buttress. The base of the buttress is partially exposed to huge avalanches from a massive ice cliff, which drops down from a side chute off Cathedral Glacier. See CD photo (Chapter 2) CD-G13. When this ice face breaks, the avalanches are truly massive. However, if one stays to the right of the buttress on the approach and remains at the very base of the buttress at the beginning of the climb, then the climbers will be out of the line of the avalanche path.

The route from the top of the granite face of the south buttress follows the spine of the southeast ridge. The ridge at the top of the south buttress is very narrow. See CD photo (Chapter 2) CD-G14. This narrow spine is followed until it climbs over a small sub-peak, which is located directly above the southeast buttress route. From this point onward the south buttress and the southeast buttress routes are identical. See CD photo (Chapter 2) CD-G15. Shortly after crossing the summit of the sub-peak on the southeast ridge crest there is a good level spot on the ridge where Camp I can be placed. See CD photo (Chapter 2) CD-G15.

The remainder of the climb to the summit of Mt. Kennedy follows the same route as described for the southeast buttress. As of this writing there are no recorded ascents of the magnificent granite formation of the south buttress. This is a big wall climb in a remote and alpine environment. Consequently, big wall gear including haul bags and a portaledge will be needed as well as the typical alpine equipment needed to complete the ascent to the true summit.

Weisshorn Mountain
11,620 feet (3,542 m)

A mountain which is not only beautiful but also has numerous challenging routes, most of which have never been climbed, is the Weisshorn. This spectacular mountain has several fine ridge climbs which rise to the narrow triangular summit pyramid. See photo 1H. This mountain sits along the eastern edge of the Kennedy Massif escarpment. The Weisshorn can be easily reached from either Cathedral Glacier or South Lowell Glacier. The United States map for the Weisshorn is USGS Mt. St. Elias Alaska-Canada, scale 1:250,000. The Canadian map for the Weisshorn is Mt. Kennedy 115 B/7, scale 1:50,000.

Southeast Ridge

The first ascent of the Weisshorn was done on the southeast ridge. This route can easily be reached from Cathedral Glacier. A good base camp can be placed at 8,500 feet (2,591 m) on Cathedral Glacier directly below the icefall leading to the basin below the Weisshorn. See CD photo (Chapter 2) CD-H01. The climb from base camp to the foot of the summit pyramid of the Weisshorn ascends this 1,700 foot (518 m) icefall. See CD photo (Chapter 2) CD-H02.

The climb through this icefall is difficult and complicated, as the icefall is massively broken. A good route through the icefall can usually be found by starting just left of the center of the icefall and climbing up and to the left across good snow ramps. The icefall leads to the large and sheltered basin below the summit pyramid of the Weisshorn. See CD photo (Chapter 2) CD-H02. A good high camp can be placed in this large sheltered basin at 10,500 feet (3,200 m).

The first ascent of the Weisshorn Mountain began in the high sheltered basin. The route ascended easy snow slopes on the southeast face until the climb intersected with the southeast ridge. This ridge is then followed along its narrow and corniced crest to reach the summit. The ascent route can be descended. Some fixed rope is useful along the crest of the southeast ridge particularly where it is narrow and corniced. Some snow protection is useful for fixing the rope. A large supply of wands are required to make

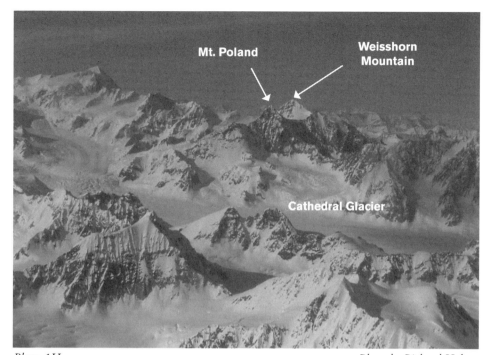

Photo 1H   Photo by Richard Holmes

a good route through the icefall leading off Cathedral Glacier. Ref. *AAJ* 1975, pp. 141-144. *CAJ* 1975, pp. 71-72 and *CAJ* 1977, p. 67.

South Ridge

A beautiful and direct unclimbed route is the south ridge of the Weisshorn. This ridge can be reached from the high basin that lies directly below the summit pyramid of the Weisshorn. The same high camp that is used to climb the southeast ridge can be used to climb the south ridge as well. *See CD photo (Chapter 2) CD-H03.*

The route up the south ridge follows the small indistinct crest of the south ridge, which splits the south face of the Weisshorn. The climb ascends this crest which is comprised mostly of snow. About two-thirds of the way to the top a corniced ice bulge is ascended on its right side by climbing on the snow slopes of the south face. The ascent route can be used as the descent route. As of this writing there are no recorded ascents of this ridge.

West Ridge

The west ridge of the Weisshorn is a long serpentine snow covered ridge. This ridge can be reached from a camp in the high basin below the summit of the Weisshorn. *See CD photo (Chapter 2) CD-H04.* The route up the west ridge begins on the broad low angle snow slopes of the west face. The snow slopes of the west face are followed about halfway up the summit pyramid.

At the halfway point on this route the climbing proceeds from the snow slopes onto the narrow crest of the west ridge. The snow crest of the west ridge can be followed to the summit of the Weisshorn. The ascent route can be used as the descent route. As of this writing there are no recorded ascents of the west ridge of the Weisshorn.

East Ridge
Left Side

The east ridge of the Weisshorn is a long narrow ridge which curves elegantly upward to the small pyramidal summit of the Weisshorn. *See CD photo (Chapter 2) CD-H05.* The east side of the Weisshorn can be reached by following South Lowell Glacier until it reaches the base of the icefall at the terminus of the east ridge.

The lower part of the east ridge can be ascended on either of two forks. The left side is a lower angle ascent but requires a climb through a complicated and active icefall. *See CD photo (Chapter 2) CD-H06.* The icefall can then be ascended by staying to the left side as the climb proceeds through the crevasse fields. The icefall is ascended into a basin on the east side of the Weisshorn to a point below the left fork of the east ridge. A good camp can be placed at 8,500 feet (2,591 m) in this basin. The climb out of the basin onto the east ridge ascends a rock shoulder covered with loose crumbly diorite rock. This rock shoulder is ascended until it reaches a prominent snow covered sub-peak at 10,000 feet (3,048 m). A good site can be found here to dig in tent platforms for Camp I.

The route above Camp I follows the relatively broad snow covered east ridge for several rope lengths. This broad snow shoulder is followed until the ridge rises sharply. The ridge at this point also becomes quite narrow. This narrow snow and ice ridge crest is followed over its length to reach the summit of the Weisshorn.

The ascent route can be used as the descent route. Some snow protection including half-length pickets can be used for moving belays. As of this writing there are no recorded ascents of this route.

East Ridge
Right Side

The lower section of the east ridge can be ascended from its right side as well. This branch of the lower east ridge is much shorter and much steeper than the left branch. However, the right branch offers the opportunity to avoid having to climb through the active icefall. *See CD photo (Chapter 2) CD-H07.*

The east ridge of the Weisshorn is reached by following South Lowell Glacier until you are directly below the east ridge. The narrow rocky crest of the right branch of the lower east ridge is ascended. At the halfway point of this route the climb begins to ascend snow and ice slopes. This narrow crest is followed until it reaches the snow covered sub-peak at 10,000 feet (3,048 m) where Camp I is located. The remainder of the climb is the same as described for the left side of the east ridge of the Weisshorn.

The left side of the east ridge probably provides an easier descent route. Some rock protection will be needed to protect the lower section of this climb. As of this writing there are no recorded ascents of this route.

Northeast Ridge

Another interesting but well-hidden part of the east side of the Weisshorn is the northeast ridge. This ridge is a narrow ridge crest which rises out of South Lowell Glacier. *See CD photo (Chapter 2) CD-H08.* The northeast ridge is actually just another branch of the main east ridge as the two routes intersect at mid-height on the mountain.

The northeast ridge can be reached from South Lowell Glacier. The lower portion of the ridge is relatively broad and can be ascended on easy snow slopes. Roughly two-thirds of the way up this route the climb narrows to follow the rocky ridge crest. This rocky crest is followed until it intersects the main branch of the east ridge at 10,500 feet (3,200 m). The snow slopes to either side of this rocky crest are steep and unstable. Therefore, it is best to remain directly on the ridge crest. A good camp can be placed on the snow platform where the northeast ridge intersects with the main east ridge route. The remainder of the climb to the summit is the same as that described for the east ridge of the Weisshorn. The left branch of the east ridge is probably the easiest descent route. Some rock protection will be needed along the rocky section of the narrow northeast ridge. As of this writing there are no recorded ascents of this route.

Mt. Poland
11,500 feet (3,505 m)

Another spectacular mountain with narrow challenging ridges is the slightly smaller southern neighbor of the Weisshorn, the highly angled narrow crested peak of Mt. Poland. Mt. Poland sits directly across the high basin from the Weisshorn. Mt. Poland was named in honor of the Polish climbers who were killed in an avalanche near the base of the mountain. The two mountains make a great combination climb. *See CD photo (Chapter 2) CD-I01.* The United States map for Mt. Poland is USGS Mt. St. Elias Alaska-Canada, scale 1:250,000. The Canadian map for Mt. Poland is Mt. Kennedy 115 B/7, scale 1:50,000.

Northeast Ridge

The route to reach Mt. Poland from Cathedral Glacier is the same as that described for the Weisshorn. A good base camp can be set up at 8,500 feet (2,591 m). *See CD photo (Chapter 2) CD-I02.* The route to Mt. Poland is the same as that described for the Weisshorn. The route must ascend a 1,700 foot (518 m) icefall to reach a high basin where a good site can be found to establish Camp I at 10,500 feet (3,200 m). The first ascent team ascended Mt. Poland by its northeast ridge and northeast face. *See CD photo (Chapter 2) CD-I03.* The ascent route can be used as the descent route. Some snow protection is useful. A large selection of wands is needed to establish a route through the icefall to get into the high basin below the summit pyramid of Mt. Poland. Ref. *AAJ* 1977, p. 200. *CAJ* 1977, pp. 66-67.

South Side

An interesting area for climbing on Mt. Poland is on its exposed rocky southern side. This area is easily reached from Cathedral Glacier where a good base camp can be set up at 8,000 feet (2,438 m). *See CD photo (Chapter 2) CD-I04.* A small icefall can be ascended by following easy snow ramps on the far left side of the icefall. A small snow basin sits above the icefall at 9,000 feet (2,743 m) just below the 2,000 foot (610 m) south face of Mt. Poland. A good site can be found in this small basin to establish Camp I. From this high camp several climbing rocks can be pursued.

West Ridge

The west ridge of Mt. Poland is easily accessible from the basin on the south side of the mountain. The west ridge can be accessed on a broad snow buttress on the south side of the west ridge. *See CD photo (Chapter 2) CD-I05.* Easy snow slopes are ascended on the snow buttress to about mid-height on the buttress where a small ice face is encountered. The ice face can be passed on snow slopes on its right-hand side. The climb then follows a narrow rocky ridge crest to reach the crest of the main west ridge.

The rocky crest of the west ridge is followed at this point. The ridge is horizontal for several rope lengths. The ridge then becomes very narrow and rises sharply. The route proceeds over mixed rock and snow climbing along the spine of the west ridge. The ridge ends at the small pyramidal summit of Mt. Poland.

The ascent route can be used as the descent route. A small selection of rock protection including small camming devices can be used to protect the crumbly diorite rock on this route. Some snow protection including pickets and deadmen is useful on the route as well. There is no need for fixed line on this route. As of this writing there are no recorded ascents of this climb.

South Ridge

The main feature of the 2,000 foot (610 m) south face of Mt. Poland is the south ridge. The south ridge is an exposed rock ridge that winds up from the high snow basin to end at the summit. The south ridge is easily accessed from Camp I by ascending a small rock face directly above the camp. *See CD photo (Chapter 2) CD-I06.*

The route proceeds along the narrow crest of the south ridge over mixed rock and snow. The ridge then rises steeply as a rock buttress is encountered. The route proceeds up the buttress and to the left onto a snow face. Above the snow face the route moves back to the right onto the narrow ridge crest. This crest is followed on mixed rock and ice for the remaining distance to the summit of Mt. Poland.

The easiest descent from the summit is down the west ridge. A good selection of camming devices will be needed on this route for rock protection. Some snow protection including half-length snow pickets will be useful on this route as well. Fixed line is not needed on this route. This is a very good route for an alpine style ascent. As of this writing there are no recorded ascents of the south ridge of Mt. Poland.

Ulu Mountain
10,160 feet (3,097 m)

At the southeast corner of the Kennedy Massif is a small but spectacular peak called Ulu Mountain. This is really two mountains with the southern summit being barely 200 feet (61 m) higher than its northern neighbor, Ulu North Peak. Both peaks have long slender ridges, which drop precipitously down from the summit to the glaciers below.

The long sharp ridges give the mountain an appearance which makes it resemble the Eskimo utility knife, known as an Ulu. Consequently, the mountain has officially been named Ulu Mountain.

Both Ulu Mountain and Ulu North Peak can be reached easily on their east side from Lowell Glacier. The west side of the mountain can be easily reached from Cathedral Glacier. These peaks are not very high, so altitude plays no problem in their ascent. There are many unclimbed ridges on both Ulu Mountain and Ulu North Peak, which are easily accessible from the glaciers below these peaks. In fact, as of this writing there is currently only one recorded ascent of Ulu Mountain. These two peaks have apparently been overlooked because of their proximity to larger and more famous mountains. Consequently, there are numerous possibilities for excellent climbs and first ascents on both Ulu Mountain and Ulu North Peak. The United States map for Mt. Poland is USGS Mt. St. Elias Alaska-Canada, scale 1:250,000. The Canadian map for Mt. Poland is Ulu Mountain 115 B/2, scale 1:50,000.

Ulu Mountain
North Ridge

There is a large glacial basin that separates Ulu Mountain from Ulu North Peak on the eastern side of these peaks. This glacial basin is easily reached from Lowell Glacier. A smooth tongue of the glacier can be followed to gain access to the glacial basin separating Ulu Mountain from Ulu North Peak. See photo 1J.

The glacial basin can be followed to the very end near the base of a small snow ramp. A good site can be found at the base of the snow ramp to place Camp I. *See CD photo (Chapter 2) CD-J01.*

The climb from Camp I proceeds up the gentle snow ramp to a large saddle that separates Ulu Mountain and Ulu North

Photo 1J

Photo by Richard Holmes

Peak. The route from the col follows the sharp but low angle rocky north ridge to the narrow pointed summit of Ulu Mountain. The ascent route can be used as the descent route. No fixed rope is required for this climb. A good selection of wands to mark the trail up the glacial basin is useful in the event that the descent has to be made in poor weather conditions. This route was the first ascent route of Ulu Mountain and remains the only recorded ascent of either Ulu Mountain or Ulu North Peak. Ref. *AAJ* 1973, p. 435.

East Ridge

Immediately to the left of the large glacial basin which separates Ulu Mountain and Ulu North Peak, is the imposing east ridge of Ulu Mountain. This route is comprised of narrow ridge climbing on a thin corniced ridge as well as face climbing. *See CD photo (Chapter 2) CD-J02.*

The east ridge of Ulu Mountain can be easily accessed from Lowell Glacier. The route proceeds up a large snow basin to the foot of the east ridge, where a good site can be found to establish Camp I. The route above Camp I proceeds up a snow covered rock face for a few rope lengths to reach a narrow col on the crest of the east ridge.

The route from the col proceeds along the crest of the east ridge until the ridge merges with the east face. The route proceeds up a rounded snow covered shoulder over unstable snow slopes. At the top of the snow shoulder the route proceeds up and left along the interface between the east face and the narrow indistinct rib at the left-hand margin of the east face.

At the top of the east face the route emerges onto the narrow and slightly corniced crest of the east ridge. This narrow ridge crest is followed to the summit of Ulu Mountain. Some snow and ice protection is needed for this route. The use of ice screws and half-length pickets is helpful on this route. No fixed line is really needed for this climb and this route can be climbed alpine style in two days. If no fixed line is left in place the north ridge is the easiest descent route. If fixed line is used, the ascent route can be used as the descent route to facilitate removal of the fixed line. As of this writing there are no recorded ascents of this route.

South Rib

Directly in the middle of the large expanse of the snow covered south face is the narrow and elegant south rib. This route can be accessed from the terminus of the Cathedral Glacier. *See CD photo (Chapter 2) CD-J03.*

The beginning of the climb ascends a low angle blocky rock buttress. After several rope lengths the buttress merges with the south face and the narrow south rib rises out of the snow covered south face. The crest of the south rib is followed along its entire length and the route finally ends directly at the summit of Ulu Mountain.

Some camming devices will be useful for protection of the rocky buttress. Ice screws, some pickets and deadmen will also be useful for running belays on this climb. No fixed line is necessary. The route can be done in a day in an alpine style ascent. The ascent route can be used as the descent route. There are currently no recorded ascents of this route.

West Ridge

The west ridge is a large rocky low angle ridge, which rises out of the Cathedral Glacier. *See CD photo (Chapter 2) CD-J04.* The base of the ridge can be accessed from the South Lowell Glacier. A large snow basin proceeds off the South Lowell Glacier where the west ridge can be accessed directly.

From the snow basin the crest of the west ridge can be accessed from any one of a number of small snow couloirs. *See CD photo (Chapter 2) CD-J05.* The ridge crest can be followed over the top of a small sub-peak and down into a shallow col. The route proceeds over mixed snow and rock climbing on a narrow ridge crest until the climb reaches the foot of a rocky buttress.

The route proceeds up onto this wide rocky buttress. The route involves mostly low angle rock climbing. The route at the top of the rock buttress intersects the narrow crest of the west ridge. This ridge rises to a steeper angle and also becomes considerably more narrow. This narrow rocky ridge crest is followed to the summit.

The ascent route can be used for the descent. Some pitons and camming devices are useful for rock protection and snow pickets will be useful for belays on the snow. This climb can be done in a long day as an alpine ascent. As of this writing there are no recorded ascents of this route.

Northwest Ridge

A very interesting and challenging route on Ulu Mountain is the northwest ridge. This ridge can be accessed directly of Cathedral Glacier. The climb starts on a small rock step and then proceeds onto the narrow rocky crest of the northwest ridge. This rocky ridge crest is followed until the rock intersects a snow rib about 500 feet (152 m) below the summit. *See CD photo (Chapter 2) CD-J06.*

The route then proceeds up this distinct snow rib which ends directly at the summit of Ulu Mountain. Camming devices are useful for rock protection on this route. Pitons may be needed to secure fixed line on the small rock step at the base of the climb. Snow pickets will be useful on the snow ridge near the summit. The ascent route can be used as the descent route. As of this writing there are no recorded ascents of the northwest ridge.

Ulu North Peak
9,960 feet (3,036 m)

Immediately adjacent to Ulu Mountain is the pointed summit of Ulu North Peak.

This mountain is very similar to Ulu Mountain and is a mere 200 feet (61 m) lower than its adjacent southern neighbor. There are several steep and well defined ridges running down from the summit of Ulu North Peak. There has been virtually no activity on Ulu North Peak so that most of the ridges on this beautiful mountain are awaiting first ascents.

South Rib

There is a large glacial amphitheater which separates Ulu Mountain from Ulu North Peak. This amphitheater is an easy way to gain access to several climbs on either peak. This amphitheater can be accessed from easy snow ramps off South Lowell Glacier. *See CD photo (Chapter 2) CD-K01.*

The most direct route up the south and east side of Ulu North Peak is the south rib. This rib can be gained by following the glacial amphitheater all the way to the back of the amphitheater where a small col can be found. This col separates Ulu Mountain from Ulu North Peak. A good camp can be placed at the back of the amphitheater below the col. *See CD photo (Chapter 2) CD-K02.*

The col can be gained by climbing an easy snow ramp out of the amphitheater. The route follows the forty degree mixed rock and snow ridge directly to the summit of Ulu North Peak. Some camming devices will be useful for rock protection on this climb. Short pickets and ice screws will be useful for snow protection although no fixed rope is required. The climb can be done in a day from the high camp below the col. The ascent route can be used as the descent route. As of this writing there are no recorded ascents of this climb.

Southeast Rib

A short but interesting climb on Ulu North Peak is the southeast rib. This climb begins in the basin that separates Ulu North Peak from Ulu Mountain. The approach to this climb follows the same glacier approach as the south rib of Ulu North Peak. *See CD photo (Chapter 2) CD-K03.* A good camp can be placed in the basin at the foot of the southeast rib above the icefall.

The route then follows the narrow crest of the southeast rib over mixed ice and snow for about 1,500 feet (457 m) until it intersects with the main crest of the east ridge. The remainder of the climb follows the east ridge to the summit.

Some ice screws and half-length snow pickets are useful for protection on this route. The route can be done in one day from a camp in the high basin. No fixed rope is needed for this climb. The ascent route can be used as the descent route. As of this writing there are no recorded ascents of this route.

East Ridge

The east ridge of Ulu North Peak is a beautiful and sinuous spine of rock and ice that rises 4,500 feet (1,372 m) out of the glacier to end at the very summit of the mountain. *See CD photo (Chapter 2) CD-K04.* The route can be reached by a side branch off the main Lowell Glacier.

The route begins directly off the glacier on easy snow slopes. The route climbs the snow slopes weaving between rock outcrops until the crest of the ridge is reached. *See CD photo (Chapter 2) CD-K05.* The narrow but low angle ridge crest is followed until a sub-peak is reached at 7,000 feet (2,134 m). The route then drops down 400 feet (122 m) into a deep saddle where a good site can be found to place Camp I at the foot of the upper part of the east ridge. *See CD photo (Chapter 2) CD-K06.*

From the saddle, the route proceeds up the narrow icy crest of the east ridge for nearly 3,000 feet (914 m). The ridge along this section is almost entirely ice with very little exposed rock. Some fixed rope along this section will facilitate an easier ascent and a more rapid descent. The route then levels out abruptly at a point where the east ridge intersects with the south east rib. *See CD photo (Chapter 2) CD-K05.* A small but useful site can be found on the exposed south face to establish Camp III.

The remaining 400 feet (122 m) of elevation gain to the summit are obtained by following the narrow crest of the summit ridge from Camp II to the true summit. The climbing along this section is level but very narrow.

The ascent route is the best descent route. Fixed rope and ice protection is needed on this route that would make a very adventurous alpine style ascent. This is not an easy route to descend in bad weather. However, the climb could be done alpine style in two days in good weather. An alpine style ascent could utilize the south rib as a good descent route. As of this writing there are no recorded ascents of this route.

West Ridge

The west side of Ulu North Peak has some interesting routes that are easily accessible from Cathedral Glacier. *See CD photo (Chapter 2) CD-K07.* One of these routes is the west ridge. This route can be started directly off Cathedral Glacier at 7,500 feet (2,286 m).

The route begins on the obvious sharp crest of the rock ridge that comprises the west ridge of Ulu North Peak. The climb follows this rocky crest for slightly more than 2,000 feet (610 m) until the west ridge intersects with the north ridge of Ulu North Peak.

A good camp can be dug into the south slopes at the intersection of the west and north ridges. The remainder of the climb ascends the narrow crest of the north ridge for several rope lengths until it reaches the true summit of Ulu North Peak.

This climb can be done alpine style in three days. Some rock protection is needed for the lower section of the ridge. A few deadmen are helpful for the belay on the snow sections high on the ridge near the summit. The ascent route can be used as the descent route. Fixed rope is not needed for this climb particularly if an alpine style ascent is made. There are no recorded ascents of this route at this time.

Northwest Ridge

Immediately adjacent to the west ridge is the northwest ridge of Ulu North Peak. This climb can be started directly off Cathedral Glacier. The easiest approach to begin this climb is directly up a low angle ridge, which is comprised of mixed rock and snow. This low angle ridge is ascended for nearly 2,000 feet (610 m) until it reaches a steeper section of rock about 500 feet (152 m) below the intersection with the north ridge.

This short section of rock is exposed rock with no snow covering, but it is generally not too steep. This blocky ridge is ascended along its crest until it intersects with the main north ridge. A good camp can be placed at the intersection of the northwest ridge and the north ridge.

The route to the top of the northwest ridge can be followed along the crest of the north ridge for about one mile (1.6 km) over the narrow but low angle north ridge until the summit of Ulu North Peak is reached. This route is a good climb for an alpine style ascent. Both rock and snow protection should be taken on this climb to secure running belays. Fixed rope is not needed for this climb. The ascent route can be used as the descent route. The northwest ridge has no recorded ascents as of this writing.

North Ridge

The north ridge of Ulu North Peak is an interesting and enjoyable climb which requires very little technical expertise. This route can be started directly off Cathedral Glacier at about 8,300 feet (2,530 m). The best approach to begin this climb is to ascend

Cathedral Glacier until an obvious set of crevasses force the climb to the right just below the north ridge. The route ascends easy snow slopes until the snow face ends below a saddle in the north ridge. *See CD photo (Chapter 2) CD-K07.*

A small rocky spur can be ascended from the snow face to reach the saddle on the crest of the north ridge of Ulu North Peak. The route becomes a little steeper as it ascends an exposed rock face. This short section of exposed rock ends on the narrow snowy crest of the north ridge. The remainder of the climb ascends the low angle but very narrow snow covered crest of the north ridge. This ridge crest winds slightly up and to the left over a distance of a mile and a half (2.4 km) until the ridge reaches the true summit of Ulu North Peak.

A good base camp can be made in the saddle at the beginning of the climb of this ridge. The remainder of the climb can be done in an alpine style ascent. A good bivouac site can be found about 300 feet (91 m) below the summit of Ulu North Peak on a snow plateau.

Both snow and rock protection is needed for the rock face at the beginning of the climb. Snow and ice protection is useful for belays higher on the climb. This climb can be done alpine style in two days from the saddle camp. As of this writing there are no recorded ascents of this route.

Igloo Peak
6,500 feet (1,981 m)

Roughly one quarter of a mile (0.40 km) to the west of Cathedral Glacier near its intersection with South Lowell Glacier is a fascinating little peak known as Igloo Peak. This little mountain derives its name from its obvious resemblance to an ice igloo. An igloo is a temporary snow and ice shelter occasionally used by the Inuit Indians of North America. See photo 1L. Igloo Peak can serve as a good warm-up climb before ascending the larger peaks in the Kennedy Group. Igloo Peak can also serve as an interesting distraction during unsettled weather which may delay climbing on the larger peaks. The United States map for Mt. Poland is USGS Mt. St. Elias Alaska-Canada, scale 1:250,000. The Canadian map for Igloo Peak is Mt. Alverstone 115 B/6, scale 1:50,000.

North Ridge

The first and only recorded ascent of Igloo Peak was by the north ridge. The north ridge can be easily reached from Cathedral Glacier. *See CD photo (Chapter 2) CD-L01.* A steep snow face can be ascended to reach a narrow col below the peak. The steep and narrow crest of the north ridge is climbed over mixed rock and ice to reach the rounded summit. The first ascent team descended the eastern snow slopes and the rock face at the base of the east face. This climb can be done easily in an alpine style ascent in one day. Ref. *CAJ* 1977, p. 67.

East Face

The east face of Igloo Peak is also a good ascent route. The route begins on a short blocky rock face. *See CD photo (Chapter 2) CD-L02.* This is ascended to reach the easy snow slopes of the east face. The snow slopes are ascended to reach the summit. The ascent route can be used as the descent route and was used as the descent route for the first ascent of the mountain.

West Ridge

The west ridge of Igloo Peak is a short and fun climb. The west ridge is easily ascended from snow slopes on either side of the ridge. *See CD photo (Chapter 2) CD-L03.* The route proceeds up a small rock spur to reach the main west ridge of Igloo Peak. The

Photo 1L   Photo by Richard Holmes

route traces the narrow but low angle crest of the west ridge. The climbing is over mixed rock and ice but is generally not steep. This ridge ends directly at the summit of Igloo Peak. The east ridge can be used as a descent

Pinnacle Peak
12,186 feet (3,714 m)

Directly across the upper reaches of Lowell Glacier from Mt. Kennedy stands a relatively small but very spectacular peak known as Pinnacle Peak. This peak is well named as its sharp pointed summit makes it look like the lightning rod of the St. Elias Mountains. The routes on Pinnacle Peak can generally be done in a day or two but they are still fun and challenging climbs. The United States map to this region is USGS Mt. St. Elias Alaska-Canada, scale 1:250,000. The Canadian maps are Mt. Kennedy 115 B/7, scale 1:50,000 and Mt. Alverstone 115 B/6,

scale 1:50,000.

West Ridge

The first ascent of Pinnacle Peak was done via the snow and ice slopes of the west ridge. The west ridge can be approached from two directions. The most direct approach is from the basin that sits to the north of Pinnacle Peak, at the head of the south arm of the Kaskawulsh Glacier. This basin leads to the broad low angle hanging glacier that sits on the north side of the mountain. See photo 1M.

The hanging glacier is easy to ascend and can be climbed on skis. The route proceeds up the glacier to the west col, which is about 2,000 feet (610 m) below the summit. From the col the climb proceeds up the narrow snow covered ridge to the summit. The west ridge is not steep but may be corniced.

The other approach to climb the west ridge is from the south. In a basin below the south face of Pinnacle Peak a route can be

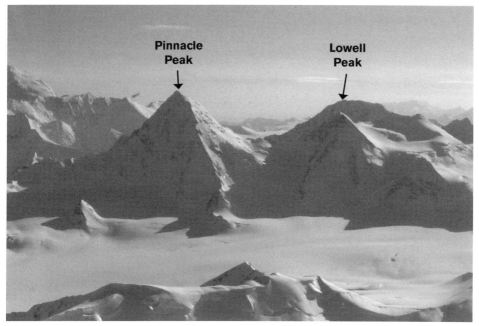

Photo 1M   Photo by Richard Holmes

climbed up an obvious couloir to reach the west col. See photo 2M. This 800 foot (244 m) couloir leads directly to the west col. The remainder of the west ridge route is the same as described for the approach from the north side. Ref. *AAJ* 1966, pp. 149-150.

Northwest Face

A challenging and unclimbed route on Pinnacle Peak is the northwest face. The northwest face is comprised entirely of snow and ice. This route can be reached from the hanging glacier on the north side of the mountain. *See CD photo (Chapter 2) CD-M01*. The route proceeds about two-thirds of the way to the west col, to a point just above a large field of seracs.

Above the serac field the route proceeds directly up the snow and ice slopes of the northwest face. There is not much route finding involved. The only deviations that must be made will be to avoid a few overhanging seracs encountered on the face.

The easiest descent route is down the west ridge route. As of this writing there are no recorded ascents of the northwest face. This 3,000 foot (914 m) route can be climbed and descended in an alpine style climb in one day.

North Ridge

The most spectacular line on Pinnacle Peak is the north ridge. This climb can be reached from the basin on the north side of the mountain. The route generally stays just to the right of the crest of the north ridge. *See CD photo (Chapter 2) CD-M02*. The route ascends snow and ice which averages about 45 degrees in angle. The route occasionally goes further to the right out onto the north face to avoid sections of steep or loose rock. However, the route stays adjacent to the crest of the ridge for a majority of the climb.

This beautiful 3,000 foot (914 m) ridge has seen a few ascents. They have all been alpine style ascents and have not involved

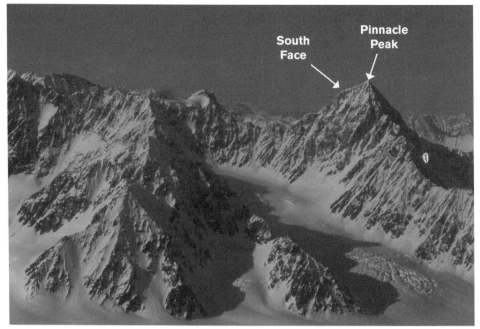

Photo 2M *Photo by Richard Holmes*

the placement of any fixed rope. The easiest descent is down the west ridge route. Ref. *AAJ* 1975, pp. 144-145. *CAJ* 1975, p. 75.

Northeast Face

A spectacular and rugged looking feature of Pinnacle Peak is the northeast face. This long and steep face presents a significant climbing challenge. This face has apparently been climbed, although there are no details of the ascent currently available. See CD photo (Chapter 2) CD-M03.

The route should be done under cold conditions early in the season to utilize the snow and ice on the face when the face is most likely to be in a frozen condition. The climb starts in the middle of the face and climbs an obvious couloir directly up the middle of the face. This route is fairly steep as the face is 45 degrees in angle, or steeper, along its entire length. The couloir in the middle of the face will avoid the overhanging rock cliffs found on either side of the face.

Approximately 500 feet (152 m) below the summit of the peak, the climb moves to the left to avoid an overhanging rock face. The route then proceeds up the remainder of the face to the summit. The west ridge route is the easiest descent off the mountain after climbing this route. Due to the potential for avalanches on this face, an alpine style ascent is probably the best approach. Ref. *AAJ* 1995, p. 173.

East Ridge

The east ridge of Pinnacle Peak is a long and beautiful ridge crest curving up and to the left towards the summit. This route is of moderate technical difficulty and is challenging enough to be very rewarding but it never involves severe climbing. See CD photo (Chapter 2) CD-M04.

The east ridge can be reached from a basin on the southeast side of the mountain off Lowell Glacier. A good camp can be established high in this basin. The route above this basin proceeds up easy snow slopes to gain the crest of the ridge. The narrow ridge is followed until it begins to level out. A good platform can be dug into the ridge crest to establish Camp II.

The route beyond Camp II is narrow but fairly level. The ridge crest is followed until the ridge becomes steeper. The climb is slightly steep at first and becomes even steeper as it proceeds. Directly beneath the very steep final 1,000 foot (305 m) rock pillar is a small step which provides a convenient place to establish Camp III.

The route above Camp III includes about 1,000 feet (305 m) of fairly steep climbing over mixed rock and snow. Some fixed rope will be useful here to facilitate both the ascent and the descent. This route is good to the very last step as the rock is steep all the way to the very top. The steep rock pillar ends directly at the summit pyramid.

This route may take five to ten days of climbing depending upon conditions and the skill of the team. The first ascent party used 1,600 feet (488 m) of rope. This is a very good climbing route as it involves some technical rock climbing but the route never becomes too severe at any point. Ref. *AAJ* 1975, pp. 144-145. *CAJ* 1975, p. 73.

South Ridge

The most significant feature of Pinnacle Peak is the south ridge. This long and serrated rock ridge rises out of Lowell Glacier and curves elegantly up and to the right to end at the exact summit of Pinnacle Peak. This is an arduous route and it is technically challenging, particularly the final 900 foot (274 m) rock headwall. However, the climbing is never extreme. Fixed rope would certainly facilitate the ascent as well as the descent. Consequently, an expedition style climb is a good tactic for this ridge. However, for a strong pair of climbers the south ridge would make an excellent alpine style ascent.

The south ridge is most easily reached off Lowell Glacier by an obvious snow couloir. *See CD photo (Chapter 2) CD-M05.* At the top of the couloir on the ridge crest a good site can be found to dig in tents for Camp I.

The route past Camp I snakes along the ridge crest. The crest of the south ridge alternates from snow cover to exposed rock. The ridge is nearly horizontal as it does not gain much elevation for about one half mile (0.8 km). The horizontal ridge then ends at the base of where the ridge becomes noticeably steeper. At the end of the horizontal section of ridge a good site can be found to dig in a tent platform to establish Camp II.

The route above Camp II is quite steep and most of the technical climbing exists in this area. From Camp II the route climbs the snow face directly above the camp. The snow face merges with the narrow ridge crest which is climbed up and to the right for several rope lengths. This section of ridge is very narrow and corniced. Consequently, fixed line will be of great value in facilitating passage across this section.

The route proceeds along a narrow ridge for several more rope lengths. The climb then surmounts a small rock tower before leveling out again. This level section is very short and ends at the base of the final 900 foot (274 m) headwall. The headwall begins on a rock face of dark metamorphic rock. The face then merges with a snow face which is climbed to the base of an overhanging rock face. The overhanging rock face can be bypassed on its left side via a steep snow couloir. The snow couloir then merges with the final snow face which is climbed to the summit of Pinnacle Peak.

This is a long and demanding route. The route might require between 1,000 to 1,500 feet (305 to 457 m) of fixed line if climbed by siege tactics. If fixed line is used the route can be descended more easily. If the route is climbed by an alpine style ascent the west ridge provides the easiest descent. The route will require some snow and ice protection and a selection of about fifty pieces of rock protection including camming devices and pitons. As of this writing there are no recorded ascents of this ridge.

South Couloir

A very interesting alternative to the south ridge is the south couloir. This route can be accessed from Lowell Glacier via a side glacier just to the right of the main bulk of the south ridge. See CD photo (Chapter 2) CD-M06. At the head of this basin a good site can be found to establish Camp I.

Above Camp I the route climbs through an obvious and active icefall. The large bergschrund can be passed near its top on the left side. The icefall leads into a large basin where Camp II can be located. The advantage of the south couloir over the south ridge to this point is the increased skill required in climbing the icefall. Also, the long horizontal traverse of the lower south ridge is eliminated altogether.

Above Camp II the route proceeds directly overhead through an obvious snow couloir to reach the crest of the south ridge. At the base of the steep headwall, Camp III can be located. The remainder of the route follows the same path as the south ridge route. As of this writing there are no recorded ascents of the south couloir variation.

South Face

The south face of Pinnacle Peak is a massive blocky triangular shaped rock face comprised of dark metamorphic rock covered with a little sprinkling of snow. There are many possible lines up this face but at this time there are no recorded ascents on the south face. The most obvious line on the south face follows a snow couloir which winds up the face and to the left to reach the summit. See CD photo (Chapter 2) CD-M07.

The south face can be reached by a side glacier off Lowell Glacier. A good site can be used at a safe distance from the face to establish Camp I. The route climbs up a low angle snow face into the obvious snow couloir at the right-hand margin of the south face. The route bypasses a rock outcrop in the couloir to the right. The couloir ends in a large triangular shaped patch of snow. A good site can be found here to dig in tent platforms for Camp II.

Above Camp II the snow couloir becomes more narrow and steep. This couloir is followed until it reaches a small snow face a few rope lengths below the summit. The snow face is then followed to the summit of Pinnacle Peak.

This narrow couloir is the same couloir used to avoid overhanging rock cliffs on the south ridge route. Consequently, at mid-height in this narrow upper snow couloir the south face and the south ridge routes merge. Some fixed rope will be useful in the upper reaches of the narrow couloir. A small rack of rock protection is useful but mainly snow and ice protection will be needed on this route. This is a challenging and exposed route directly up the south face and would make an excellent ascent. As of this writing there are no recorded ascents of the south face of Pinnacle Peak.

Lowell Peak
11,480 feet (3,499 m)

Immediately to the west of Pinnacle Peak is the impressive summit of Lowell Peak. The southern escarpment of this mountain is a large rocky outcrop and presents many fine climbing opportunities. Most of the climbing possibilities on this escarpment have not seen a single ascent. Therefore, this area is rich in opportunities for first ascents. The United States map to this region is USGS Mt. St. Elias Alaska-Canada, scale 1:250,000. The Canadian maps are Mt. Kennedy 115 B/7, scale 1:50,000 and Mt. Alverstone 115 B/6, scale 1:50,000.

Southeast Ridge

Rising out of Lowell Glacier is the massive and convoluted complex of the southeast ridge of Lowell Peak. The easiest way to gain access to the southeast ridge is off a small side glacier from Lowell Glacier. *See CD photo (Chapter 2) CD-N01.* A good site can be found to establish Camp I at the base of the southeast ridge.

The route above Camp I follows the low angle rocky ridge crest to the top of a sub-peak on the main crest of the southeast ridge. A good site for Camp II can be dug into the snow slopes on the back side near the top of the sub-peak. The route from Camp II drops down onto the crest of the southeast ridge and follows the narrow and sometimes corniced ridge crest. This narrow ridge traverses horizontally until it becomes steeper at the base of the final headwall. A good spot to dig in Camp III can be found at the top of a large snow face.

The route above Camp III becomes noticeably steeper but is never severe. The route follows this narrow ridge crest until it reaches the summit of Lowell Peak. This final headwall may require some fixed line to facilitate the ascent as well as the descent.

A good rack of both snow and ice as well as rock protection will be useful on this route. The ascent route can be used as the descent route. As of this writing there are no recorded ascents of the southeast ridge of Lowell Peak.

South Ridge

The south ridge of Lowell Peak is an imposing rock buttress coupled with a narrow snow and ice ridge. The south ridge can be accessed directly off Lowell Glacier. *See CD photo (Chapter 2) CD-N02.* A good site for Camp I can be found at the base of the south ridge.

The route begins on the left side of the ridge following an obvious snow couloir for several rope lengths. The couloir ends at the base of the first rock buttress. The first rock buttress can be climbed on its right-hand side up blocky cliffs to reach a small level platform. The route above the first rock buttress climbs a snow face on the right side of the second buttress to reach the top of the buttress. At the top of the second rock buttress the ridge becomes horizontal. A good spot can be found at the beginning of this level section of ridge to establish Camp II.

The route above Camp II follows the narrow and corniced ridge crest gradually upwards to end at the very summit of Lowell Peak. The route can be descended if fixed line is used. Alternatively, the west ridge can be used as an easier descent if an alpine style ascent is made. A good selection of rock protection will be useful for the two rock buttresses. Some snow and ice protection is useful for the horizontal ridge crest. As of this writing there are no recorded ascents of the south ridge of Lowell Peak.

Southwest Ridge

The southwest ridge can be reached off Lowell Glacier. *See CD photo (Chapter 2) CD-N03.* A narrow ridge can be followed off Lowell Glacier to reach the upper basin. The upper basin provides a good spot to place Camp I.

The route from Camp I follows the narrow rocky ridge crest of the southwest ridge for several rope lengths. The rocky ridge then merges with the summit plateau. The summit plateau provides easy snow slopes leading to the summit of Lowell Peak. There is no need to use fixed line on this route. A small rack of rock, snow and ice protection is useful. The route from Camp I to the summit can be ascended and descended easily in one day. As of this writing there are no recorded ascents of the southwest ridge of Lowell Peak.

West Ridge

From the upper basin below the southwest ridge of Lowell Peak a good site can be found to establish Camp I. *See CD photo (Chapter 2) CD-N04.* From Camp I the west ridge of Lowell Peak can be ascended. The route ascends a small snow couloir to reach the crest of the west ridge. A low angle rock ridge is climbed to reach the summit plateau. The summit plateau provides easy snow slopes to reach the summit.

A small rack of rock and snow protection can be used on this climb. The west ridge of Lowell Peak can be climbed easily in one day from Camp I. The ascent route can be used for the descent route. As of this writing there are no recorded ascents of the west ridge of Lowell Peak.

The Lowell Traverse

A very interesting variation on climbing Pinnacle Peak would be to climb Pinnacle Peak and subsequently to climb Lowell Peak by traversing the ridge that connects Pinnacle Peak with Lowell Peak. The easiest beginning to this climb would be to obtain the west col by either its northern or southern approach. *See CD photo (Chapter 2) CD-N05.* The west ridge of Pinnacle Peak can be climbed easily from the col.

After traversing back down to the col the climb proceeds up a snow couloir onto a small peak midway between Pinnacle Peak and Lowell Peak. *See CD photo (Chapter 2) CD-N06.* The climb goes over this small peak and onto a large snow plateau. A good camp can be placed on the level part of this plateau. The climb proceeds past the plateau onto the crest of the ridge leading to Lowell Peak.

The ridge past the plateau is very narrow, rocky and in some places corniced. The ridge goes over another rocky peak and drops down into a col on the northwest corner of Lowell Peak. The level snow field in this col is a good place to bivouac if necessary.

The climb to the summit of Lowell Peak goes up a steep narrow ridge out of the col. This ridge intersects the southeast ridge of Lowell Peak which is followed the remainder of the distance to the summit. Lowell Peak can easily be descended down its south side to reach Lowell Glacier. This would be a fun and challenging traverse. The summit of two peaks could be reached on such a climb. This traverse could probably be done most easily in an alpine style climb. An alpine ascent would facilitate the speed with which the climb could be done. As of this writing there is no record of this traverse being attempted.

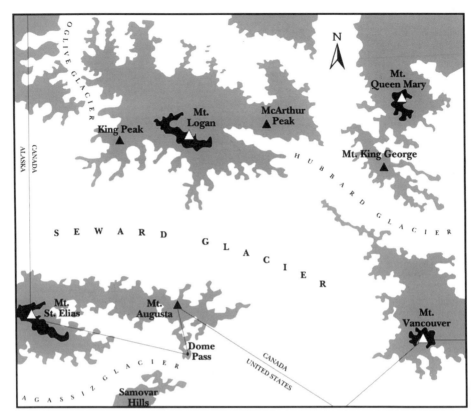

The St. Elias Group

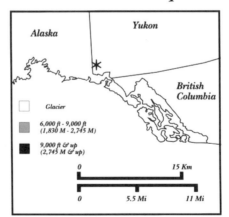

CHAPTER 3

THE ST. ELIAS GROUP

Introduction

The St. Elias Mountain massif and its satellite peaks are a linear east west group of spectacular spire shaped ice covered mountains rising precipitously out of the Pacific Ocean. Mt. St. Elias was originally spotted by the ubiquitous Russian seafaring captain Vitus Bering. His name now adorns a large ice sheet in the Wrangell-St. Elias Mountain complex. This great stretch of spectacular peaks is visible from many miles out to sea on a clear day. From the top of these ice laden summits, one can see well into the interior of the St. Elias Range. Mt. Lucania is easily visible on a clear day some seventy miles (113 km) away.

Mt. St. Elias is the second highest mountain in Canada and the fourth highest mountain in North America, yet there remain five major ridges which have yet to see a first ascent. Analogously, most of the satellite peaks adjacent to Mt. St. Elias have numerous unclimbed ridges beckoning a first ascent team. Remarkably, Mt. Malaspina does not appear to have any ascents at all.

The adjacent peak of Mt. Augusta cannot really be considered a satellite peak of any other mountain as it towers over Seward Glacier, reaching the respectable height of 14,070 feet (4,289 m). Yet, there are several first ascent possibilities on Mt. Augusta as well. In fact, most of the routes on Mt. Augusta have been climbed only once or twice.

In summary, Mt. St. Elias and its adjacent peaks are in a remote and wild part of the St. Elias Mountains. These mountains are not only spectacular in size and appearance but many in fact possess the greatest number of first ascent possibilities in the entire Wrangell-St. Elias complex.

Mt. St. Elias
18,008 feet (5,489 m)

Mt. St. Elias, the mountain for which the entire range is named, on a clear day provides one of the most glorious alpine spectacles possibly imaginable. Mt. St. Elias is covered to the very base with ice and snow and sends its glistening slopes rising to more than 18,000 feet (5,486 m) into a steel blue sky. Mt. St. Elias is easy to underestimate; despite its huge size the clear air and the optical illusion of perspective make St. Elias look closer and smaller than it really is. In fact, the summit is just over 18,000 feet (5,486 m) high and is some twelve miles distant from tidewater. The intervening distance from the sea is comprised of extraordinarily rugged and complex terrain.

The south side of Mt. St. Elias falls directly into Tyne Sound such that the climbing routes on the south side of Mt. St. Elias start at no more than 3,000 feet (914 m) above sea level. Consequently, routes on the south side of Mt. St. Elias gain at least 15,000 feet (4,572 m) before reaching the summit. This is the largest elevation gain needed to reach a summit on any mountain anywhere in the world.

On the feast day of St. Elias in 1741, Captain Vitus Bering sighted this huge mountain from his ship. He christened the peak after the patron saint of the day and Mt. St. Elias gained its name. Nearly forty years later the great British sea captain, James Cook, while on the third of his notable voyages of discovery, also sighted the mountain. He assumed correctly that this was Mt. St. Elias and also made note of it in his logbook. From that point onward Mt. St. Elias was labeled on all seafaring maps.

The true elevation of Mt. St. Elias was in dispute for quite some time. In 1786, the French explorer Jean-Francois de Galaupe, Count de La Pérouse assigned an elevation of 12,672 feet (3,862 m) to Mt. St. Elias. In 1791, Alejandro Malaspina, a great Spanish explorer, after whom the great piedmont glacier south of Mt. St. Elias was named, determined the mountain to be 17,850 feet (5,441 m). Russian hydrographic charts published in 1847 claimed the correct elevation to indeed be 17,850 feet (5,441 m). However, a British Admiralty chart published in 1872 again shrank the mountain to 14,972 feet (4,563 m). The United States Coast and Geodetic Survey of 1874 raised the elevation to 19,100 feet (5,822 m). This elevation was accepted as the correct height until the early 1890's.

All of this attention finally aroused the interest of mountaineers, who were ultimately the first Caucasians to venture into the Wrangell-St. Elias area. In 1886, Fredrick Schwatka, who had made the first successful descent of the Yukon River, lead a climbing expedition to Mt. St. Elias which was sponsored by *The New York Times*. The Schwatka expedition landed on a beach in Icy Bay. They had supplies for just ten days, which shows how vastly they underestimated the struggle ahead.

They followed the Yahtse River, which spills out of the Malaspina Glacier about ten miles from the coast. Yahtse was in fact the name given to Mt. St. Elias by native North American Indians before the European explorers arrived. Schwatka and his team eventually reached the head of the Malaspina Glacier and found the distinctive moss covered sandstone outcrops which rise above the glacier. Schwatka named this formation the Chaix Hills, in honor of the president of the Swiss Geographical Society. Schwatka and his team ultimately were only able to reach the modest height of 7,300 feet (2,225 m) before he departed, claiming that no man would ever set foot on the summit of this mountain.

The next attempt was made in 1888 by a much more experienced climbing team. The leader of this expedition was an Englishman, Harold Topham. The team was comprised of climbers from the United States and Europe. They stockpiled forty days' worth of food for their climb. Since this team had no official backing they made their way to the mountain the best that they could. They used local Tinglit Indian guides, whom they had hired in the nearby coastal village of Yakutat. They proposed to follow the same route taken by Schwatka and his team.

Topham and his team struggled up the Yahtse River and to the head of Malaspina Glacier. They then climbed to the head of Tyndall Glacier before running out of supplies. They ultimately reached an altitude of 11,460 feet (3,493 m). Topham also commented on the great complexities of the south side of Mt. St. Elias and suggested that an approach from the north might be a more practical alternative for future expeditions.

That was in fact what happened when the next expedition appeared in 1890. This team was led by the renown geologist, Professor Israel Russell. Russell's team had the impeccable sponsorship of the National Geographic Society and the United States Geological Survey. Russell and his team reached the head of Malaspina Glacier and then moved up onto a small side glacier, which they named Marvine Glacier. At the head of the Marvine Glacier they located Pinnacle Pass, named after the many spires and pinnacles on the adjacent cliffs. After they descended Pinnacle Pass they reached the largest and grandest of the alpine glaciers discovered during the expedition. They named it Seward Glacier in honor of William Seward, the American Secretary of State responsible for the purchase of Alaska for the United States.

Beyond the Seward Glacier was another opening, which they called Dome Pass, so named because of its bold snow covered domes rising out of the crest of the divide. Dome Pass gave way to Newton Glacier, which led directly to Mt. St. Elias. Russell found that Newton Glacier occupied a steep-walled, avalanche prone valley. Professor Russell led his team through this valley up Newton Glacier to a high camp below the saddle that connects Mt. St. Elias and Mt. Newton, now named Russell Col in honor of Professor Russell's pioneering expedition. At this point Russell and his team were low on supplies and the weather turned bad. Consequently, the expedition ended with a high point of 9,500 feet (2,896 m). However, they had now found a way to reach the mountain from the north and a climbing route to the summit which appeared feasible.

Professor Russell was back for another attempt in 1891. They followed the same route as they had used the previous year. Two climbers ultimately reached the Russell Col at 12,280 feet (3,743 m). From the col they could see well inland and for the first time realized the vastness of the icefields that were present. The climbers went on to reach 14,500 feet (4,420 m) before reluctantly turning back.

In 1897, the breakthrough finally occurred when a well organized and now legendary team, led by the Duke of Abruzzi, arrived to climb Mt. St. Elias. Luigi Amedeo di Savoia-Aosta, the Duke of Abruzzi, was born in Spain just two weeks before his father abdicated the throne of Spain in 1873. Upon returning to his father's native Italy, he became a sailor in the Italian Navy at the age of six. He was the commander of a vessel by age twenty. His travels took him to India where he became interested in the Himalayas. He led a successful trip to the Karakorum Range in Pakistan in 1909. Then his team successfully ascended Bride Peak, with an elevation of 25,105 feet (7,652 m).

He then set his sights on the still unclimbed Mt. St. Elias. He arrived in the United States by steamship to New York harbor. The team traveled across the United States by train to Seattle, and then took a ship to Alaska, arriving in the small coastal fishing village of Yakutat. The expedition led by the Duke of Abruzzi had several of Italy's finest climbers and Vittorio Sella, a skilled photographer, whose magnificent photographs provided the only photographic record of the Duke's expedition as well as the first quality photographs of the St. Elias Mountains.

The Abruzzi Expedition proposed to follow the same route pioneered by Professor Russell. The team expected to reach the Russell Col and then proceed to the summit. This is in fact what the team accomplished. This has now become the standard approach to climb the Abruzzi Ridge, named in honor of the first ascent made by the Duke. This route will be described in more detail later.

The remote location of Mt. St. Elias

has not allowed it to escape the effects of the modern world, however, including global warming. Mt. St. Elias is now "closer" to the ocean than ever before. Tyndall Glacier, at the foot of the south side of the mountain has melted considerably. Consequently, the glacier has retreated into the newly created fjord and has lost nearly six miles since it was first photographed in the 1930's. Tidewater is now only twelve miles from the summit of Mt. St. Elias.

In addition to all the early attempts, Mt. St. Elias has seen many more recent climbs. The mountain is large and varied in its climbing challenges. The south ridge provides the highest elevation gain of any route on any mountain in the world. It is necessary to ascend more than 15,000 feet (4,572 m) from the base of the south ridge to the summit.

The great south face of Mt. St. Elias has seen only one ascent. This massive and glacially active face is an extreme climb and provides one of the great mountaineering challenges on any mountain anywhere. There are, however, numerous climbs that follow safer approaches to the summit along narrow spines of rock. Mt. St. Elias has seen many ascents and is well-known to most climbers, however it still remains one of the best sources of first ascents in the entire Wrangell-St. Elias Mountain Range. There are at least five major ridges on Mt. St. Elias, which remained unclimbed. As of this writing, the long sinuous crest of the southeast ridge has never been climbed. The narrow and exhilarating south ridge has never been ascended and there are no records that it has ever been attempted. The south buttress leading directly to the Mira Face on the south side of the mountain has never been climbed. The spectacular south buttress ridge leading over The Hump and connecting with the Boundary Route has never been climbed either. Finally, the north spur connecting with the northwest ridge has never been climbed, although it has been attempted.

In short, Mt. St. Elias provides an excellent climbing challenge with many types of ascents available. The mountain is in the most remote corner of the St. Elias Range and provides a very commanding view of the ocean as well as the vast inland icefields. Mt. St. Elias is an enjoyable and rewarding mountaineering challenge.

The United States maps to this region are USGS Mt. St. Elias Alaska-Canada, scale 1:250,000, and USGS Bering Glacier Alaska-Canada, scale 1:250,000. The Canadian map is Newton Glacier 115 C/7, and 115 C/2, scale 1:50,000.

Abruzzi Ridge

The Abruzzi Ridge was named in honor of the Duke of Abruzzi who made the first ascent of the ridge as well as Mt. St. Elias itself in 1897. This well financed team of skilled European climbers pioneered a route to Mt. St. Elias from the sea and ultimately completed the ascent of the Abruzzi Ridge. The marvelous photographs taken by their expedition photographer, Vittorio Sella, provided insight into the topography of the St. Elias Mountains as well as an excellent record of the climb itself.

The Abruzzi Ridge is the most direct and least technical route that can be used to ascend Mt. St. Elias. However, this ridge is not without its own difficulties. Abruzzi Ridge can be approached via Newton Glacier. The Newton Glacier sits in a steep-walled canyon and is prone to massive avalanches that pour off the north face of Mt. St. Elias. See photo 10.

The first ascent team ascended Newton Glacier and placed an advanced base camp on the glacier opposite the east ridge of St. Elias. *See CD photo (Chapter 3) CD-001.* The route then ascends the steep and crevassed snow slopes leading to the Russell Col. This is an active avalanche zone subject

Photo 10 *Photo by Richard Holmes*

to massive avalanches of snow and ice that fall from the north face of Mt. St. Elias. The larger avalanches will bury anything in the valley at the head of the Newton Glacier. Consequently, it is best to ascend and descend this section of the climb in the early morning hours when the snow is most firm.

A good camp can be placed on the Russell Col at 12,280 feet (3,743 m). The first ascent team went directly up the remaining 5,000 feet (1,524 m) to the summit. However, it might be a good idea to place a high camp at about 15,000 feet (4,572 m) on the ridge to ensure success on summit day. Also, a high camp will provide refuge if bad weather suddenly moves in.

This approach to climbing the Abruzzi Ridge was the standard ascent until the early 1970's when a new variation was introduced. Today some climbers find it easier and safer to ascend the north ridge of Mt. Newton to reach the Russell Col. *See CD photo (Chapter 3) CD-002.* This route begins on the Seward Glacier at the base of the north ridge of Mt. Newton. The route ascends easy snow slopes to reach the crest of the north ridge. The crest of the north ridge is followed to the summit of Mt. Newton at 13,811 feet (4,210 m).

From the summit of Mt. Newton the route descends 1,600 feet (488 m) down the narrow and corniced ridge crest leading from the summit of Mt. Newton to the Russell Col. The advantage of this approach is that it avoids all of the avalanche danger found on Newton Glacier. The disadvantage of this route is that the narrow ridge crest leading from Mt. Newton to the Russell Col is very narrow and corniced. The final 1,500 feet (457 m) is the most difficult part. Although it is completely horizontal, it is razor edged and double corniced. In fact, in some years the snow and ice on this ridge is so unstable that it cannot be traversed at all. Therefore, the choice of routes needed to reach the Russell Col will depend upon the time of year and the snow conditions found during that year. The earlier in the year this route is climbed the greater the chances for success. Generally, the month of May provides the best chance for good snow and ice conditions. Ref. *AAJ* 1971, pp. 111-112; *AAJ* 1998 pp. 233-234. *CAJ* 1972, pp. 4-6; *CAJ* 1984, pp. 81-82.

The East Ridge

The east ridge of Mt. St. Elias is one of the most beautiful lines on any mountain in the entire St. Elias Range. It is a long slender crest rising elegantly out of Newton Glacier and rising nearly 9,000 feet (2,743 m) to the pinnacle shaped summit of the mountain. The ridge is easy to access off Newton Glacier and represents a moderately difficult technical challenge. The climb has been done in one week and can be done with a minimum of fixed line.

The first ascent of the east ridge of Mt. St. Elias took place in the summer of 1972 following many attempts in the previous years. The climb begins directly off Newton Glacier at the foot of the east ridge. See photo 20. The route follows the rounded crest of the ridge on easy snow slopes until the ridge becomes noticeably steeper. Camp I can be placed on level ground at 11,000 feet (3,353 m).

The first ascent team climbed the narrow crest of the ridge directly above Camp I. This involves following a narrow ridge crest which is double corniced over very unstable and loose snow slopes. This corniced section is very difficult and time-consuming. A new variation has been used to avoid this narrow portion of the ridge crest.

Immediately above Camp I, the route moves to the right of the ridge onto the north face. This 45 degree face is climbed for about ten rope lengths to regain the ridge above the narrow crest. From there the ridge begins to broaden and a good place can be found at 12,000 feet (3,658 m) to establish Camp II.

The north face variation has the

Photo 20

Photo by Richard Holmes

advantage of avoiding the narrow double corniced section of a knife-edged ridge between 11,000 to 12,000 feet (3,353 to 3,658 m). However, this variation does present its own problems. The face is steep as it has an average angle of 45 degrees. This section of the climb ascends directly below large menacing overhanging seracs. Consequently, this one section of the climb should be done during the very cold early morning hours when the snow is generally more solid. This will minimize avalanche dangers.

Above Camp II the ridge becomes narrow and icy again. However, this section is not as narrow or corniced as the lower sections. The ridge is usually climbed just to the left of the main crest at the interface between the snow and rock and generally does not need any fixed line. This narrow section ends at 15,000 feet (4,572 m) on a broad snow shoulder. A good tent platform can be dug in here at 15,000 feet (4,572 m) to establish Camp III.

The route above Camp III follows the ridge crest until it gives way to a large snow face. *See CD photo (Chapter 3) CD-003.* The snow face is followed to the final summit ridge, which is climbed up and to the right to reach the true summit of St. Elias. The ascent route can be used as the descent route.

This route can be done in as little as seven to ten days. There is not much need for fixed rope, but this will depend upon the snow conditions at the time of the ascent. This is a beautiful line on a ridge which provides moderate technical challenges but is never too severe. Ref. *AAJ* 1973, pp. 299-302. *AAJ* 1985, p. 182. *CAJ* 1973, pp. 10-13.

Southeast Ridge

One of the premiere first ascent possibilities in the entire St. Elias Mountain Range is the southeast ridge of Mt. St. Elias. The southeast ridge is a long slender and steep ridge curving up and to the right to end directly at the summit. See photo 3O. This ridge has been attempted on a few occasions but has not yet seen a successful ascent. This beautiful ridge could be climbed in an expedition style climb but the lack of large campsites high on the ridge would facilitate space for only a single two-man tent at any one time.

Another intriguing and more rewarding possibility would be to climb the southeast ridge in tandem with the east ridge of St. Elias. The east ridge of Mt. St. Elias is a good warm-up climb since it is not as technically difficult and this would be a great way to acclimatize to high altitude. After descending the east ridge, an alpine style ascent of the southeast ridge would be a great second climb. The east ridge could then be used as the descent route and you could already have wands in place to help with the descent if the weather turned bad.

Either way, the southeast ridge remains unclimbed to this day. An ascent of this ridge would require excellent technical skills and good judgement to overcome the climbing challenge of this spectacular alpine ridge.

The best place to start the climb is probably about 100 yards (91 m) up the left side of the ridge. *See CD photo (Chapter 3) CD-4O.* The left or south side of the ridge has some exposed rock. These small rock buttresses represent a good way to get on to the ridge crest and avoid the narrow ridge crest that exists at the foot of the ridge.

Once on the southeast ridge a short section of narrow ridge must be ascended to reach a large flat snow platform. A short distance past the large snow platform is a rounded snow shoulder. A good site can be located on this large platform to establish Camp I. This is the highest point at which a good secure camp can be placed on a relatively large flat area on the southeast ridge.

Above Camp I the climb becomes very steep and the crux of the climb is encountered. The climb begins on a narrow crest of snow that is corniced. This steep ridge crest is climbed until it merges with a steep ice face. This face is climbed on the left side to avoid overhanging rock in the middle of the face. *See CD photo (Chapter 3) CD-005.*

The ice face ends at a narrow ridge crest which is almost horizontal. This narrow and corniced crest is traversed to reach a large rounded snow dome at 15,000 (4,572 m). It provides an excellent place to dig in a platform for a tent to establish Camp II.

The climb proceeds from the magnificent location of Camp II onto a horizontal ridge crest. The crest is narrow but can be climbed fairly easily on its left side. *See CD photo (Chapter 3) CD-006.* At the end of the horizontal traverse the climb ascends the final summit ridge. The summit ridge involves mixed rock and ice climbing but it is not difficult or very steep. It ends directly at the summit of Mt. St. Elias. The ascent route can be used as the descent route if an expedition style climb was attempted. It will be much easier to descend with fixed rope in place. An alpine style ascent would necessitate a descent down the east ridge, which is much easier to descend. As of this writing the southeast ridge of Mt. St. Elias has not been climbed.

South Ridge

The second of the five great unclimbed ridges on Mt. St. Elias is the south ridge. Since this climb starts on the south side of the mountain, the climb will entail significant elevation gain. This climb will require ascending nearly 13,000 feet (3,962 m) of ridge before reaching the summit. This is a long and circuitous route covering every type of climbing imaginable. There is some face climbing as well as traversing over narrow ridge crests. There is an ice face as well as exposed rock. Altogether, this interesting

Photo 30 *Photo by Richard Holmes*

climb represents a good mountaineering challenge and has still not been climbed. The climb begins on a side glacier off Libbey Glacier. *See CD photo (Chapter 3) CD-007*. The route follows the narrow ridge over mixed rock and snow for several rope lengths. A short horizontal section of snow is traversed to reach a rounded snow ridge which leads to the top of a snow dome. A good camp can be dug into the top of this snow dome at 12,000 feet (3,658 m) to make Camp I.

The route then descends from the snow dome into a saddle where a horizontal snow ridge is traversed. *See CD photo (Chapter 3) CD-008*. The saddle gives way to a narrow rock ridge, which is climbed along its crest. The rock ridge then merges with a snow face, which is climbed up and to the right to reach the crest of the southeast ridge. *See CD photo (Chapter 3) CD-009*. A good camp can be dug into a snow dome at 15,000 feet (4,572 m). This is also the site of Camp II on the southeast ridge route.

From this point onwards the south ridge and the southeast ridge routes merge. The south ridge route follows the same horizontal traverse as described earlier. *See CD photo (Chapter 3) CD-010*. The route proceeds up the summit ridge above the traverse and ends directly at the summit. If this climb is done in an expedition style then the ascent route can be used as the descent route. If an alpine style climb is done the east ridge is probably the easiest descent.

South Face

The most notable geologic feature of Mt. St. Elias is the great south face. This massive 15,000 foot (4,572 m) face stands defiantly overlooking the Gulf of Alaska. The face is too steep to possess any glaciers; however, it is covered with many pocket glaciers. These smaller pocket glaciers are very active, continuously avalanching in a symphony of thunderous roars. The face is one complete and total avalanche zone with some avalanches sweeping half of the face at one time and rolling all the way down, a half mile (0.8 km) onto Libbey Glacier. There are no safe routes on this face as any potential route will be subject to continuous avalanche danger.

Nonetheless, there has been one ascent of this face. The climb follows the only line of weakness in the face ascending through a snow chute at mid-height on the face. This chute is the only potential line through the otherwise unbroken rock cliff, which spans the entire face halfway up. Any climb on this face will have to involve climbing early in the season when the snow and ice are still frozen solid. The only recorded ascent of this face approached the mountain from the head of Libbey Glacier where Camp I was placed at the base of the south face. The route proceeds up gentle snow slopes on an indistinct buttress where Camp II was placed just above a rock outcrop. *See CD photo (Chapter 3) CD-011*.

The route proceeds up the snow slopes above Camp I towards an obvious snow chute. This is the only line of weakness through an otherwise unbroken wall of rock that girdles the entire face at mid-height. The route proceeds up the chute to the crest of a narrow rib where Camp III was placed at 11,500 feet (3,505 m) in a snow cave. The chute is best done early in the morning or late at night as all the avalanches from the upper face are channeled through this chute. *See CD photo (Chapter 3) CD-012*.

The route above Camp III is the technical crux of the climb. The route proceeds straight up a steep 65 degree ice face. The route moves to the right around an overhanging rock face. The route continues up the steep ice face directly below overhanging ice seracs, which avalanche with considerable frequency. The first ascent team moved onto the upper snow face just left of the overhanging ice seracs and placed Camp

IV at 13,100 feet (3,993 m). *See CD photo (Chapter 3) CD-O13.*

The route above Camp IV follows a snow face which is at a lower angle than that encountered in the middle of the face. The climb moves to the right to miss large crevasses in the upper face. The first ascent team placed Camp V at 14,400 feet (4,389 m) below the crest of the southeast ridge. *See CD photo (Chapter 3) CD-O13.* The route then merges with the southeast ridge and the climb to the summit is the same as that for the southeast ridge route.

The ascent route was used as the descent route. The climb can really only be done in an alpine style ascent. An expedition climb would expose the climbers to unnecessary avalanche dangers. This route has excellent mountaineering challenges. However, it can not really be considered a safe or enjoyable climb. Ref. *AAJ* 1980, pp. 481-486. *AAJ* 1985, pp. 20-29.

Southwest Ridge

The southwest ridge of Mt. St. Elias was the scene of the first attempts to climb the mountain. The 1886 Schwatka and the 1888 Topham expeditions made attempts on the southwest ridge of St. Elias with only limited success. Although the Abruzzi Ridge yielded the first ascent of Mt. St. Elias, it was nearly a half-century later when the first successful ascent was made of the southwest ridge of Mt. St. Elias.

In 1946, an expedition from the Harvard Mountaineering Club organized a trip to climb Mt. St. Elias via the southwest ridge. The team had an ambitious list of objectives which included: (1) the first ascent of Mt. St. Elias by an American team, (2) the first ascent of the mountain by the southwest ridge, (3) the first ascent of Haydon Peak, (4) the first ascent of Haydon peak as well as Mt. St. Elias by a woman and finally, (5) the first use of air support to supply the expedition high on the mountain.

This well organized team was in fact successful in all of their objectives. The use of aircraft to drop supplies high on the mountain greatly facilitated their movement. This air support enabled the team to reach the summit of Haydon Peak in addition to the main summit of St. Elias. The team also enjoyed the luxury of fresh baked goods, as freshly baked apple pies were included in one of the air drops!

The climb of the southwest ridge of Mt. St. Elias generally begins at the head of the Tyndall Glacier, in a basin below the foot of the main mass of the southwest ridge. An excellent level snowfield exists here at 4,300 feet (1,311 m) to create Camp I. The first ascent team chose to climb a rock ridge which is comprised of very loose frost fractured shale. *See CD photo (Chapter 3) CD-O14.* The route proceeds up the right-hand edge of the shale ridge. The climb then proceeds up the snow face above the ridge to the crest of the main southwest ridge. *See CD photo (Chapter 3) CD-O15.*

The shale rock is very fractured and very sharp and is tough on climbing ropes. During some recent ascents a new variation has been established to the left of the shale ridge. *See CD photo (Chapter 3) CD-O16.* This variation avoids the shale and ascends an obvious snow bowl left of the shale ridge. The problem with this variation is that it requires that the climber traverse below large and unstable seracs which avalanche with uncertain frequently. This may create more problems than it solves, consequently, ascending the shale ridge may be the lesser of two evils. Once on top of the ridge, the route proceeds up a gentle snow slope to the base of the Haydon Bench. A good camp site can be dug into the snow slopes at the base of the bench at 8,000 feet (2,438 m) to establish Camp II. *See CD photo (Chapter 3) CD-O17.*

The rock above Camp II climbs the snow face to the right of a rock outcrop to get onto the Haydon Bench. The Haydon Bench is a long slender snow plateau that rises gently up and to the right ending at the base of Haydon Peak at Haydon Col. The route proceeds along this bench to the base of Haydon Peak where a good place can be found at 10,300 feet (3,139 m) to establish Camp III. *See CD photo (Chapter 3) CD-O18.*

From this point a short detour can be made to climb the 11,945 foot (3,641 m) summit of Haydon Peak, which was ascended by the team that made the first ascent of the southwest ridge of St. Elias. The slopes of Haydon Peak are unstable and slab avalanches are common. Consequently, the best approach is to ascend the narrow but obvious ridge up and to the left to reach the summit of Haydon Peak. This ascent should take about three hours and the descent will take about one hour. *See CD photo (Chapter 3) CD-O19.*

The route above Camp III climbs into Haydon Col. The snow slopes in this area are loose and unstable and this remains the one area with the greatest danger of avalanches. The best approach in this area is to stay far below the summit slopes of Haydon Peak and work your way up into Haydon Col. *See CD photo (Chapter 3) CD-O20.*

The steep icy ridge above Haydon Col is the technical crux of the climb. The steepest slopes on this section reach 65 degrees in angle. Occasionally, the slope will have a steep bergschrund lip that must be ascended but generally the slope is just icy and fairly steep. *See CD photo (Chapter 3) CD-O21.* The route goes through the rock bands that span the entire south side of the mountain. The best approach is to make your way to the right side of the ice face just above Haydon Col. Just below the overhanging seracs, work back to the left where there is a gap in the seracs. Depending on the conditions that year a serac may have to be climbed directly. *See CD photo (Chapter 3) CD-O21.* The route then goes through an obvious chute in the granite rock band. The route through the rock is much easier than it looks from below. The route then proceeds up the steep snow face to reach the top of an obvious snow dome. The top of this snow dome is a good place to establish Camp IV at 13,500 feet (4,115 m). Some fixed line through the ice seracs just above Haydon Col will facilitate the ascent with heavy packs. It may also facilitate the descent particularly if the weather turns bad.

The route above Camp IV follows the obvious but narrow ridge crest directly above camp. The snow faces on either side of the ridge crest are avalanche hazards and are heavily crevassed. *See CD photo (Chapter 3) CD-O22.* The ridge crest averages about 45 degrees in angle and is a little icy; however, fixed line is generally not needed here. Immediately above the icy ridge the slope flattens out. There is a good sheltered spot here to establish Camp V at 15,500 feet (4,724 m). Some teams skip this camp and go all the way to the summit from Camp IV, but this creates a very long summit day. This approach can also be dangerous if the weather turns bad. Consequently, establishing a high camp at 15,500 feet (4,724 m) is probably the safest approach.

The final stretch to the summit follows the obvious ridge crest. The route begins on a low angle rock ridge and then turns to snow and ice. The last two pitches on the climb involve climbing on or around large ice mushrooms. Although these look difficult from below, the approach to surmounting them is obvious when you get on them. Two large ice mushrooms must be climbed directly just below the summit, making the last pitch of this magnificent climb almost the single hardest pitch of the climb. *See CD photo (Chapter 3) CD-O23.*

The southwest ridge of Mt. St. Elias is a seven mile (11.3 km) mountaineering adventure. Nearly 15,000 feet (4,572 m) of climbing must be surmounted to reach the summit, making this the largest elevation gain on any route on any mountain anywhere in the world. This is more than compensated for when reaching the tiny pyramidal summit of Mt. St. Elias, which is barely large enough for two people to stand on simultaneously.

This is a popular route but it should not be underestimated. It is very long and the moderate technical difficulties preclude the southwest ridge from being an easy walk up. The technical demands are not serious but they are continuous. There are significant objective hazards present on the avalanche slopes below Haydon Col. This area should be traversed during the coldest hours of the day to minimize the danger.

There is a sufficient amount of hiking across broad snow slopes, particularly on the Haydon Bench, to warrant carrying snowshoes and sleds all the way to Haydon Col. There is no real advantage to using skis as they are bulkier and harder to pack and carry. Some fixed line is useful to fix the more difficult pitches. The shale ridge at the base of the climb might be fixed if necessary. The ice slopes above Haydon Col will probably require fixed line. An extra lightweight 9mm rope is useful as the descent off the summit ice mushrooms frequently requires a rappel.

The team should have plenty of food and fuel to wait out storms on this long and arduous route. There should be a good solid shovel available for each person on the team to facilitate digging good tent platforms and for digging out the snow after storms.

Remarkably, the southwest ridge route yielded the first winter ascent of Mt. St. Elias. This was a feat of great endurance on a long route under the tremendously rigorous conditions of an Arctic winter on an Alaskan giant. It should be noted that a well prepared team can enjoy a magnificent climb on the southwest ridge, which is rapidly becoming a classic alpine route on a beautiful mountain. Ref. *AAJ* 1947, pp.257-268. *AAJ* 1997, pp. 49-52. *CAJ* 1947, pp. 44-56.

South Buttress

The third of the five unclimbed ridges on Mt. St. Elias is the south buttress. The south buttress starts at the very head of the Tyndall Glacier. *See CD photo (Chapter 3) CD-O24.* The route begins by climbing an obvious and narrow ridge crest to the top of a snow dome at 9,500 feet (2,896 m). The top of the snow dome provides sufficient space for tent platforms to establish Camp I.

The route then dips down into a little saddle and then climbs up onto a narrow ridge crest which alternates between snow and rock. The ridge is narrow and corniced and the traverse of this section will be facilitated with the use of fixed rope.

The ridge crest finally ascends a steep rib, which protrudes from the south buttress of Mt. St. Elias for several rope lengths. This ridge ends on a broad smooth snow face. The snow face is climbed to reach an obvious snow dome. This snow dome is actually the top of The Hump, 12,375 feet (3,772 m), which is a small sub-peak on the south side of Mt. St. Elias.

The route from the summit of The Hump merges with the Boundary Route of Mt. St. Elias and then climbs the Mira Face to reach the summit ridge of Mt. St. Elias. The route possibilities on the Mira Face are discussed in more detail in the description for the Boundary Route.

The south buttress route does in fact climb the south buttress of Mt. St. Elias; however, the lower part of this route is actually the south ridge of The Hump. In either case, the south ridge of The Hump in connection with the Mira Face has not been completed as of this writing.

West Ridge

The west ridge of Mt. St. Elias is the fourth of the unclimbed ridges of Mt. St.

Elias. This climb is actually the south ridge of Mt. Huxley, 12,375 feet (3,772 m) of which sits astride the west ridge of Mt. St. Elias. Consequently, an ascent of the west ridge of Mt. St. Elias would in fact be climbing Mt. Elias' west ridge but would also be the first ascent of the south ridge of Mt. Huxley.

The climb starts at the head of Tyndall Glacier. *See CD photo (Chapter 3) CD-O25.* The route climbs the obvious south ridge of Mt. Huxley. It starts up the rock buttress until it reaches the narrow ridge crest of the south ridge. The narrow south ridge is climbed until a short rock step is climbed.

Above the rock step the route proceeds up a broad snow face until it ends directly below the west ridge of Mt. St. Elias. The top of the face can be climbed on a narrow rocky ridge, which ascends the final distance to reach the top of the west ridge of Mt. St. Elias. A short traverse brings one to the top of Mt. Huxley.

The broad snow slope of the west ridge of Mt. St. Elias is traversed from the summit of Mt. Huxley to reach the base of the Mira Face. At this point the west ridge of St. Elias merges with the Boundary Route. The climb to the summit of Mt. St. Elias and ascent of the Mira Face is discussed in more detail in the section under the Boundary Route. As of this writing the south ridge of Mt. Huxley and the combination with the west ridge of Mt. St. Elias to the summit has not yet been climbed.

The Boundary Route

Mt. St. Elias sits astride the boundary that demarcates the eastern edge of Alaska and the western edge of the Yukon Territory. In order to better understand the topography of this area, an expedition was mounted in 1913 to survey the area around Mt. St. Elias as well as to make an attempt to climb the mountain.

The route that the team chose to climb was the glacier that hugs the western escarpment of Mt. St. Elias. The team ascended the heavily crevassed glacier on the west side of the mountain to reach a large plateau at 13,500 feet (4,115 m). The team ultimately was stopped at 16,000 feet (4,877 m) due to bad weather. This route is now known as the Boundary Route after the pioneering climb of the 1913 Boundary Survey Team. The Boundary Route is now a well-established and challenging mountaineering climb.

The climb begins at the northwest corner of the mountain on Columbus Glacier. *See CD photo (Chapter 3) CD-O26.* The standard route goes directly up the glacier that hugs the northwest side of Mt. St. Elias. The route starts out to the right and then weaves back towards the left side. The route then moves further up the glacier towards the right side again. The crux of the lower glacier is a series of bergschrunds at 10,500 feet (3,200 m) that must be crossed to reach the top of the glacier. *See CD photo (Chapter 3) CD-O27.* A good site can be found just above the bergschrunds to establish Camp I at 11,000 feet (3,353 m).

The standard route does have the difficulty of surmounting some difficult bergschrunds. In addition to the bergschrunds the lower part of this route is constantly threatened by avalanches from seracs hanging off the west face of St. Elias. Consequently, an alternative approach can be utilized. This approach starts on the Columbus Glacier but climbs an obvious and smooth snow ramp that ascends just to the right of Windy Peak, 12,500 feet (3,810 m). *See CD photo (Chapter 3) CD-O28.* The route reaches the top of a crevasse field and then turns left to follow a corridor that reaches a saddle behind Windy Peak. A good spot can be found here at 11,500 feet (3,505 m) to establish Camp I. A short detour can be made here to make the one hour ascent of Windy Peak.

Both the standard route and the route

to the right side of Windy Peak merge in a saddle just above it. The route above Windy Peak follows the smooth upper glacier to the bench at 13,500 feet (4,115 m). A good spot can be found just below the bench at 13,500 feet (4,115 m) to place Camp II. It is best to place the camp just below the crest of the bench to protect it from the wind. This bench is exposed to the full force of the wind on the south side of Mt. St. Elias as well as the tremendous snowfall that accumulates here. So it is imperative to place the camp in a wind protected area and build snow walls around the tent. Also, it is wise to have snow shovels available to dig out accumulated snow that may fall in a long storm.

The route then proceeds from the bench up the 3,000 foot (914 m) western escarpment of Mt. St. Elias to reach the long summit ridge. The 3,000 foot (914 m) high western escarpment of Mt. St. Elias is now known as the Mira Face. This name is derived from the nickname of the famous Czech climber, Miroslav Smid, known to his friends as Mira. Mira made an ascent of this face using an interesting variation. Mira subsequently died later that same year (1993) while rock climbing in Yosemite National Park. Consequently, the name Mira has been applied to the upper section of this climb in his honor.

The Mira Face has been ascended by three variations. The first complete ascent of this face was done on the rock buttress directly above the high bench. *See CD photo (Chapter 3) CD-O29.* This fifty degree buttress was ascended over mixed rock and ice. The rock climbing consists of some low fifth class climbing. The buttress is moderately steep and provides very enjoyable climbing in an unbelievably exposed and exciting location. Fortunately, the climbing on this buttress is never too severe in difficulty.

The use of fixed line will facilitate the ascent and will make the descent vastly easier and faster, particularly in bad weather. The climb from the top of the Mira Face then traverses the two and one half mile (4 km) ridge to the base of the pyramidal summit of Mt. St. Elias.

The rock buttress remained the only route up the Mira Face until the summer of 2000, when two new routes were pioneered on the face. The first variation placed on the Mira Face climbs the fifty degree snow face directly up the middle of the face. The climb is entirely on snow and ice except for one small chute through a rock band at mid-height on the face. The exit off the face climbs an exciting 55 degree snow face on the last pitch below the summit ridge. This variation connects with the summit ridge just to the right of the rock buttress and then makes the long two and one half mile (4 km) traverse to the summit pyramid. *See CD photo (Chapter 3) CD-O30.*

The next variation was put up by Miroslav Smid himself, on an indistinct rock buttress on the right-hand side of the Mira Face. *See CD photo (Chapter 3) CD-O31.* This variation connects with the long summit ridge and then requires the traverse along this ridge to the base of the summit pyramid.

The variation chosen on the Mira Face will depend on the snow conditions of that year and the skills of the team making the ascent. A small camp can be placed at the top of the buttress at 16,500 feet (5,029 m) to create Camp III. A high camp at this location will greatly facilitate the summit push. The traverse to the base of the summit pyramid is mainly horizontal but it does cover two and one half miles (4 km) at an elevation over 16,000 feet (4,877 m). This is quite an exhausting summit day. The final climb to the summit follows the obvious ridge on the western edge of the summit pyramid.

The ascent route can be used as the descent route. Some fixed rope can be used on the Mira Face if desired to facilitate the descent. This is an excellent climb involving

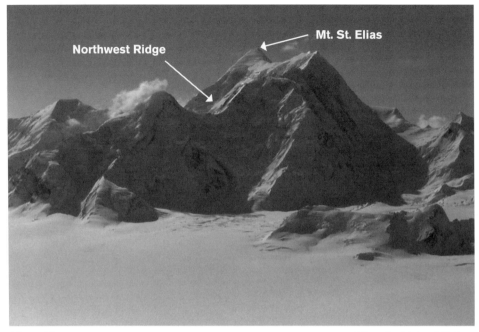

Photo 40 *Photo by Richard Holmes*

a mix of glacier travel and face climbing. Interestingly, the Mira Face has been used as a ski descent. This is an impressive achievement considering the steep angle of the face and the texture of the snow at this high altitude. Ref. *AAJ* 2001, pp. 223-224. *CAJ* 1980, pp. 88-89.

The Northwest Ridge

The north side of Mt. St. Elias is dominated by the steep and imposing northwest ridge. This long and complicated route saw its first ascent in the summer of 1965. See photo 40. This route involves a great deal of climbing along the slender crest of the northwest ridge crest. The climb also involves some very interesting rock climbing on two pronounced rock gendarmes.

The climb ends with the traverse across the upper west ridge to reach the pyramidal summit of Mt. St. Elias with full views of the Pacific Ocean and the interior icefields. Although the first ascent team predicted this marvelous climb would become a well-traveled route on Mt. St. Elias, the challenging nature of the route has somehow unfortunately precluded very many ascents of this beautiful and satisfying ascent.

The climb can begin at the very foot of the northwest ridge. *See CD photo (Chapter 3) CD-O32*. However, this entails climbing over a 13,200 foot (4,023 m) sub-peak and then descending to a large col at 12,000 feet (3,658 m). *See CD photo (Chapter 3) CD-O33*. To avoid ascending and descending this unnecessary elevation the first ascent team chose to climb from Camp I on the Seward Glacier up a side glacier on the south side of the northwest ridge. The route bypasses a crevasse field on its left-hand side. The route then ascends up into the col, which involves easy snow climbing except for one bergschrund about 200 feet (61 m) below the col. The bergschrund can be bypassed on its left side. The col provides an excellent place to establish Camp II at 12,000 feet

Photo 50 Photo by Richard Holmes

(3,658 m).

The crux climbing on the northwest ridge is the 1,500 foot (457 m) ridge above Camp II. The ridge averages fifty degrees in angle and sometimes reaches sixty degrees in angle but is never less than 45 degrees. See photo 50.

Most of this ridge is hard packed snow. The conditions will vary from year to year as some years it is hard ice. The rock climbing on the ridge is not too steep but the rock is rotten and crumbly. Fixed rope is best used along this section to secure the ascent and facilitate the descent. *See CD photo (Chapter 3) CD-O34.*

A good spot can be found at the top of the steep ridge at 13,500 feet (4,115 m) to create Camp III. *See CD photo (Chapter 3) CD-O34.* The first ascent team climbed the remaining 500 feet (152 m) of vertical elevation to reach a large snow plateau at 14,000 feet (4,267 m) where they placed Camp IV. The route above the snow plateau at 14,000 feet (4,267 m) goes up the ridge crest over mixed rock and snow. This section of the climb involves the most rock climbing on the entire route. The route also involves climbing two rock gendarmes. The first gendarme is fairly easy but the second one involves rock climbing on crumbly rock which is up to sixty degrees in angle. The route then enters a small col at 15,000 feet (4,572 m) where Camp V is placed on a narrow section of the ridge. *See CD photo (Chapter 3) CD-O35.*

The route above Camp V follows moderate angle slopes on hard packed snow. The route ascends 1,500 feet (457 m) to reach the long northwest ridge, which traverses the two and one half mile (4 km) long summit plateau. The route ascends the western edge of the summit pyramid. *See CD photo (Chapter 3) CD-O36.*

The ascent route can be used as the descent route. The placement of fixed rope will greatly facilitate the descent of this

Photo 60 *Photo by Richard Holmes*

complex route. This is a magnificent climb requiring moderate technical difficulty yet is never too steep or overwhelmingly difficult. Despite predictions that this route would become a frequently repeated route there is no record of a successful second ascent of this climb. Ref. *AAJ* 1966, pp.19-24.

North Spur

The fifth of the five great unclimbed ridges on Mt. St. Elias is the north spur. See photo 6O. This is a challenging snow and ice ridge which connects with the northwest ridge route at the broad summit plateau at 14,000 feet (4,267 m). This route has been attempted at least twice and both attempts were unsuccessful. Remarkably, the reason for the failure of both attempts was identical: earthquakes. Significant earthquakes occurred during both known attempts on this route causing a significant number of avalanches to occur and thus making the conditions unsafe for climbing. The chances are that the next time a team attempts this route it will probably be relatively earthquake free. After all, the third time is a charm.

This route begins at the foot of the ridge on the Columbus Glacier. See photo 7O. The route ascends easy snow slopes for several rope lengths until the ridge becomes steeper. A very narrow ridge crest is followed until the ridge becomes broader again.

The rounded snow shoulder on the broad section of ridge is followed. This section of ridge has several wide crevasses that must be crossed. The broad section ends at the only level spot on the ridge at 12,800 feet (3,901 m). This is a good spot to make an equipment and food cache. This section of ridge is too unstable to establish a safe camp. Consequently, it is best to rappel back down to the glacier and use base camp as a safe campsite.

After ascending the fixed line back to the food cache the route ascends some difficult bergschrunds. Above the bergschrunds the route broadens out again. The broad shoulder leads to a narrow ridge which is ascended until it intersects with the broad snow plateau at 14,000 feet (4,267 m). The route over this plateau is the same as that described for the northwest ridge route. The north spur route can be descended if fixed line is left in place. As of this writing there have been no successful ascents of the north spur.

Mt. St. Elias Satellite Peaks

Directly east of Mt. St. Elias is a series of intermediate sized peaks that run in a straight line from Mt. St. Elias to Mt. Augusta. These mountains are not tall by St. Elias standards but they present a maze of challenging ridges and snow faces. These peaks are fun climbs and can be done as a warm-up before doing the larger peaks in the area. Additionally, many of the ridges on these peaks have never been climbed so this group of mountains is a rich source of first ascents. The United States map to this region is USGS Mt. St. Elias Alaska-Canada, scale 1:250,000. The Canadian map is Newton Glacier 115C/7 & 115 C/2, scale 1:50,000.

Mt. Newton
13,811 feet (4,210 m)

The climb of Mt. Newton has been discussed with the ascent of the Abruzzi Ridge of Mt. St. Elias. The standard ascent of the Abruzzi Ridge of Mt. St. Elias utilizes the north ridge of Mt. Newton. The north ridge of Mt. Newton is the only feasible ascent of this mountain. The south side of Mt. Newton is subject to continuous avalanche dangers from seracs falling from the north face of Mt. St. Elias.

Photo 70 *Photo by Richard Holmes*

The north ridge of Mt. Newton rises out of the Seward Glacier. *See CD photo (Chapter 3) CD-P01*. The north ridge can be accessed easily, on low angle snow slopes. The snow face rises to the crest of the north ridge, which is followed to reach the summit. The climb of the north ridge of Mt. Newton involves 3,000 feet (914 m) of climbing. This climb can be done easily in one day from a camp on Seward Glacier. The ascent route can also be used as the descent route. Ref. *AAJ* 1965, pp. 303-308.

Mt. Jeannette
12,408 feet (3,782 m)

West Ridge

Directly to the east of Mt. Newton is Mt. Jeannette. Mt. Jeannette is a long horizontal peak possessing a long slender summit ridge. Rising out of the long horizontal summit ridge are three separate summits, each nearly equal in height. However, the western summit adjacent to Mt. Newton is the highest of the three summits. *See CD photo (Chapter 3) CD-Q01*. Mt. Jeannette can be reached from its north side directly off Seward Glacier. *See CD photo (Chapter 3) CD-Q02*. The most direct route to the true summit of Mt. Jeannette is the west ridge. This can be accessed from a small side glacier off Seward Glacier. *See CD photo (Chapter 3) CD-Q02*. This low angle snow and ice ridge can be climbed directly to the summit of Mt. Jeannette. This route can be done in a single day from a camp on the Seward Glacier. The ascent route can be used as the descent route. As of this writing there is no recorded ascent of the west ridge of Mt. Jeannette.

North Ridge

Immediately to the east of the true summit of Mt. Jeannette is the north ridge. *See CD photo (Chapter 3) CD-Q03*. The north ridge can be accessed directly off Seward Glacier. The route climbs the crest of the narrow north ridge to reach the rounded snow covered dome of a sub-peak on the ridge.

The route then proceeds across a narrow horizontal traverse and continues up a narrow snow crest to meet the long east-west horizontal summit ridge of Mt. Jeannette. A short traverse along the summit ridge brings one to the true summit of Mt. Jeannette. The ascent route can also be used as the descent route. As of this writing there are no recorded ascents of the north ridge of Mt. Jeannette.

North Col

The central peak of the three summited Mt. Jeannette is the highest point at 12,000 feet (3,658 m) and can be reached from its north side. Descending directly from the central peak is a beautiful rocky ridge. *See CD photo (Chapter 3) CD-Q04*. This ridge can be accessed off Seward Glacier on a small side glacier that approaches a col on its left side. The crest of the ridge can be reached from this col.

The route ascends from this col on a narrow ridge of mixed ice and rock. The ridge abruptly becomes steeper and climbs on exposed rock. *See CD photo (Chapter 3) CD-Q05*. The rock ridge gives way to the rounded snow covered dome of the central summit of Mt. Jeannette. This route can be done in a day from Seward Glacier. The ascent route can also be used as the descent route. As of this writing there are no recorded ascents of the north col route of Mt. Jeannette.

North Rib

Rising out of the Seward Glacier at the extreme eastern edge of the long horizontal summit ridge of Mt. Jeannette is the north rib. *See CD photo (Chapter 3) CD-Q06*. This slender rib rises out of Seward Glacier and curves elegantly up and to the left to reach the eastern most summit of Mt. Jeannette,

11,909 feet (3,630 m).

The rib can be accessed off Seward Glacier. The route ascends low angle rock and proceeds along the snow covered crest of this narrow rib. The route ascends the broad slopes of the upper part of the north rib to reach the easternmost summit of Mt. Jeannette. *See CD photo (Chapter 3) CD-Q07*. This climb can be done in one day from Seward Glacier. The ascent route can also be used as the descent route. As of this writing there are no recorded ascents of the north rib of Mt. Jeannette.

East Buttress

There is a large snow covered col at the extreme eastern edge of Mt. Jeannette. *See CD photo (Chapter 3) CD-Q08*. Rising above this col is a rounded snow covered buttress that rises up the east side of Mt. Jeannette to reach the long horizontal summit ridge of the Mt. Jeannette complex. A good camp can be placed in this col east of Mt. Jeannette. The east buttress is ascended on broad snow and ice slopes to reach the eastern most summit of Mt. Jeannette. *See CD photo (Chapter 3) CD-Q09*. From the eastern summit it is possible to traverse the length of the long two mile (3.2 km) summit ridge to reach the true western summit. The east buttress climb was the route of the first ascent of Mt. Jeannette.

The ascent to the top of the eastern summit can be done in one day. The long traverse to the true western summit and back might add another day to the climb. Alternatively, a traverse can be made across the summit ridge and the north ridge of the main peak of Jeannette can be descended. The return trip can then be made along the Seward Glacier back to base camp. Ref. *AAJ* 1969, pp. 380-381.

Southern Escarpment

The south side of Mt. Jeannette offers numerous climbing challenges. The approach to the basin below the south side of Mt. Jeannette is the same as the approach to the Russell Col on the Abruzzi Ridge of Mt. St. Elias. The route ascends Agassiz Glacier and ultimately Newton Glacier. This approach brings one to a good base camp just below the southern escarpment of Mt. Jeannette, which is directly across from the base of the southeast ridge of Mt. St. Elias. *See CD photo (Chapter 3) CD-Q10*.

South Ridge

Descending directly from the summit of Mt. Jeannette is the south ridge. This long elegant ridge of snow and rock rises in nearly a straight line to end at the true summit of Mt. Jeannette and can be easily reached from Newton Glacier. *See CD photo (Chapter 3) CD-Q11*. The base of the south ridge is ascended on easy snow slopes. The route rises on a rounded snow shoulder until it levels out at mid-height. The route then follows the narrow crest of this ridge which is comprised mostly of snow and occasionally has some exposed rock. The route ends directly at the true summit of Mt. Jeannette.

The ascent route can also be used as the descent route. There is no need to use fixed rope for this climb. The climb can be done in a long day or in two days with a bivouac midway up the ridge. There are no recorded ascents of this route as of this writing.

Central Buttress

Between the true summit of Mt. Jeannette and the central summit of Mt. Jeannette is a very small sub-peak. A large well-defined rock buttress rises out of Newton Glacier to reach the top of this little sub-peak. *See CD photo (Chapter 3) CD-Q12*.

The central buttress can be reached from the Newton Glacier. The base of the buttress can be ascended on easy snow slopes. The rock face near the base of the buttress can be ascended through a narrow couloir that splits the face. The couloir leads to a broad snow face above it that can be ascended to the base of a narrow rock ridge. A good site can be found at the top of the snow face to create Camp I. The route past Camp I leads up an increasingly steep and narrow couloir to gain the narrow and rocky crest of the buttress. Fixed line will be useful in the narrow couloir and on the rock ridge. The use of fixed line will also facilitate a more rapid descent.

The rock ridge gives way to a narrow snow ridge. This narrow snow crest is followed the remainder of the way to the top of the buttress. The ascent route can be used as the descent route. This is a beautiful climb on an exposed rock buttress. Nonetheless, there are no recorded ascents of this route.

South Ridge
Middle Peak

Rising up the south face of the middle peak of Mt. Jeannette is an indistinct ridge crest. This ridge is not as well-defined as the south ridge leading to the main summit. Additionally, this ridge is subject to some noticeable avalanche hazards. This route can be reached from Newton Glacier. *See CD photo (Chapter 3) CD-Q13.* The route ascends a low angle rock buttress. The buttress is climbed until it reaches an ice cliff. The loose seracs of the ice face can be climbed to overcome this ice cliff and reach a level snow platform where Camp I can be placed.

The route above Camp I follows the indistinct snow ridge along its narrow crest. The ridge crest has some ice seracs that must be climbed to reach the upper snow face. It is a flat snow face which leads directly to the top of the central summit of Mt. Jeannette. The upper snow face is subject to snow slab avalanche danger.

The south ridge of the central summit of Mt. Jeannette is an interesting climb but is does have slightly more objective hazards than the adjacent ridges. The ascent route can also be used as the descent route. As of this writing there are no recorded ascents of this route.

South Ridge
East Peak

Rising elegantly up and curving slightly left to reach the eastern summit of Mt. Jeannette is an interesting rock ridge. *See CD photo (Chapter 3) CD-Q14.* The south ridge of the eastern summit of Mt. Jeannette can be reached off Newton Glacier. The route ascends a broad snow face and then ascends a narrow couloir to reach a small sub-peak at the base of the eastern summit of Mt. Jeannette. A good spot can be found on the back side of this sub-peak to place Camp I.

The route descends down the sub-peak into a narrow couloir. A very narrow rock ridge is traversed across the col. The ridge rises out of the col on the other side onto a narrow rock ridge. The rock ridge is ascended until it gives way to a snow covered ridge.

The narrow snow covered ridge is ascended until it intersects with a broad snow face. The low angle slopes of the face are ascended to reach the eastern summit of Mt. Jeannette. The ascent route can be used as the descent route. Alternatively, the east buttress can be descended to reach Seward Glacier. As of this writing there are no recorded ascents of the south ridge of the eastern summit of Mt. Jeannette.

Mt. Bering
11,844 feet (3,610 m)

Towards the eastern end of the long east-to-west oriented range of peaks that lie between Mt. St. Elias and Mt. Augusta is Mt. Bering. *See CD photo (Chapter 3) CD-R01.* Mt. Bering is a relatively small peak as it sits in the shadow of Mt. Logan and Mt. St. Elias. However, Mt. Bering is not only a fun climb but it is a good warm-up before attempting the larger peaks around it.

Mt. Bering has seen very little climbing activity and as such has numerous ridges available to provide first ascents. Many of these ridges are not only interesting climbs but they can be done in one or two days from a camp on either Seward Glacier or from a camp on Newton Glacier.

West Ridge

Mt. Bering can be reached easily from Seward Glacier. A good spot can be found to place an advanced base camp in the Bering/Jeannette Col. *See CD photo (Chapter 3) CD-R02.* From the advanced base camp it is a short and easy climb up the west ridge to the summit of Mt. Bering. The west ridge is a rounded snow shoulder with little technical difficulty. *See CD photo (Chapter 3) CD-R02.* The climb can be done without fixed rope in one day from the col. The west ridge was the route used for the first ascent of Mt. Bering. Ref. *AAJ* 1978, pp. 542-543.

North Ridge

An interesting alternative is to climb the north ridge of Mt. Bering. The north ridge can be ascended directly off Seward Glacier. The base of the ridge can be ascended on broad low angle snow slopes. *See CD photo (Chapter 3) CD-R03.* The route proceeds up a narrow snow crest over a small sub-peak rising out of the ridge crest.

The route drops down into a col and follows a rounded horizontal ridge. The route then follows a narrow snow crest until it reaches the west ridge of Mt. Bering at mid-height. The remainder of the route to the summit is the same as that for the west ridge of Mt. Bering.

The west ridge is probably the easiest descent route for Mt. Bering. The north ridge can be done without fixed rope in one day. As of this writing there are no recorded ascents of the north ridge of Mt. Bering.

Northeast Ridge

A very exciting ridge climb is the northeast ridge of Mt. Bering. *See CD photo (Chapter 3) CD-R04.* This long sinuous ridge can be reached from Seward Glacier. The route begins on easy snow slopes directly above the glacier. The snow gives way to exposed rock on a narrow ridge crest. The rock is ascended to reach the top of a small tower on the ridge.

The route descends from the rock tower down into a col and follows the narrow snow covered ridge. The ridge begins to rise gently and intersects a broad snow face. The snow face is ascended to reach a sub-peak northeast of Mt. Bering. The route from the sub-peak follows the easy snow slopes of the rounded snow ridge that connect it to the true summit of Mt. Bering.

The west ridge of Mt. Bering is probably the easiest descent off the mountain. There is no need for fixed rope on the northeast ridge. The climb can be done in two days with one bivouac on the ridge. As of this writing there are no recorded ascents of the northeast ridge of Mt. Bering.

Southwest Ridge

The south side of Mt. Bering can be reached via Newton Glacier. From Newton Glacier the southwest ridge of Mt. Bering is easily accessible. *See CD photo (Chapter 3) CD-R05.* The southwest ridge of Mt. Bering can be ascended from the col that separates Mt. Bering from Mt. Jeannette. This moderate angle ridge is snow covered and is narrow but it is not very steep. The southwest ridge of Mt. Bering intersects the west ridge of Mt. Bering at mid-height. The remainder of the climb to the summit follows the west ridge route.

The southwest ridge can be descended easily. There is no need for fixed rope on this climb. The southwest ridge of Mt. Bering can be done in one day with one camp on the ridge. As of this writing there are no recorded ascents of the southwest ridge of Mt. Bering.

South Ridge

An interesting climb is the south ridge of Mt. Bering. This climb can be approached from the amphitheater created where the Agassiz and Newton Glaciers meet. From this amphitheater a long narrow glacier can be ascended to reach a small basin on the south side of Mt. Bering. A good advanced base camp can be placed in the basin below Mt. Bering. *See CD photo (Chapter 3) CD-R06.*

The south ridge can be reached from the basin below Mt. Bering. The climb ascends a small col to reach the ridge crest of the south ridge. The route ascends a narrow snow ridge to reach a sub-peak. The route then follows the easy snow ridge to the summit of Mt. Bering.

This climb can be done without fixed rope. The climb can be done in one day from the advanced base camp in the basin below Mt. Bering. The south ridge can be used as the descent route.

Mt. Malaspina
12,388 feet (3,776 m)

Rising out of the Seward Glacier is the magnificent snow encrusted summit of Mt. Malaspina. *See CD photo (Chapter 3) CD-S01.* This beautiful mountain is sandwiched between the summits of Mt. Augusta to its east and Mt. Bering to its west. Mt. Malaspina is a snow and ice encrusted rock fortress. The only feasible route to climb Mt. Malaspina is off Newton Glacier on its south side.

South Ridge

The south side of Mt. Malaspina offers the only feasible and accessible climb of this mountain. The north side of Malaspina faces the Seward Glacier and is comprised of steep rock cliffs, which are overhung with ice seracs. Fortunately, the south side of the mountain, which rises out of the Newton Glacier, offers a very interesting and straightforward climbing opportunity. *See CD photo (Chapter 3) CD-S02.*

The base of the south ridge can be reached from Newton Glacier. A narrow but low angle snow ridge can be ascended into a small snow basin. From the left side of the basin a rounded snow shoulder can be climbed to reach a small but level plateau. The plateau offers the opportunity to create a site for Camp I.

From Camp I the route follows a narrow but low angle snow ridge to reach the true summit of Mt. Malaspina. There is a ridge connecting the summit of Mt. Malaspina with the summit of Mt. Bering. A team of climbers has attempted to make this traverse but poor snow conditions and overhanging cornices on this ridge prevented them from being successful. However, a traverse can be made down into a col from the summit of Mt. Malaspina to reach a ridge which connects with the summit of Mt. Baird.

The south ridge of Mt. Malaspina can be used as the descent route. There is no need to use fixed rope on this climb. The summit can be reached easily in one day from Camp I. As of this writing there are no recorded ascents of the south ridge of Mt. Malaspina. In fact, there are no recorded ascents of Mt. Malaspina at all. Apparently this summit still awaits its first ascent.

Mt. Baird
11,644 feet (3,549 m)

Standing in a small cirque surrounded by Mt. Augusta, Mt. Malaspina and Mt. Bering is the rounded summit of Mt. Baird. *See CD photo (Chapter 3) CD-T01.* Mt. Baird can be easily reached from Seward Glacier. The mountain offers several short but interesting climbs to reach its summit. As of this writing all but one of the ridges on Mt. Baird are unclimbed.

East Ridge

From Seward Glacier the route ascends the easy snow slopes leading to a col between Mt. Augusta and Mt. Baird. *See CD photo (Chapter 3) CD-T02*. The only difficulty reaching the col is avoiding the few crevasses that lead up to it. The col provides a good spot to place Camp I at 9,184 feet (2,799 m). From the col, the summit of Mt. Baird can be easily reached by climbing the easy snow slopes of the east ridge which can be used as the descent route. There is no need to use fixed rope on this climb. The east ridge was the route of the first ascent of Mt. Baird. In fact, the one and only recorded ascent of Mt. Baird was on the east ridge with a base camp on Seward Glacier. Ref. *AAJ* 2001, p. 232.

East Ridge
South Side

An interesting but cumbersome alternative to climbing the east ridge from Seward Glacier is to climb the east ridge from its south side, off Newton Glacier. *See CD photo (Chapter 3) CD-T03*. The east ridge can be reached from a side branch of Newton Glacier. A steep and narrow ridge can be climbed to the right of a large, dangerous and active icefall. This ridge ultimately reaches the col between Mt. Augusta and Mt. Baird. The remainder of the climb follows the east ridge of Mt. Baird. This approach is subject to significant avalanche hazards in its lower sections. There are no recorded ascents of this variation of the east ridge route.

North Ridge

The north ridge of Mt. Baird can be reached easily from a camp on Seward Glacier. *See CD photo (Chapter 3) CD-T04*. The route ascends easy snow slopes to gain the ridge which then narrows and becomes much steeper as it rises. The route ascends the interface of exposed rock on the east side of the ridge, and snow on the west side of the ridge.

The route then ascends a small exposed rock step. Above the rock step the route regains the narrow snow covered ridge. The ridge becomes broader as it rises and ends directly at the true summit. If fixed rope is used to ascend the rock step then the ascent route can be used as the descent route. If no fixed rope is used then the east ridge is probably the easiest ascent route. The climb can be done in two days with one bivouac on the ridge. As of this writing there are no recorded ascents of the north ridge of Mt. Baird.

West Ridge

A short but interesting climb of Mt. Baird is via its west ridge. *See CD photo (Chapter 3) CD-T05*. The west ridge of Mt. Baird can be gained from Seward Glacier in a small basin between Mt. Baird and Mt. Malaspina. The base of the west ridge can be gained just left of a small icefall. The west ridge of Mt. Baird begins as an indistinct but steep snow and ice ridge. The lower section of this ridge is a constant 55 degrees in angle. Some fixed line may be useful here to aid in the ascent and facilitate a rapid descent. This section of the climb can be done without fixed line and would be a very enjoyable and challenging climb with light packs if an alpine style ascent is to be made.

The steep section of climbing ends on a large and level snow plateau. This plateau is a good spot to place Camp I. *See CD photo (Chapter 3) CD-T06*. Above Camp I the route ascends the steep snow face above the plateau to reach the narrow summit ridge. The narrow but horizontal summit ridge is climbed to reach the true summit of Mt. Baird. The easiest descent is down the east ridge route. The ascent route can be used as the descent route if fixed line is used. As of this writing there are no recorded ascents of the west ridge of Mt. Baird.

Baird-Malaspina Traverse

An interesting addition to climbing any route on Mt. Baird would be to make the traverse over to the summit of Mt. Malaspina. From the summit of Mt. Baird the traverse begins by dropping down into a broad snow col between the two mountains. *See CD photo (Chapter 3) CD-T07.*

The route then ascends the steep snow face above the col. The face gives way to a narrow ridge crest. The narrow ridge crest is followed to the summit of Mt. Malaspina. The traverse can be down-climbed and the east ridge of Mt. Baird is the easiest descent route. The traverse will add two days to the climb of Mt. Baird. As of this writing there are recorded ascents of a traverse between Mt. Baird and Mt. Malaspina.

Mt. Augusta
14,070 feet (4,289 m)

At the extreme eastern edge of the long east-west horizontal ridge which descends from Mt. St. Elias is Mt. Augusta. Although Mt. Augusta anchors the eastern edge of the satellite peaks that flank Mt. St. Elias, Mt. Augusta is not a satellite peak of any other mountain.

Mt. Augusta is a beautiful, steep pyramidal shaped mountain that is unique in its own right. This mountain is characterized by steep and narrow ridges which lead to its summit. Mt. Augusta has twin summits of nearly equal height with the eastern summit being the highest.

There are many narrow ridges that can be climbed, all of which represent a good climbing challenge. There are no truly easy routes up this peak. There are, however, some very challenging routes, particularly on the south face. The mountain is intermediate in height but is not extremely tall. Consequently, the steep mountain challenges of Mt. Augusta can be enjoyed without concern for any altitude difficulties. The United States map of Mt. Augusta is USGS Mt. St. Elias Alaska-Canada, scale 1:250,000. The Canadian map is Corwin Cliffs 115 C/8 & 115 C/1, scale 1:50,000.

West Ridge

The shortest and most direct route to the summit of Mt. Augusta is the west ridge. This route can be accessed from Seward Glacier and begins as a glacier route on easy snow slopes. See photo 1U. The route proceeds off the Seward Glacier onto snow slopes below the north face. The route moves up the snow slopes to the right towards a col between Mt. Baird and Mt. Augusta. The col can be reached by passing a crevasse field on its left side. A good spot can be found to dig in a tent platform to create Camp I in the col at 7,800 feet (2,377 m).

The route proceeds from the col up the west ridge on a broad triangular snow face. The ridge crest is then reached and becomes very narrow. This narrow section of ridge crest can be passed by climbing on the snow face to the left of the ridge. *See CD photo (Chapter 3) CD-U01.*

The narrow ridge crest then ends at the base of a steep triangular ice face. This face represents the crux of the climbing on the west ridge. The best way to ascend the face is at the far right-hand side of the face at the interface between the snow and rock. *See CD photo (Chapter 3) CD-U02.* The top of the ice face gives way to a very narrow ridge crest, which can also be climbed along the snow and rock interface. The ridge then becomes a horizontal traverse along a very narrow crest. The ridge crest can be followed and the cornices on the north side of this ridge crest should be avoided. The ridge eventually blends into the broad summit pyramid which is followed to the true summit.

Photo 1U — Photo by Richard Holmes

There are no good places for camps above the Mt. Augusta and Mt. Baird Col. However, a bivouac can be made if necessary below the broad summit pyramid. The west ridge can be used as the descent route although the north ridge can be used for the descent also. This route is not difficult but it does involve some short sections of very challenging climbing. As of this writing there are no recorded ascents of the west ridge of Mt. Augusta.

North Rib

The north side of Mt. Augusta presents a large formidable face with many hanging glaciers split by long narrow ridges. One of these ridges, the north rib, splits the right-hand side of the north face. The north rib is an indistinct rib of snow and ice which leads to the crest of the west ridge and ultimately to the summit of Mt. Augusta.

The north rib can be approached from the Seward Glacier. The route begins on the slopes of the north face above the bergschrund. *See CD photo (Chapter 3) CD-U03.* The north face is climbed until the indistinct crest of the north rib is reached. The route proceeds along the crest of the north rib. The first ascent team made a bivouac about halfway up the rib at 11,000 feet (3,353 m). The route continues up the rib until it intersects with the west ridge. The route then follows the narrow crest of the west ridge. There is plenty of room on the right side of the west ridge to avoid the cornices overhanging the north face. The west ridge is followed to the summit.

The first ascent team descended the north ridge route. The first ascent team used one bivouac at 11,000 feet (3,353 m) on the north rib and completed the climb in two long days. If an alpine style ascent is done then there is no need to used fixed rope. The north rib is an exhilarating and moderately difficult climb. Ref. *AAJ* 1988, pp. 76-79.

Photo 2U   Photo by Richard Holmes

North Ridge

The north side of Mt. Augusta is dominated by the impressive north ridge. This massive ridge descends directly from the summit in a long serpentine fashion curving down and to the right to meet Seward Glacier. This ridge is challenging but not difficult. The difficulty on this ridge will be determined by the snow conditions present during the climb. The route can consist of easy snow slopes or it can be plagued by numerous crevasse fields. This ridge was the route of the first ascent of Mt. Augusta and can be climbed with one intermediate camp at mid-height on the mountain.

The route begins directly off Seward Glacier. The route can be accessed on easy snow slopes from either the right side or the left side of the ridge. The route ascends the snow slopes to reach the top of a small pyramid. The route then moves onto the crest of the north ridge. See photo 2U. The steep ridge crest rises to a point where the ridge becomes nearly horizontal. The horizontal crest can be traversed until it meets the base of the summit pyramid. A platform can be chopped out at the base of the summit pyramid to make a high camp.

The route above the high camp follows the obvious ridge crest. The ridge is narrow at first but becomes broader as you climb higher. The route ends at the summit of Mt. Augusta. The ascent route can also be used as the descent route. This is an interesting and enjoyable climb on a spectacular looking mountain. This was the route used for the first ascent of Mt. Augusta. Ref. *AAJ* 1953, pp. 416-423.

Northeast Buttress

The northeast corner of Mt. Augusta is characterized by a massive and sprawling array of ridges. There is one prominent buttress amongst these ridges that provides the possibility for an interesting ascent and this is the northeast buttress. This route can

Photo 3U   Photo by Richard Holmes

be reached from Seward Glacier directly to the west of the north ridge. *See CD photo (Chapter 3) CD-U04*. The route proceeds up a smooth ramp on a broad low angle face to reach a narrow ridge crest. A good spot can be found at the top of the snow ramp at 10,000 feet (3,048 m) to create Camp I.

The route from Camp I follows the very narrow ridge crest over mixed rock and ice. This ridge then merges with the true east ridge. The east ridge is followed along a narrow but horizontal traverse until it reaches the base of a large snow pyramid. This pyramid is climbed on easy and broad snow slopes. The top of this snow pyramid is known as Mt. Eaton, elevation 11,000 feet (3,353m). There is ample space on the gentle snow slopes of the south side of Mt. Eaton to dig in tent platforms for Camp II.

The remainder of the route follows the narrow ridge past Mt. Eaton to the summit of Mt. Augusta. The ascent route can be used as the descent route. Alternatively, the north ridge can be used as the descent route. As of this writing there are no recorded ascents of the northeast buttress of Mt. Augusta.

East Ridge

The east ridge of Mt. Augusta is a long curving ridge comprising the entire eastern mass of the mountain. The route ascends this ridge and surmounts three small subsidiary peaks on the way to the true summit of Mt. Augusta. The east ridge was the route used to make the fourth ascent of Mt. Augusta.

The east ridge can be accessed directly off Seward Glacier. See photo 3U. The route ascends a small snow ramp to reach a large snow plateau and a ridge crest above the plateau across low angle snow slopes. A short snow face is ascended to reach a broad section of the east ridge. There is plenty of space on this broad shoulder to dig in a platform to establish Camp I at 9,500 feet (2,896 m). This camp commands excellent views of Seward Glacier to the north and the Corwin

Cliffs which drop away precipitously on the south side of the east ridge.

The route past Camp I continues up the broad snow shoulder which ascends the first of three subsidiary peaks on the east ridge. The route proceeds along a broad and horizontal snow shoulder until it reaches the base of another snow pyramid. A snow face is ascended to reach the top of this snow pyramid which is the second of three subsidiary peaks on the east ridge.

The route past the second peak follows easy snow slopes until it reaches the base of the third peak on the ridge. This is Mt. Eaton, elevation 11,000 feet (3,353 m). A good spot can be found on the south side of Mt. Eaton to dig platforms for Camp II. *See CD photo (Chapter 3) CD-U05.*

The route past Mt. Eaton drops down into a col. The ridge crest in the col is narrow and corniced. *See CD photo (Chapter 3) CD-U06.* The route past the col follows the snow slopes on the upper part of the south face of Mt. Augusta. A small rock step can be passed on its left-hand side. The ridge ends at the summit of Mt. Augusta.

The first ascent team descended the north ridge route. The ascent route can be used as the descent route if fixed rope is left in place. This is an interesting route but is not technically difficult. Ref. *AAJ* 1994, p. 153.

South Ridge

The great south face of Mt. Augusta is a towering 9,000 foot (2,743 m) triangular shaped rock and ice cliff which is split by several steep jagged ridges dropping from the summit to Augusta Glacier nearly two miles (3.2 km) below. The most dramatic of these ridges is the south ridge, which is a serrated spine of rock and ice rising dramatically up the south face to end directly at the true summit of Mt. Augusta. See photo 4U.

The south ridge is a long, steep and challenging climb. The first ascent of this route was done in an alpine style climb in good weather over a period of five days. Alternatively, the route can be done in an expedition style climb with fixed ropes, which will facilitate the descent down the mountain. There are very few spots low on the route that can be used for tent platforms so that bivouacs may be required. Consequently, an expeditionary style climb may have no real advantages over an alpine style ascent except that a rapid retreat in poor weather might be facilitated by fixed lines.

The south ridge can be gained from the Augusta Glacier at an obvious col. The route can be reached from either the east or the west side of the ridge. The east side may be somewhat easier as there is a low angle rock rib running up to meet the col. *See CD photo (Chapter 3) CD-U07.*

The route then ascends a narrow but low angle section until the steep part of the south ridge is encountered. The rock face that is encountered can be passed on its right by climbing steep couloirs filled with snow and ice. These gullies are climbed until the top of a tower is encountered. A small but adequate bivouac can be placed at the top of the tower. *See CD photo (Chapter 3) CD-U08.*

The route then drops down from the tower and crosses a heavily corniced section of the ridge. A narrow section of rock ridge is encountered which becomes steeper the further it goes. Another rock tower is then encountered. This tower can be climbed on its right side on the snow slopes on the main south face.

The route drops down from the tower onto a horizontal traverse, which is heavily corniced. A large overhanging cornice can be passed on the right side to gain a large snow platform at 8,500 feet (2,591 m). This is the only good spot on the ridge for a campsite. Consequently, Camp I can be placed here. This campsite is about halfway up the climb. *See CD photo (Chapter 3) CD-U09.*

The route from Camp I follows the

Photo 3U   Photo by Richard Holmes

main crest of the south ridge. The angle becomes less severe as the ridge rises. The narrow portions of the ridge can be passed on snow slopes on the right side of the ridge. The ridge then merges with the east ridge just below the summit. The low angle snow slopes are followed to the summit.

This route has been done in an alpine style ascent. The route can be done in expedition style with several bivouacs and one good camp at 8,500 feet (2,591 m). If fixed line is used the ascent route can be descended. If an alpine style ascent is done the north ridge route will provide the easiest descent. This is a long, enjoyable and challenging climb no matter what technique is used to ascend it. Ref. *AAJ* 1991, pp. 111-117.

South Buttress

The other major route on the great south face of Mt. Augusta is the south buttress. *See CD photo (Chapter 3) CD-U10.*

The south buttress can be approached from a side branch off the upper Agassiz Glacier. The route ascends a small rounded snow dome to reach the base of the main crest of the south buttress.

The difficult climbing begins on the narrow crest of the lower south buttress. This ridge crest is narrow and fairly steep. The climbing can be done mostly on the snow slopes to the left of the ridge. This ridge crest is ascended for nearly one half of the climb. This ridge crest is ascended until it reaches a large hanging glacier about halfway up the climb. A good camp can be placed on this plateau. *See CD photo (Chapter 3) CD-U11.*

The route past the hanging glacier climbs easy but avalanche prone snow slopes reach the base of a large steep rock and ice buttress. *See CD photo (Chapter 3) CD-U12.* The buttress can be ascended directly up the center of the rock face. However, this is not only a difficult climb but it will also require a very difficult horizontal traverse once the buttress has been ascended.

To circumvent this buttress a snow face can be climbed to the left of the buttress. *See CD photo (Chapter 3) CD-U12.* The face is climbed on its right side and an easy snow gully is finally ascended to exit the lower portion of the south buttress to reach the upper part of the climb. The snow face and the snow gully are somewhat avalanche prone. Consequently, this part of the climb should be done in the cold early morning hours. This snow face should be climbed as quickly as possible to minimize the time that is spent in avalanche prone areas.

Once the upper part of the face is reached the route ascends easy snow slopes for several rope lengths until it reaches the upper rock buttress. The upper rock buttress guards the western summit of Mt. Augusta. Fortunately, there is a broad snow gully that can easily be climbed to ascend the rock buttress to reach the western summit of Mt. Augusta. *See CD photo (Chapter 3) CD-U12.*

The route from the western summit of Mt. Augusta to the true summit follows the horizontal summit ridge. This ridge is narrow but there is ample room on the south side of the ridge to follow easy snow slopes to reach the true summit of Mt. Augusta.

There is only one really good place to camp on this route and that is on the hanging glacier halfway up the route. Consequently, there is no real advantage to an expeditionary style climb as compared to an alpine style ascent. This route would make an excellent alpine climb.

The route is challenging but never really difficult. The avalanche prone nature of the snow slopes around the hanging glacier encourages a team to climb past this area rapidly, so an alpine ascent might be preferable to the slow methodical nature of an expedition. As of this writing there are no recorded ascents of the south buttress of Mt. Augusta.

Southwest Rib

The only other potential route on the south face of Mt. Augusta is the southwest rib. This is a narrow rib at the far left-hand side of the south face of Mt. Augusta. *See CD photo (Chapter 3) CD-U13.* This route can be reached from a small branch at the head of the Agassiz Glacier.

The route ascends a snow buttress just to the right of a large and active icefall. It is important to minimize time spent below the base of this icefall due to the avalanche hazards. The route then ascends the narrow ridge crest of the southwest rib. The climb can be ascended on the snow slopes on the left side of the ridge.

The angle of the ridge decreases as it rises higher. The southwest rib eventually intersects the west ridge of Mt. Augusta. The west ridge route of Mt. Augusta is then followed to the true summit of the mountain. The west ridge also provides access to a col, which would allow a traverse to the summit of Mt. Baird if time and conditions permit. As of this writing there have been no recorded ascents of the southwest rib of Mt. Augusta.

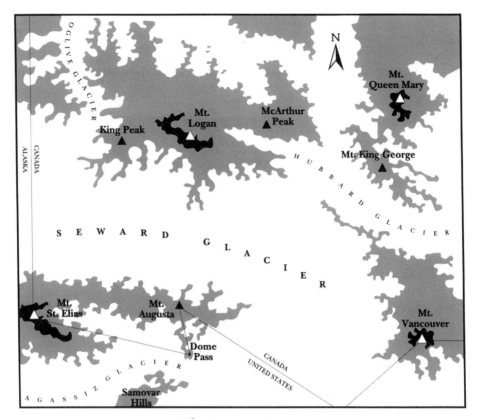

The Logan Group

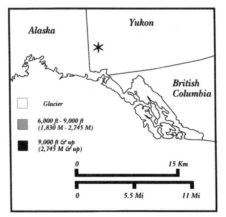

CHAPTER 4

THE LOGAN GROUP

Introduction

Mt. Logan is the crown jewel of the St. Elias Mountains. This monolithic peak is not only the tallest mountain by far but it is also the most massive. In fact, Mt. Logan has more bulk than any other mountain in the Western Hemisphere.

From the 10,000 foot (3,048 m) level on Mt. Logan the mountain is sixteen miles (26 km) from east to west and it is eight miles (13 km) from north to south. Mt. Logan has five summits ranging from 18,300 feet (5,578 m) to 19,545 feet (5,957 m). The 17,000 foot (5,182 m) high plateau is over twelve miles (19 km) in length. The mountain has a circumference of over 100 miles (161 km) and is guarded by 10,000 feet (3,048 m) high walls of rock and ice. This is truly a massive mountain of great proportions and Mt. Logan is truly a worthy climbing objective.

Mt. Logan was not the first of the lofty peaks to be climbed in the St. Elias Range. The first great peak climbed in this range was Mt. St. Elias. This is simply due to geography. Mt. St. Elias was first observed by the great Danish sea captain Vitus Bering, in July of 1741. Mt. St. Elias is adjacent to the coast and as such is visible far out to sea. Bering commented, "I do not recall any mountains this big in Siberia and Kamchatka."

The result was that Mt. St. Elias received the initial attention from climbers. Mt. Logan was clearly seen and its immense height and bulk was not fully realized until Professor Israel Russell visited Mt. St. Elias on a geology expedition in 1890. Professor Russell named Mt. Logan in honor of the first director of the Geological Survey of Canada, Sir William Logan. Professor Russell estimated with uncanny accuracy the height of Mt. Logan to be about 19,800 feet (6,035 m).

The interest in Mt. Logan was reignited when the 1913 International Boundary Survey team did a survey of the Alaska and Canada border along the 141st meridian. The border survey also provided the first close-up photographs of Mt. Logan. In 1922, Professor A.P Coleman, a former President of the Canadian Alpine Club, suggested the possibility of studying whether it was feasible to climb Mt. Logan.

The initial investigation took form in 1923 under the direction of Lt. Col. W. W. Foster who was the current President of the Canadian Alpine Club. Lt. Col. Foster selected A.H. MacCarthy to begin a study of the feasibility of climbing Mt. Logan. A.H. MacCarthy was already renown for his ascent of the beautiful and spectacular Mt. Robson in the Canadian Rockies. A.H. MacCarthy had also been a captain in the United States Navy and as such was a capable leader of men.

Also selected as the co-leader was H.F. Lambert, who had been part of the 1913 International Boundary Survey team. His intimate knowledge of the area was very valuable in the initial efforts to organize the Mt. Logan expedition.

One of the first things that must be addressed when attempting to climb a mountain is how to get there. It was known that there are three possible approach routes to Mt. Logan. The first is to enter from the east, from the city of Whitehorse, in the Yukon Territory. This trip would entail a hike up the Slims River Valley and onto Kaskawulsh Glacier. This approach would then enter unknown and unmapped territory. This would entail hiking over terrain that had never been seen or explored and the exact distances involved were unknown. Consequently, due to the unknown nature of this area this approach was rejected.

The second approach, which is in fact the shortest, would involve approaching from the sea, from the small town of Yakutat, Alaska. This approach would cover some of the same area covered by the expedition led by the Duke of Abruzzi. The descriptions of this approach were so appalling that the added distance beyond where the Duke had already traveled caused this approach to be rejected as well.

The third and final approach was from the northwest, starting in the small Alaskan town of MacCarthy. This city was named after someone else other than the expedition leader A.H. MacCarthy. This approach would entail traveling over extremely rough terrain for a distance of nearly 150 miles (241 km). However, this approach did have the benefit of having been previously attempted. Enough information was gleaned from hunters and miners that a feasible approach route could be established. Consequently, it was determined that the approach would take place from the northwest.

The vast quantity of supplies that would be used on such an undertaking was truly staggering. Therefore, it was determined that supply caches would have to be established in the late winter and early spring prior to the initiation of the expedition.

From late February to mid April of 1925 A.H. MacCarthy and Andrew Taylor began the massive task of creating supply caches which would be used by the climbing team in early summer. They used horses and dog sleds to haul the gear and were able to travel fairly easily over the snow covered ground and along the frozen rivers. They ultimately deposited 19,860 pounds (9,028 kg) of supplies that they felt would last the team for two months. They deposited 65 gallons (246 liters) of gasoline weighing 400 pounds (181 kg). The cost for these supplies and the expedition in total was $11,500.

The 1925 expedition to attempt the first ascent of Mt. Logan was finally ready. The climbing team was confirmed and the members included A.H. MacCarthy (leader), H.F. Lambert (co-leader), Allen Carpe, Andrew Taylor, W.W. Foster, N. Read, and two men with the last names of Morgan and Hall. The team assembled initially in Seattle, Washington. They then traveled by steamer the 1,600 miles (2,575km) to Cordova, Alaska. From Cordova the team traveled by railroad the final distance to MacCarthy, Alaska.

Finally, on May 12th, the team left MacCarthy to begin the expedition. They traveled up the river valleys using the supplies deposited in the winter by MacCarthy and Taylor and finally reached Ogilvie Glacier. They were able to overcome the small icefall at its base and enter what we now know as the King Trench.

The ascent of the smooth glacier within the King Trench was made quite easily. The team was disappointed to find that an icefall blocked easy access onto the upper plateau. The route from the top of the King Trench turns sharply to the left and the first ascent team was able to overcome the icefall by following a narrow but smooth ice ramp to the top of the icefall. This narrow passage is now known as the MacCarthy Gap. This ice ramp led the team to the upper plateau.

Mt. Logan is adorned by several summits and several of these summits are nearly equal in height. The team ascended what they thought to be the highest summit, which is now known as the west summit. Once on this summit they were immediately struck with the realization that the central or true summit was in fact slightly higher than the one they were currently standing on. Undeterred by this misfortune the team set off to ascend the true summit. Finally, on June 23rd, 1925 at 8 PM, the team reached the true summit of Mt. Logan.

The team descended the route successfully and uneventfully. They retreated down the river valleys using the supplies laid in the previous winter by MacCarthy. Finally, when they were nearly within reach of their home base at the little town of MacCarthy, the team encountered a small crisis. Everybody on the team had developed frostbite on their toes to such an advanced extent that they could no longer walk. Consequently, they fashioned makeshift log rafts and floated the final distance down the Chitina River to the town of MacCarthy where their adventure had begun nearly three months earlier.

Considering all of the unknown aspects of Mt. Logan such as its exact height, which of the many summits is the true summit and whether there really was a feasible route that could be climbed to reach the upper plateau, this expedition must be considered a spectacular success. It is almost unprecedented in the history of climbing such a large mountain in such a remote location with so little information available,

would be successfully climbed on its first attempt. Notwithstanding, many previous first ascents on other great peaks, it has been commented that the first ascent of Mt. Logan might be the most arduous mountaineering adventure ever undertaken.

Today we know the King Trench route as the standard glacier route to reach the summit of Mt. Logan. The altitude of the peak is well-known, the best locations and exact elevations of the camps on the route are well-established. Nonetheless, this historic route still provides an excellent climbing challenge on one of North America's greatest peaks.

Despite the size and significance of Mt. Logan, the Logan massif is comprised of more than just Mt. Logan alone. There are two other great peaks that are part of this enormous complex: Mt. King and Mt. McArthur. Mt. King rises out of the southern flank of Mt. Logan. In fact Mt. King comprises the southern edge of the great King Trench route. Mt. McArthur rises from the eastern edge of the Logan Massif and is linked to Mt. Logan through the Cantenary Ridge. Mt. McArthur looks like a giant piece of wedding cake that was cut in half. The northern half of Mt. McArthur is a smooth snow covered face with the beautiful and well-known north ridge rising to reach the summit. In stark contrast the southern escarpment is very steep and is a rock monolith. Some of the finest alpine style climbs are found on the south face of Mt. McArthur.

Both Mt. King and Mt. McArthur are significant peaks in their own right. These two peaks are dwarfed by the size and immensity of their nearest neighbor, Mt. Logan. Nonetheless, both of these peaks comprise worthy mountaineering challenges in their own right. The Logan group of peaks has more climbing opportunities in this one group than in any other spot in the entire Wrangell-St. Elias complex of mountains.

There is a worthwhile mountaineering challenge in this group of peaks for every level of skill and interest.

Mt. Logan
19,545 feet (5,957 m)

Mt. Logan was named in honor of the first director of the Geological Survey of Canada, Sir William Logan. Mt. Logan is the highest peak in the Wrangell-St. Elias complex of mountains and in fact, it is the tallest mountain in Canada. Mt. Logan was the scene of one of the great mountaineering epics of all times, namely, the expedition to make the first ascent of this great peak.

Mt. Logan has numerous serrated and corniced ridges descending from its massive summit plateau. This peak has some of the most challenging climbs that exist anywhere in North America. An ascent of Mt. Logan will provide not only lasting memories of a great wilderness experience but will also provide a challenge to any mountaineer wishing to test their skills on a great peak.

The United States map for this peak is USGS Mt. St. Elias Alaska-Canada, scale 1:250,000. The Canadian maps for Mt. Logan are McArthur 115 C/9, scale 1:50,000 and King Peak 115 C/10, scale 1:50,000.

The King Trench

The King Trench was the route used for the first ascent of Mt. Logan. Although the first ascent of the King Trench and Mt. Logan as well was an epic adventure, the route now enjoys the status of a moderate glacier route. The route is not technically difficult but should not be underestimated, however, as there are some difficult icefalls to negotiate and the route does lead to the summit of the highest mountain in Canada. Storms can blow in from the Gulf of Alaska quickly and with great ferocity. The temperature that will be experienced on the upper plateau will be well below freezing. Consequently, the team should be well prepared physically and mentally before challenging this route.

Because the King Trench route is not a technically difficult one, it has been the scene for numerous adventures on Mt. Logan. The King Trench route was used to make the first winter ascent of Mt. Logan in the late winter of 1986 and was the route used for the first ski descent of Mt. Logan. The first all female ascent of Mt. Logan climbed the King Trench. When a traverse is made of Mt. Logan by climbing a route on the east or north side of the mountain the traverse is usually completed by descending the King Trench.

The usual drop off for a team beginning the King Trench route is fifteen miles (24 km) west of the United States and Canadian border at 8,600 feet (2,621 m) on the east end of the Jefferies Glacier. The King Trench route can be done in twelve days if the weather and the snow conditions are favorable. The pickup for the climbing team after the climb is usually at 7,800 feet (2,377 m) on Quinto Sella Glacier.

Generally a good base camp can be established on the broad reaches of the lower King Trench at 8,200 feet (2,499 m). The route must ascend a short icefall that can be passed on its right side by a snow ramp. A good site can be found at the top of the icefall to place Camp I at 10,500 feet (3,200 m). See photo 1V.

The route past Camp I is comprised of broad and easy snow slopes. The route ascends an icefall which is encountered at 12,300 feet (3,749 m). This icefall can be passed on the left side by climbing a steep snow ramp. The remaining 600 feet (183 m) up to the King Col is easy but it is steep. The King Col camp can be placed at 13,500 feet (4,115 m). This camp is well protected from the wind.

From the King Col camp the route now

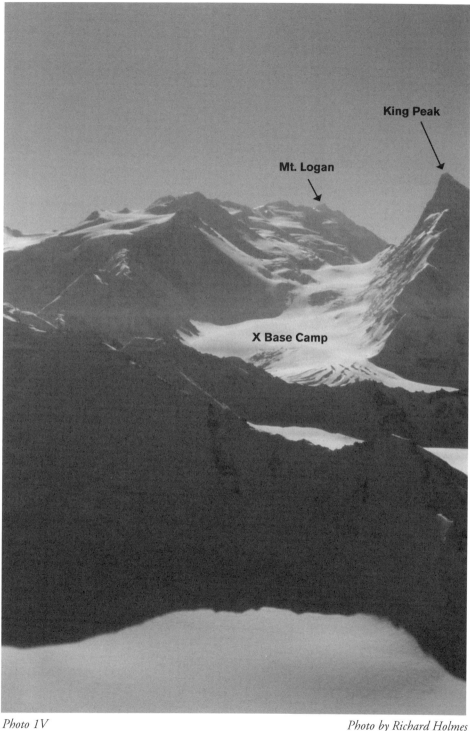

Photo 1V *Photo by Richard Holmes*

Photo 2V Photo by Richard Holmes

enters the crux of the climb. The first ascent team named this section the MacCarthy Gap. The route turns sharply to the left and climbs through a steep broken serac field. The first part of this climb goes up a headwall on its north side for about 500 feet (152 m). The seracs can be passed on their right side by climbing a snow ramp. The ramp leads to level ground at 15,000 feet (4,572 m), just east of Queen Peak, one of the many false summits passed on the way to the true summit. See photo 2V. The route proceeds past Queen Peak to a large broad flat area where a camp can be established at 16,300 feet (4,968 m).

The route continues towards the northeast until a col is reached at 18,000 feet (5,486 m). The snow slopes at the top of the col become steep until the small rocky col is reached. The route goes through the col and descends slightly to gain the main summit plateau at 17,500 feet (5,334 m). A good camp can be placed at 17,500 feet (5,334 m) on the summit plateau.

The route proceeds along the summit plateau passing the western summit on its north or right-hand side. The route then goes southeast a short distance from the western summit toward the central or true summit of Mt. Logan. The central summit is ascended on a diagonal snow ramp to reach the top.

There are a lot of broad open slopes on the King Trench route, with a great deal of deep snow. Consequently, it is essential to use skis or snowshoes on this climb. It is wise to carry several hundred wands to mark the route and the camps in the event that bad weather occurs during the descent. The King Trench is not a difficult climb but it will reward the successful climber with a sense of great accomplishment in reaching the summit of the highest mountain in Canada. Ref. *AAJ* 1974, p.154; *AAJ* 1974, p. 155; *CAJ* 1987, p.75.

West Ridge

The dominant feature on the west side of Mt. Logan is the long and serrated west

Photo 3V *Photo by Richard Holmes*

ridge. This three mile (4.8 km) long ridge is the longest approach that can be used to reach the upper plateau on Mt. Logan, and it provides virtually every type of climbing that one can imagine.

The ridge is knife-edged in many places. Some parts of the ridge are double corniced. The ridge occasionally widens out to broad snow slopes. It is wise to stay well below the cornice line of the most heavily corniced sections of the ridge as these cornices can break away easily. See photo 3V.

The first ascent team chose to gain the ridge crest by climbing a narrow snow and ice couloir. *See CD photo (Chapter 4) CD-V01.* This narrow couloir is 2,700 feet (823 m) high and involves snow and ice climbing. The couloir has 27 roped climbing pitches in it of which ten were fixed with rope by the first ascent team. There is steep climbing in the couloir with ice up to sixty degrees in angle. There is loose snow and rock in the couloir so it is best to climb the couloir in the cool early morning hours.

Once on the ridge crest a good camp can be made below a small peak on the ridge. The ridge does not gain much elevation for the three miles (4.8 km) that it traverses to reach the summit plateau. The climbing along the ridge crest involves corniced and knife-edged sections. Additionally, four rock gendarmes must be climbed or circumvented. *See CD photo (Chapter 4) CD-V02.*

The three mile (4.8 km) long ridge eventually intersects with the summit plateau. The point where the ridge intersects the plateau contains the crux climbing pitch. This pitch involves ice climbing up to 75 degrees in angle. Once the steep ice pitch is surmounted the climb traverses the summit plateau.

The distance across the summit plateau from the point where the west ridge intersects the plateau to the true summit of Mt. Logan is nearly ten miles (16 km). The route proceeds up the plateau and around the left side of Queen Peak. The route then intersects the King Trench route and follows the standard

Photo 4V

Photo by Richard Holmes

route across the plateau to the summit. The plateau is flat and long with occasional deep snow. Consequently, it is best to bring small plastic sleds on the climb to carry gear across the plateau. The sleds will also be useful on the descent as well.

The first ascent team climbed the western summit. The team then descended the King Trench route. This is a very long route but it does possess some very interesting climbing. The route has the added advantage that it is seldom climbed so there will be few people on this route. The descent is easily done by using the King Trench route. Ref. *AAJ* 1979, pp. 118-121. *CAJ* 1979, pp.81-82.

Amenity Ridge

Directly around the corner from the west ridge on the north face of Mt. Logan is Amenity Ridge. This is a long, narrow and highly serrated ridge. A good route has been established on this ridge which reaches the summit plateau slightly east of the west ridge route. See photo 4V.

Amenity Ridge can be seen from a great distance away as you approach Mt. Logan by aircraft. The pilot of the first ascent team commented that, "this ridge seemed to have all the amenities of a good route with good climbing." The first ascent team agreed and subsequently named the route Amenity Ridge.

There are two approaches to gaining the main ridge crest of Amenity Ridge. One approach is to climb a 4,100 foot (1,250 m) high mixed rock and ice spur to gain the ridge crest. See photo 5V. The second approach is to climb a steep icy spur on the east side of the main ridge which ascends to meet the main ridge crest at mid-height. See photo 6V.

The first ascent team chose to climb the steep icy spur that rises to meet the ridge crest. See photo 6V. *See CD photo (Chapter 4) CD-V03.* The base of the steep icy spur is constantly bombarded with avalanches from the upper slopes of the north face. Consequently, the base camp should be

144 *The Logan Group*

Photo 5V *Photo by Richard Holmes*

placed some distance away and to the north of the base of Amenity Ridge.

The climb ascends the steep, narrow and icy spur along its crest for 4,100 feet (1,250 m) to reach the main ridge crest. Snow and ice protection using pickets and flukes will be useful on this spur for belays and anchoring ropes. A site can be secured about halfway up the icy spur near a bergschrund to place Camp I. Another good site can be found at the top of the icy spur to create Camp II.

The next 2,000 feet (610 m) of the ridge is a traverse, which is the crux of the climbing. This section of the ridge is blocked by a steep ice gendarme named the "Cocks Comb." The next section of the ridge past the Cocks Comb is very narrow and serrated and is sardonically named the "Cakewalk." The narrow section of ridge ultimately gives way to a broader snow shoulder. *See CD photo (Chapter 4) CD-V04.*

At the point where the intersection of the ridge crest meets the summit plateau, the route encounters a steep icefall. The route through the icefall is tricky and interesting. The route goes over and through large crevasses. The route emerges above the icefall on the summit plateau. *See CD photo (Chapter 4) CD-V05.*

On the summit plateau the difficult nature of the climb is over. The Amenity Ridge route then intersects with the top of the west ridge route. The standard trudge across the ten miles (16 km) of summit plateau to the true summit can be facilitated by using plastic sleds to help distribute the loads that need to be carried the remainder of the distance.

The first ascent team descended the King Trench route, as this is the most direct route off the mountain. This is a seldom-climbed route and is a moderately difficult one. It will require fixed rope, rock and snow protection. Large snow flukes and half-length pickets will probably be the best form of protection for anchoring fixed line. Some large pitons and camming devices will be needed for the lower sections of the rock

Photo 6V *Photo by Richard Holmes*

and ice buttress. Ref. *AAJ* 1980, p. 559. *CAJ* 1980, pp. 5-8.

Northwest Ridge

Immediately to the west of the beautiful Amenity Ridge is a large blocky ridge known as the northwest ridge. This bulky ridge rises in a stairstep fashion to meet the summit plateau at 15,500 feet (4,724 m). See photo 7V.

A good base camp can be placed some distance from the base of this ridge to provide easy access to it but also to provide a safe distance from the avalanches that roll down the north face of Mt. Logan. The ridge can be accessed on its left side on a steep spur.

This icy spur is climbed along its ridge crest up and to the left. The ridge becomes narrow and corniced. The cornices can be safely passed on the right-hand side. When the cornices are passed a large broad platform can be reached at 12,000 feet (3,658 m). This large platform is a good place to secure Camp I. *See CD photo (Chapter 4) CD-V06.*

The route above Camp I follows an easy section of ridge which is fairly broad. The broad section of ridge then merges with steep and unstable snow slopes. These unstable snow slopes should be climbed during the coldest hours of the early morning to ensure their stability. At the top of the snow slopes at 14,500 feet (4,420 m) is a broad platform where Camp II can be placed.

The route above Camp II follows easy but moderately steep snow slopes. The northwest ridge is spared the difficulty of ascending an ice cliff, as all other north face routes must do. The northwest ridge follows wide but steep snow ramps to reach the summit plateau. *See CD photo (Chapter 4) CD-V07.*

The route merges with the summit plateau at about 15,500 feet (4,725 m). At this point the route follows the standard hike across the summit plateau to reach the true summit. The King Trench can be used to descend the mountain. Snow flukes, snow pickets and ice screws will be needed to

Photo 7V *Photo by Richard Holmes*

secure fixed rope on this climb.

Colorado Route

Directly in the middle of the north face of Mt. Logan is the steep and slender Colorado Ridge. The Colorado Ridge is perhaps the most beautiful and direct line to rise up and meet the summit plateau of any ridge on the entire mountain. This is not a particularly long route but it is very direct. This ridge does not wander from side to side at all but rises directly to the summit plateau. See photo 8V.

The route can be easily accessed at its base on the left-hand side. There is an easy snow ridge which can be climbed to gain the main crest of the ridge. The main ridge crest is very narrow and is followed for several rope lengths. The climb is mostly snow and ice with a few rock gendarmes that must be climbed along the way. A good spot can be found to secure Camp I where a small icy spur rises up to meet the main ridge crest. This is the widest spot on this section of ridge but it will still entail some digging to get a good tent platform. *See CD photo (Chapter 4) CD-V08.*

The route then follows the narrow ridge crest above Camp I. The crest is narrow and corniced in places. The climbing is stimulating but not extreme. The steepest section involves about half a rope length of ice which is up to 75 degrees in angle.

About three-quarters of the way up the ridge a large ice cliff protrudes to the right side of the ridge. A good spot can be found here to secure Camp II beside a large bergschrund. The tent should be securely attached to the main ridge crest.

The route past Camp II follows alternating narrow and broad sections of the ridge. Finally the ridge merges with the summit plateau. A steep and interesting icefall guards the exit off the ridge onto the summit plateau. The route ascends about 150 feet (46 m) of steep honeycombed ice to finally get onto the plateau. *See CD photo (Chapter 4) CD-V09.* The route from the

Photo 8V   Photo by Richard Holmes

Photo 9V   Photo by Richard Holmes

top of the icefall goes directly across the plateau past the west summit toward the true summit of Mt. Logan. The King Trench can be used as the descent route.

This route is narrow and constantly steep. However, it is never severely steep, although fixed rope will be useful for carrying loads and securing the tents to the ridge crest at the campsites. Snow flukes and pickets will be useful for securing rope. Long ice screws are essential to climb the icefall at the top of the ridge. Ref. *AAJ* 1975, p. 140. *CAJ* 1983, pp. 82-84.

Centennial Ridge

In the middle of the north face of Mt. Logan is a large concave cirque adorned with massive hanging ice cliffs. This cirque is delineated with a ridge on either side of it that rises up in a wishbone pattern to meet at 15,000 feet (4,572 m), a short distance below the northeast summit.

The right-hand ridge of this wishbone is Centennial Ridge. See photo 9V. This ridge acquired its name because the first ascent of this route was done slightly after the United States and Canada had celebrated their Centennials. Centennial Ridge is a beautiful climb of moderate difficulty. It involves a little bit of steep ice climbing with a great deal of route finding challenges. The climb is not done very frequently and provides a good alternative to the east ridge of Mt. Logan which is roughly the same difficulty, but which is climbed with great frequency. Centennial Ridge provides a fun challenge in a remote cirque on the north side of Mt. Logan. The climber will be rewarded with a great climb as well as spectacular views looking deep into the interior of the St. Elias Range.

The climb generally starts at the base of the wishbone cirque bound by the confluence of Independence Ridge on the left and Centennial Ridge on the right. See CD photo (Chapter 4) CD-V10. However, this approach involves not only some extra climbing over small summits but it is also _bject to frequent avalanches cascading down the north face of Mt. Logan from the wishbone cirque.

A good but seldom-used alternative is to start the climb from a high plateau on the west side of Centennial Ridge. A small snow ramp can be found here which provides easy access onto the ridge crest. See CD photo (Chapter 4) CD-V11. The route follows the crest of Centennial Ridge. The climbing on the lower part of the ridge involves slogging through deep wet snow. One short narrow section is encountered which is heavily corniced. This section can be passed on the left-hand side. Immediately past the narrow section the route broadens onto a wide but sloping shelf. A good site can be found here to dig in a good campsite. See CD photo (Chapter 4) CD-V12.

The route above this camp climbs beyond a small ice cliff, which can be passed on its right-hand side. The route passes a short section of corniced ridge to reach a truly massive and level snow plateau at 12,000 feet (3,658 m). The route past the plateau follows an obvious snow ramp onto the upper part of the route.

The upper part of Centennial Ridge is a wide snow shoulder which is buffeted by the wind. The climbing is easy and follows the low angle snow slope to an elevation of 15,000 feet (4,572 m) where Centennial Ridge intersects with Independence Ridge, coming up from the left. A good camp can be established at the point where these two ridges meet. See CD photo (Chapter 4) CD-V13.

The route above the intersection follows the narrow but low angle ridge for a short distance. The ridge then ascends the northeast summit of Mt. Logan. The route then proceeds across the summit plateau just south of the west summit to reach the true summit of Mt. Logan. The King Trench route can be used as the descent route.

The Centennial Ridge route is a fun climb and can only be considered moderately difficult. This route is seldom ascended and could provide a good alternative to the frequently climbed east ridge of Mt. Logan. The route will require some fixed rope to secure the narrow corniced sections of ridge. It is best to use snow flukes and pickets for securing fixed rope. Ref. *AAJ* 1977, pp. 196-197. *CAJ* 1977, pp. 12-15.

Independence Ridge

Independence Ridge forms the left-hand side of the wishbone formation that comprises the giant concave cirque on the north face of Mt. Logan. Unlike the adjacent Centennial Ridge, the Independence Ridge route is narrow all the way to the summit plateau. See photo 10V.

This route is very stimulating but not extremely difficult. Its moderate but challenging nature and the fact that it is not attempted very often makes it a good alternative to some of the more heavily traveled routes on Mt. Logan. The route was named Independence Ridge because it rises out of a basin at the base of the cirque which itself is named Independence Basin. Additionally, the true summit was reached on July 4th, the date celebrated as Independence Day in America, hence the name Independence Ridge.

The route starts on low angle snow slopes at the base of the toe of the ridge. The route ascends the lower section of the ridge, which resembles the shape of a shark's fin. The route climbs past narrow cornices to a point just above a steep gully coming up from the left side of the ridge. A wide spot on the ridge can be found just above the gully to establish Camp I at 9,650 feet (2,941 m). See CD photo (Chapter 4) CD-V10.

The route above Camp I follows the ridge crest. This section of ridge is very narrow and heavily corniced in places. It is best to stay below the cornice line to avoid collapsing the cornices. It will be useful to

Photo 10V *Photo by Richard Holmes*

secure fixed rope along this section of ridge to ensure climbing safety when carrying loads. The ridge reaches a point where it begins to rise over a very steep crest. Just before the ridge rises steeply and adjacent to the rock face left of the ridge, there is a good spot to place Camp II at 10,850 feet (3,307 m). A good tent platform can be dug in here just to the left of a giant cornice.

The route above Camp II rises sharply for a short distance. The ridge beyond Camp II involves more climbing on a narrow ridge with cornices. The ridge then broadens out to a much wider snow shoulder. The snow slopes are followed to a point just below a small icefall where a good level spot can be found to place Camp III at 13,000 feet (3,962 m). *See CD photo (Chapter 4) CD-V14.*

Immediately above Camp III a small icefall is climbed. The icefall is not very long or very steep. Some route finding around seracs is needed to pass this icefall. Above it the ridge is still narrow for a short distance. Eventually the ridge broadens out and the most technical sections of the ridge are completed. A good site for tents can be found on a very large shelf above a rock face. This shelf can be used to establish Camp IV at 14,500 feet (4,420 m).

The route past Camp IV follows very easy snow slopes over a gentle ridge. The route ascends into the deep basin below the northeast peak. Camp V can be established in this basin at 17,500 feet (5,334 m). *See CD photo (Chapter 4) CD-V15.*

The route past Camp V is the usual trudge across the summit plateau. The true immensity of the summit plateau can be appreciated at this point. The top of Independence Ridge is directly across the plateau from the true summit of Mt. Logan, yet it is still a six mile (9.6 km) hike to get there. The first ascent team down climbed Independence Ridge with the aid of the fixed ropes which they had left in place. However, it might be just as easy to descend the King Trench route.

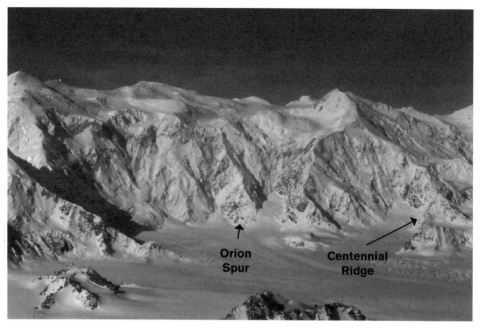

Photo 11V

Photo by Richard Holmes

Independence Ridge involves some fun and challenging climbing. It is best to climb the lower part of the ridge in the cooler early morning hours to facilitate climbing on the soft wet snow. It will be necessary to bring protection for snow and ice to secure ropes on this climb. It will be necessary to bring wands to work your way across the summit plateau. Independence Ridge is an excellent alternative to many of the more heavily traveled and popular climbs on Mt. Logan. Ref. *AAJ* 1965, p. 309-314.

Orion Spur

Nestled into the northeast side of Mt. Logan in a little basin bounded by Cantenary Ridge on the east and Independence Ridge on the west, is the Orion Spur. This spectacular little spur rises in a direct line out of the Logan Glacier to meet the summit plateau. This spur is continuously steep over its entire distance. Consequently, the Orion Spur is the shortest and perhaps most exhilarating route to get onto the summit plateau. See photo 11V.

The first ascent team did the route in five days in an alpine style climb. This climb is perfect for an alpine style ascent; however, it can be done just as easily with an expedition style climb. The Orion Spur can be accessed at its base on the right-hand side on a steep snow and ice face. The base of the Orion Spur is subject to avalanches from the icefall that sits just to the left of Independence Ridge. Therefore, it is best not to spend too much time near the base of this climb.

The route ascends the snow face for a short distance and gains the crest of the ridge. The ridge is corniced on its left side. There is ample room to climb on the right-hand side of the ridge and this will avoid the overhanging cornices on the left side. The corniced section of ridge is climbed just back from the cornice line until the ridge begins to broaden at mid-height. At mid-height the ridge broadens into a large rounded shoulder. On the large rounded snow shoulder there is

Photo 12V *Photo by Richard Holmes*

plenty of space to secure Camp I. *See CD photo (Chapter 4) CD-V16.*

The ridge above Camp I becomes narrow again. This section involves a little bit of exposed rock, however, the climb proceeds mostly on snow and ice. The ridge remains narrow but reaches a point where it becomes much steeper. At the base of the steep section there is sufficient space to dig in a platform for Camp II.

The route above Camp II follows the narrow and increasingly steeper ridge crest until it reaches the ice cliff which blocks the entrance onto the summit plateau. The route then proceeds through the ice cliff on the right-hand side on snow ramps, which avoid the exposed rock and the steep ice blocks. Some ice climbing on honeycombed ice over steep ice seracs is necessary to reach the summit plateau. *See CD photo (Chapter 4) CD-V17.*

Once the summit plateau is reached the route to the true summit travels directly across the plateau from the top of the Orion Spur. The route across the summit plateau bypasses the eastern summit on its north side traveling 3.7 miles (6 km) to reach the true summit. The King Trench route can be used as the descent route. The climb has been done alpine style in five days. The route can be done in an expedition style push as well. It will be useful to secure fixed line over the narrow section of ridge. Long ice screws will be necessary to secure belays through the honeycombed ice found in the summit ice cliff. Ref. *AAJ* 2003, pp. 243-244.

Cantenary Ridge

Swooping down from the summit plateau on the northeast side of Mt. Logan is the long and curving Cantenary Ridge. The ridge received its name because of its resemblance to a cantenary curve. This is a very long ridge as it winds its way up off Logan Glacier to reach the summit plateau.

Additionally, this ridge has more than its fair share of undulations. This is a long ridge which connects the adjacent Mt.

McArthur with the eastern side of the Logan Massif. From the summit of Mt. McArthur the ridge drops 3,000 feet (914 m) down into the McArthur Col. The ridge then rises another 2,500 feet (762 m) to reach the top of a sub-peak at 12,500 feet (3,810 m). After another short 500 foot (152 m) descent the route rises again to the top of a second sub-peak at 13,500 feet (4,115 m).

The route from the top of the second sub-peak drops precipitously another 1,500 feet (457 m) into the Cantenary Col which contains a corniced knife-edged ridge. This ridge connects Mt. McArthur with the main bulk of Mt. Logan. The ridge rises from the col another 6,500 feet (1,981 m) to the summit plateau on the eastern side of Mt. Logan.

This route is probably best done as an expedition style climb. Due to the length of the climb, the difficulties encountered and the probable need to descend using fixed rope placed on the ascent, it is best to use expedition style tactics to surmount this climb. See photo 12V.

Despite first appearances there is really no easy way to access this ridge. There are, however, three possibilities to gain the main ridge crest of Cantenary Ridge. It is possible to gain the ridge crest through a heavily broken crevasse field in the McArthur Col. Alternatively, it is possible to climb either one of the north ridges that rise to meet the sub-peaks on the lower section of Cantenary Ridge. See photo 13V.

The first ascent team initially attempted to gain the main ridge crest of Cantenary Ridge by climbing the north ridge of the taller of the two sub-peaks, known as Cantenary Peak. The north ridge of Cantenary Peak is narrow, corniced and decorated with many steep rock gendarmes. The combination of the steep rock and rotten ice towers on the narrow ridge crest forced the first ascent team to abandon their attempt on this ridge. Subsequent climbing parties have also attempted this north spur and they have met with the same unsuccessful results. Although this spur is really not the best approach to gaining the ridge crest it would make an excellent climb for a strong team. This spur can probably only be successfully climbed early in the season and during the coldest early morning hours of the day.

The first ascent team then switched their attention to the north spur of the smaller of the two sub-peaks, known as Dak Peak. This sub-peak is so named because it was named after one of the favorite foods of the first ascent team, Dak Stroganoff. The first ascent team ran into the same difficulties on the north spur of Dak Peak as they did on the north spur of Cantenary Peak. Consequently, they abandoned their attempt on Dak Peak as well.

Finally, the first ascent team switched their attention to the third and final alternative which is the McArthur Col. This is a deep col which sits between Mt. McArthur and the beginning of the Cantenary Ridge route of Mt. Logan. This col can be accessed by snow slopes through a heavily crevassed icefall. The route finding up the col is quite easy until just before the exit onto the main Cantenary Ridge crest. At this point a large bergschrund is found that traverses the entire slope. The first ascent team descended into the crevasse and used direct aid on ice screws to climb the back wall of the crevasse. The difficulties experienced in this col will probably depend upon the time of year that the route is climbed. Nonetheless, the McArthur Col is probably the most logical way to access Cantenary Ridge.

The first ascent team established their first camp in the McArthur Col at 10,250 feet (3,124 m). *See CD photo (Chapter 4) CD-V18.* The route then ascends the easy snow slopes to the top of the first sub-peak, Dak Peak. The team established Camp II on top of Dak Peak at 12,500 feet (3,810 m). The route then descends 500 feet (152 m)

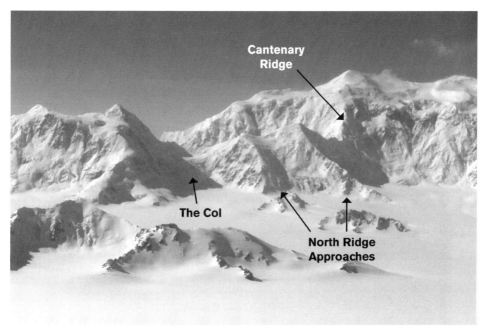

Photo 13V   *Photo by Richard Holmes*

into a small col before rising to the top of the second sub-peak, Cantenary Peak. The first ascent team dug in tent platforms just below the summit of Cantenary Peak to create Camp III at 12,900 feet (3,932 m).

The route from Cantenary Peak then descends 500 feet (152 m) before climbing again a little bit to reach Cantenary Col, which connects the initial part of Cantenary Ridge with the main bulk of Mt. Logan. The first ascent team placed a camp at the entrance to Cantenary Col at 12,000 feet (3,658 m) creating Camp IV.

The route across the col is not as difficult as it appears. The ridge is not a knife-edged ridge continuously all the way across, and there are occasional breaks in the overhanging cornices. The col was fixed with rope for safety. The team placed Camp V on the other side of the col at the base of the Logan Massif. The site selected for Camp V was located at 12,000 feet (3,658 m).

The route above the col becomes steeper and climbs some steep and rotten ice. The next good site for a tent platform is at 14,000 feet (4,267 m) where Camp VI was established. The route continues up the moderately steep but broad snow slopes to a point just below the summit plateau. Camp VII was established at 16,500 feet (5,029 m) on this broad snow shoulder. *See CD photo (Chapter 4) CD-V19.*

The route above Camp VII traverses around the southeast corner of the eastern summit of Mt. Logan and continues to the true central summit of Mt. Logan. It might be necessary to establish one high camp before completing the entire traverse over the plateau to the true summit due to the distance involved. A good spot for Camp VIII can be found at 17,500 feet (5,334 m) on the south side of the eastern summit. *See CD photo (Chapter 4) CD-V20.*

The King Trench route can be used as the descent route. However, if fixed line is secured along Cantenary Ridge during the ascent then the ascent route can be used as the descent route. The first ascent team

Photo 14V *Photo by Richard Holmes*

descended from the mountain by descending their fixed line down Cantenary Ridge.

The ascent of Cantenary Ridge is moderately difficult. It is a long route and may require securing about 4,000 feet (1,219 m) of fixed line. The route involves a great deal of ascending and descending along the lower ridge before finally reaching the summit plateau. This route is not climbed very often so it will not be a crowded climb. Ref. *AAJ* 1968, pp. 51-55. *CAJ* 1980, p. 87.

East Ridge

Rising in a spectacular ice-encrusted spire out of a small but beautiful basin formed by the southeast ridge of Mt. Logan to the south and Mt. McArthur to the north, is the magnificent east ridge of Mt. Logan. The east ridge of Mt. Logan may be one of the most beautiful ridges on the entire Logan Massif. The east ridge has a little bit of everything on it. It is a very enjoyable climb with snow faces, rock ridges and a little bit of steep ice as well. It is challenging but never severe. Yet you will really feel like you climbed something once you have successfully completed this climb.

The east ridge of Mt. Logan has become quite popular and probably receives the most attention from climbers outside the King Trench route. Fortunately, the campsites on the ridge are large enough to accommodate more than one climbing expedition at a time.

The east ridge is the climb most often done when a traverse of the mountain is made. A traverse of Mt. Logan usually involves an ascent of the east ridge of Mt. Logan and a descent of the King Trench route. The route is popular with climbers ready to challenge themselves with a technical climb on a large mountain. The east ridge is an excellent mountaineering objective. See photo 14V.

A good base camp can be established below the base of the east ridge. This small side glacier off Hubbard Glacier can be easily accessed by plane or helicopter. *See CD photo (Chapter 4) CD-V21.* The route from the base camp goes to the left or south side of the ridge. *See CD photo (Chapter 4) CD-V22.*

There is a small icefall on the left side of the ridge but there are a series of easy snow ramps that lead through it. The south side of the ridge can be climbed by an obvious and easy snow couloir that leads to the crest of the ridge. If the north side of the ridge is climbed to gain access to the ridge crest, this will involve unnecessary ice climbing on a steep ice face. Additionally, all the supplies for the entire trip will have to be carried up this steep ice face. *See CD photo (Chapter 4) CD-V23.*

The couloir on the south side of the east ridge will gain the main ridge crest by following the gentle snow slopes up this snow couloir. The route from the top of the couloir climbs another 500 feet (152 m) along the rocky ridge crest to a spot at 9,000 feet (2,743 m) where a good level spot can be found to establish Camp I. See photo 15V. The route above Camp I follows the ridge crest. The ridge is fairly narrow but there is ample room for climbing. Climbing on this section of the ridge involves easy scrambling over rock outcrops on the ridge crest. The route also involves some simple climbing on easy snow slopes. A good spot can eventually be found on a wide spot on the ridge at 11,000 feet (3,353 m) to create Camp II. *See CD photo (Chapter 4) CD-V24.*

The crux of the route can be found above Camp II. The ridge narrows dramatically and becomes much steeper. The north side of the ridge drops away on 75 degree ice slopes to the glacier far below. Fortunately, the left side of the ridge provides a straightforward approach to ascending the ridge. There is sufficient room on the left side of the ridge to provide a good climbing route just below the main crest of the ridge before it too drops off to the glacier below. *See CD photo (Chapter 4) CD-V25.* The ridge ultimately broadens

Photo 15V *Photo by Richard Holmes*

out to a nice level spot to create Camp III at 13,500 feet (4,115 m).

The ridge above Camp III begins to broaden quite a bit. There are a few steep icefaces to be climbed that are steep but short. *See CD photo (Chapter 4) CD-V26.* The route ascends the broad crest of the ridge on easy snow slopes until a good spot can be found at 15,500 feet (4,724 m) to create Camp IV. This camp is situated on a nice broad level section of ridge immediately below the lip of a large crevasse which sits below a small ice face. This camp provides spectacular views into the interior of Kluane Park. *See CD photo (Chapter 4) CD-V27.*

The route past Camp IV must surmount the small ice face immediately above the camp. Fortunately, the ice face does not have to be climbed directly. The route past the ice face traverses left around the face and crosses a small bergschrund with a good snow bridge. The route continues up easy snow slopes on a broad snow dome. *See CD photo (Chapter 4) CD-V28.*

The technical climbing on the east ridge is over at this point and the climb surmounts the rounded snow dome that ultimately leads to the summit plateau. A good camp can be found at 16,500 feet (5,029 m) to create Camp V on the edge of the summit plateau. The summit plateau is so large that an intermediate camp should be placed further along the plateau at the base of the eastern summit of Mt. Logan. This camp can be located at 17,500 feet (5,334 m), creating Camp VI. This high camp gives the climber the opportunity to reach the eastern or the true central summit in a fairly easy summit day. *See CD photo (Chapter 4) CD-V29.*

The route to the true summit from Camp VI traverses around the south side of the eastern summit. This traverse affords spectacular views down Hummingbird Ridge as well as views of the adjacent Mt. St. Elias. The route traverses the narrow ridge crest, which connects the eastern and central summits. *See CD photo (Chapter 4) CD-V30.*

The King Trench route can be descended if a traverse of the mountain is desired. The ascent route can be used as the descent route if fixed rope is left in place during the ascent. Some rock protection is useful to secure fixed ropes on this route. Large angle pitons are excellent for protection for the rock formations encountered on the east ridge. Camming devices can be used successfully as well. Some ice screws will also be needed. It will be necessary to have full-length as well as half-length pickets. The half-length pickets are perfect for securing ropes on the honeycombed ice on some of the narrowest sections of the ridge crest. Ref. *AAJ* 1958, pp.31-38. *CAJ* 1977, pp. 67-70.

Southeast Ridge
Hubsew Ridge

Descending from the southeast side of Mt. Logan is the long and sinuous southeast ridge. This ridge forms a hydrological divide between the Hubbard and Seward Glaciers. Consequently, this ridge has been nicknamed the Hubsew Ridge. This ridge is a four mile (6.4 km) long serrated ridge with spectacular rime-encrusted ice faces. *See CD photo (Chapter 4) CD-V31.*

The Hubsew Ridge rises up and to the right nearly parallel to the east ridge of Mt. Logan until the two ridges eventually meet on a large rounded snow dome at 14,000 feet (4,267 m). See photo 16V. Fortunately, the lower undulating sections of the Hubsew Ridge do not have to be climbed. The ridge can be ascended on its north side via a small col. The route to this col climbs an unstable snow face which contains many loose ice towers. Although the ascent onto the ridge crest via this snow face is tricky it is very short. *See CD photo (Chapter 4) CD-V32.*

The unstable snow face leads to the top of a small col. There is ample room to create a camp on a wide section of the ridge at the

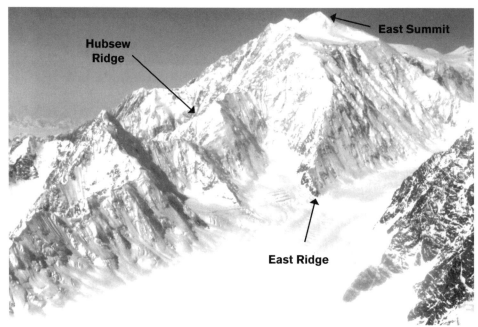

Photo 16V   *Photo by Richard Holmes*

top of this col at 10,000 feet (3,048 m). This col is just past a beautiful little peak, found lower down on Hubsew Ridge, which has been nicknamed Nice Peak due to its pleasant appearance. See photo 17V.

The first ascent team ascended the Hubsew Ridge in an alpine fashion. The team met their climbing partners, who were simultaneously climbing the east ridge of Mt. Logan, at 14,000 feet (4,267 m), where the east ridge and the Hubsew Ridges intersect. The Hubsew Ridge can be climbed alpine style but an expedition style climb will work just as easily.

The route past the col ascends easy snow slopes. The ridge begins to rise slightly and becomes narrower. The narrow section of ridge is climbed and the ridge becomes horizontal for some distance. This section of horizontal ridge is heavily corniced. It is important to exercise great caution when climbing around the cornices so as not to set off an avalanche. It would be a good approach to secure fixed rope along this narrow and corniced section of the climb in order to secure the route past the cornices. There is one wide spot on the ridge at 12,500 feet (3,810 m) where a second camp can be placed. *See CD photo (Chapter 4) CD-V33.*

The route past Camp II follows the narrow corniced ridge crest. The crux of the climbing is found along this narrow ridge crest where several short but steep ice towers must be climbed. The route follows the ridge crest as it rises to reach a round snow dome at 14,000 feet (4,267 m) where the east and the Hubsew ridges intersect. Camp III can be located here at 14,000 (4,267 m) feet on this round snow dome. *See CD photo (Chapter 4) CD-V34.*

The route past Camp III at 14,000 feet (4,267 m) on the snow dome follows the remainder of the east ridge route to the summit. The Hubsew Ridge can be used as the descent route. The King Trench route can be descended if a traverse of the mountain is desired. Some climbing teams have used as much as 4,000 feet (1,219 m)

Photo 17V *Photo by Richard Holmes*

of fixed line to secure this route along the narrow corniced section of ridge crest. Snow and ice protection are the only forms of climbing protection needed on this route. A full assortment of ice screws will be needed. Both full-length and half-length pickets are useful as well. Deadmen and deadboys are useful for belays and anchoring ropes on the soft snow lower on the ridge. Ref. *AAJ* 1968, pp. 46-50. *AAJ* 1975, p. 140. *CAJ* 1968, pp. 141-142.

Raven Ridge

Nestled into a recess on the southeast side of Mt. Logan is the beautiful formation known as Raven Ridge. This is a long thin serrated and corniced ridge which rises out of Seward Glacier and ultimately meets Hubsew Ridge on a large rounded snow dome at 14,000 feet (4,267 m).

This spectacular looking ridge can be accessed from Seward Glacier at the base of the ridge. At the toe of the ridge there are two forks. The left-hand fork is usually selected to begin the route. The left fork is climbed along its crest over several rock towers. See photo 18V.

The route continues along the narrow ridge crest until it reaches a snow face climbing to the top of a small false summit at 9,600 feet (2,926 m). This false summit has been reached on several occasions. However, as of this writing the entire ridge has not been successfully ascended.

The route past the false summit follows the ridge crest. The ridge is not steep along any portion of its length. However, the ridge is narrow and corniced. Also, there are numerous rock gendarmes that must be surmounted in order to successfully climb this ridge. The rock that comprises these towers is rather loose and rotten. Raven Ridge ultimately intersects with Hubsew Ridge on a 14,000 foot (4,267 m) snow dome. The route to the summit from the snow dome is the same as that for the Hubsew and east ridge routes. The King Trench route can be used as the descent route if a traverse of the

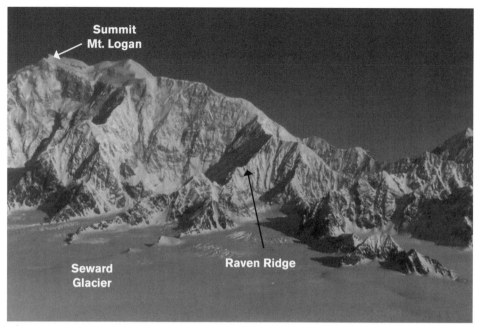

Photo 18V *Photo by Richard Holmes*

mountain is desired. Raven Ridge can be descended if fixed line is left in place during the ascent. This is the longest and most spectacular of the remaining unclimbed ridges of Mt. Logan. See CD photo (Chapter 4) CD-V35.

This climb can be done in alpine fashion; however, an expedition style climb might be easier and safer. The route will require a fair amount of fixed rope. The climb will need some rock protection to surmount the rock towers. Large angle pitons or large and mid-sized camming devices will be required to ascend these towers. An assortment of ice screws and pickets will be useful to ascend the snow and ice sections of the ridge.

An interesting alternative to beginning Raven Ridge is to climb the south spur. The south spur can be ascended from the Seward Glacier in a couloir on its south side. The south spur is a long narrow ridge which rises at a steep angle to meet Raven Ridge at 10,000 feet (3,048 m). The remainder of the route is the same for the regular Raven Ridge route. This spur has not been climbed as of this writing and is a worthwhile challenge. See CD photo (Chapter 4) CD-V36. Ref. *AAJ* 2003, pp. 244-245.

Warbler Ridge

The great south face of Mt. Logan is one of the most dramatic and awe-inspiring sights in the entire Wrangell-St. Elias complex of mountains. Not only is Mt. Logan the tallest mountain in Canada but the great south face is one of the largest escarpments as well. The south face of Mt. Logan is split by several ridges which rise out of Seward Glacier uninterrupted for nearly 10,000 feet (3,048 m) to reach the great summit plateau. On the eastern edge of the great south face rises the long and convoluted Warbler Ridge. In keeping with the traditions of the south face routes, this climb received its name when a lost little warbler flew around base camp on several occasions.

The climbing on Warbler Ridge can be divided into three portions. The first part of

Photo 8V *Photo by Richard Holmes*

the climb is associated with attempting to reach a prominent subsidiary peak of 13,448 feet (4,099 m) where the initial pyramid of the route meets the main ridge crest. It is possible to access the base of Warbler Ridge off Seward Glacier via a large and obvious snow couloir. See photo 19V.

The route ascends the snow slopes to gain a col in the ridge crest. A good spot can be found in the col to create Camp I at 9,512 feet (2,899 m). The route above the col follows the rocky ridge crest over small rock gendarmes. The route leads to the end of the rock spur where a spectacular site can be found on a large snow platform to establish Camp II.

The route above Camp II is blocked by a massive rock tower which is composed of loose and rotten rock and is very steep on all sides. Fortunately, there is a route around this rock tower so that does not have to be climbed directly. A Tyrolean traverse can be done on the southeast side of the tower to circumvent climbing directly over the tower.

This 100 yard (91 m) long Tyrolean traverse climbs horizontally around the tower and is actually the technical climbing crux of the entire climb. The route past the Tyrolean traverse leads up easier snow slopes to the top of the snow dome where a good spot can be found at 13,448 feet (4,099 m) to create Camp III. *See CD photo (Chapter 4) CD-V37.*

From the top of the snow dome the second part of the climb begins. At this point the main ridge crest is followed. As is characteristic of ridges on the south face of Mt. Logan, a large section of this ridge is horizontal. The appearance of a horizontal section by itself is not remarkable but this section of ridge is double corniced and great care must be taken to tightrope across this section without dislodging the loose overhanging cornices. The distance across this horizontal section is too great to do in a single push. Consequently, it is necessary to place camps along this unsettled section of corniced ridge crest. Unfortunately, the cornices have given way in this area resulting in fatalities. So the placement of a camp along this section must be treated with great caution and vigilance.

The route proceeds delicately along the catwalk between the cornices that fall away 2,000 feet (610 m) on either side of the ridge. Fixed rope can be used here but you must be able to release yourself from the rope immediately in case a cornice gives way. Otherwise, you may be in jeopardy of being carried away with the falling cornice. The first ascent team placed two camps along the corniced section of ridge. *See CD photo (Chapter 4) CD-V38.*

The long horizontal section is finally completed and the ridge blends into the main bulk of the mountain at 15,000 feet (4,572 m). At this point the third portion of the climb begins, which involves climbing the snow slopes of the main south face of Mt. Logan. A good spot can be found at the end of the horizontal traverse at 15,000 feet (4,572 m) to place Camp VI.

The route above Camp VI follows easy snow slopes to reach the summit plateau. A good spot can be found at the base of the eastern summit at 17,500 feet (5,334 m) to place Camp VII. The route from Camp VII can climb the eastern summit directly above camp. Alternatively, a traverse can be made along the summit plateau the remaining two miles (3.2 km) to reach the true summit. *See CD photo (Chapter 4) CD-V39.*

The King Trench route is the easiest decent route. The first ascent team descended the east ridge. Warbler Ridge is a long and serious climb. It will require a great deal of fixed rope and climbing equipment. It will be necessary to use good judgement on the long horizontal corniced section of ridge. Despite the fact that the climbing on this route is long and arduous it is really never severe. The hardest sections of climbing are 5.5 for the rock climbing and the steepest ice sections are no more than one rope length long. However, the long nature of the route and the high altitude of Mt. Logan combine to make this a serious yet rewarding undertaking. Ref. *AAJ* 1978, pp. 539-540. *CAJ* 1978, pp.8-9.

Hummingbird Ridge

One of the most spectacular and renowned climbs in the St. Elias Mountains is Hummingbird Ridge. This gigantic ridge sits squarely in the middle of the great south face of Mt. Logan and descends directly from the true summit.

Hummingbird Ridge acquired its name as a result of the pleasant but surprising brief appearance of a hummingbird, over one of the lower camps of the first ascent team. This bird must have mistaken a climber's red parka for a giant flower. The result of this nomenclature was to generate a long string of names for ridges on the south face of Mt. Logan, all containing the names of popular birds. This is not really such a bad way to name such spectacular climbs.

The true enormity of the size of Mt. Logan is perfectly exemplified by Hummingbird Ridge. This enormous ridge rises some 12,000 feet (3,658 m) out of Seward Glacier to end directly at the true summit of Mt. Logan. In the process it runs nearly ten miles (16 km) in length. Hummingbird Ridge is long and narrow with plenty of challenging climbing. The ridge has some steep rock and ice. There is a mile long horizontal traverse with double cornices. The ridge rises to meet the exact summit of Mt. Logan. The commitment necessary to climb this spectacular ridge and the skill and energy needed to succeed on this climb are now legendary in mountaineering history.

Hummingbird Ridge was fully visible to many climbers and explorers over the decades since the initial visual sighting of Mt. Logan by Professor Israel Russell in 1890. The concept of attempting a climb on

Photo 20V   *Photo by Richard Holmes*

such a long and difficult route had certainly ruminated in the minds of many would-be alpinists. Finally, in the summer of 1965 a team of strong climbers set out to challenge this formidable route. See photo 20V.

The initial obstacle that must be overcome on this climb is to reach the main ridge crest. This is no minor obstacle as the potential buttresses and couloirs that lead to the ridge crest are all 3,000 feet (914 m) in length. The first ascent team chose to ascend the west or left side of Hummingbird Ridge to gain the main ridge crest. They chose a 3,700 foot (1,128 m) long couloir and buttress system that rises off a side glacier of Seward Glacier and named it the Osod Couloir. Osod is a word from the indigenous Tlingit Indians of the area, meaning an overall prevalence of fear. This is not an uncommon feeling when attempts are made to climb such large and forbidding routes. *See CD photo (Chapter 4) CD-V40.*

The Osod Couloir is a 3,700 foot (1,128 m) long system that rises to meet the main ridge crest of Hummingbird Ridge at 12,000 feet (3,658 m). The climbing in this couloir involves steep ice and occasionally climbing the rock buttress to the left of the couloir. The rock climbing involves difficulty up to and including 5.7 rock moves.

The Osod Couloir is a direct approach to the ridge crest and has been climbed successfully. However, it should be noted that the couloir is overhung by numerous cornices which occasionally break off and avalanche down the couloir. Some of the avalanches are very large and sweep the entire couloir. Consequently, climbing in the couloir should be done during the coldest hours of the early morning to ensure that everything remains safely frozen in place.

Ever since the first successful ascent of Hummingbird Ridge, climbing teams have been searching for an alternative approach to gaining the ridge crest and therefore avoiding the dangerous avalanche problems found in the Osod Couloir. One team even attempted to climb the ridge from its very tip. This approach adds an additional five miles (8 km) to the length of the overall climb. Attempting to climb Hummingbird Ridge from its very tip has not proven to be a successful method of ascending this long route.

An interesting alternative to the Osod Couloir is to approach the climb from the east or right-hand side of the ridge. A seemingly safer and more logical approach to gaining the ridge crest is to ascend a large and obvious couloir on the east face of the ridge. This couloir does gain the ridge crest nearly 3,000 feet (914 m) lower than the Osod Couloir. It will also necessitate climbing a large blocky rock buttress directly above the couloir on the main ridge crest. However, it does have the significant advantage of being much safer than the Osod Couloir. If the east face couloir is climbed then the team can begin their expedition without the trepidation of knowing that they may be at risk of a massive avalanche at a moment's notice before ever setting foot on the main crest of Hummingbird Ridge. *See CD photo (Chapter 4) CD-V41.*

Another alternative to gaining the ridge crest has actually been attempted on the east side. This approach is the large and spectacular east buttress of Hummingbird Ridge. This climb is difficult but rewarding. The east buttress of Hummingbird Ridge reaches the main ridge crest only about 500 feet (152 m) below the point where the Osod Couloir joins the ridge. The east buttress is quite long as the ascent is over 1,500 feet (457 m). The climb on this buttress is steep and must ascend some difficult rock steps. The upper part of this buttress is an open face that is subject to frequent avalanche danger. Consequently, an alpine ascent is probably the best approach to the east buttress variation. *See CD photo (Chapter 4) CD-V42.* Each team must choose the approach that is appropriate for their level of skill and the conditions found on the ridge during that season. All of the routes eventually reach the snow dome at 13,500 feet (4,115 m).

Tent platforms along any of the lower sections of Hummingbird Ridge will have to be manufactured on the spot. This will involve moving rocks around to create a level site or a significant amount of chopping ice to create a level spot on the ridge. The placement of camps will depend more on the progress of the team than on the terrain of the ridge. Since the ridge is so narrow along much of its length and there are few good natural spots for tent platforms, the team will just have to chop out a level spot whenever it becomes necessary to camp.

From the top of the snow dome the route drops 500 feet (152 m) down into a narrow col. The route then begins one of the more notorious sections of the entire climb and perhaps one of the most notorious sections on any big mountain in North America. This is the one mile (1.6 km) long horizontal traverse along a thin delicate ridge flanked by unstable cornices on both sides. This horizontal section of ridge has been referred to as the "shovel traverse" as well as the "forward retreat." The latter name is of course in reference to the fact that once you cross the traverse it is easier to continue to the summit than to backtrack across the traverse.

The traverse is so long that it is impossible to climb all the way across it with all the supplies in just one trip. Consequently, an intermediate camp must be placed about halfway along the traverse. There is one relatively large and level spot about halfway across the traverse where a camp can be placed. However, this camp will be sitting on top of hanging cornices of questionable quality. Consequently, the tents and the supply bags as well as the climbers themselves should all be tied off to the center of the ridge. *See CD photo (Chapter 4) CD-V43.*

When the horizontal traverse is finally crossed, the ridge crest becomes much steeper. Despite the formidable appearance of this upper section of ridge it is not as difficult as it appears. However, at this point in the climb the amount of food and fuel that remain as well as the altitude and the weather conditions will become a factor in successfully completing the climb.

The steep ridge is climbed to a large rock buttress near the top of the steep section. The buttress can be passed on its right side by a traverse on snow slopes that average about 45 degrees in angle. The route continues on to the final steep section of ridge, which can be bypassed by climbing easy snow slopes to the right of the ridge. These easy snow slopes lead to the true central summit of Mt. Logan. The King Trench route is the most expedient way to descend from the summit after completing Hummingbird Ridge, although some teams have down-climbed the east ridge route. *See CD photo (Chapter 4) CD-V44.*

If Hummingbird Ridge looks big from below, its true magnitude can really be appreciated from the top. The overall size and continually steep nature of this ridge are apparent from the summit plateau. *See CD photo (Chapter 4) CD-V45.*

Hummingbird Ridge is a hallmark climb in mountaineering. The size and difficulty render this one of the most challenging climbs in all of North America. It will require a full assortment of rock and ice gear to fix the difficult pitches. The first ascent team placed their 4,000 feet (1,219 m) of rope along the ridge six times, making for an astounding total of 24,000 feet (7,315 m) of fixed rope used on the route. The horizontal traverse is a very unique feature of this climb. Once the traverse is crossed it is easier to go on with the climb than to retreat. It will take a sense of total commitment to complete this magnificent route. Ref. *AAJ* 1966, pp. 8-18.

Early Bird Buttress

Subsequent to the first ascent of Hummingbird Ridge climbers have begun searching for alternative methods of gaining the ridge crest. Access to the ridge crest is frequently blocked by cornices or troubled by avalanche slopes. One interesting alternative to gaining the main crest of Hummingbird Ridge is to climb the Early Bird Buttress.

Early Bird Buttress is an 8,000 foot (2,438 m) large, blocky ice encrusted buttress dropping down the west, left side of Hummingbird Ridge. *See CD photo (Chapter 4) CD-V46.* This buttress still suffers from some of the same difficulties as the other approach routes. There is some avalanche danger and the climbing is steep. Nonetheless, this buttress has developed a reputation of being an excellent approach to beginning the climb of Hummingbird Ridge.

The ascent of Early Bird Buttress begins by following the side glacier on the left side of Hummingbird Ridge. At the top of the Seward icefall, the base of Early Bird Buttress can be reached. *See CD photo (Chapter 4) CD-V47.* The climb begins at the base of the buttress in a little cirque. The route follows a small finger-like couloir onto the buttress. The route moves up and left around a large active ice cliff. *See CD photo (Chapter 4) CD-V48.* The route proceeds initially up the left side of the buttress and then back towards the center of the buttress. The route involves short stretches of steep rock. The climb also involves climbing on thin layers of ice which are overlaying the rock beneath. The route eventually breaks out onto an upper snow field that involves postholing through deep snow to reach the main crest of Hummingbird Ridge.

There are no good campsites or even bivouac sites below 14,000 feet (4,267 m). Consequently, other than enjoying very short rest breaks it is important to move as rapidly as possible to 14,000 feet (4,267 m) in order to obtain a good bivouac site and move past the avalanche prone sections of the lower buttress. The route intersects Hummingbird Ridge at 16,000 feet (4,877 m). The main advantage of climbing the Early Bird Buttress is that it intersects Hummingbird Ridge past the horizontal traverse, which is always a difficult section to climb.

Early Bird Buttress suffers from avalanche prone slopes and overhanging ice cliffs lower on the buttress. This is probably not the preferred route if an expedition style climb is desired. This route would subject the climbing team to a great deal of avalanche activity during the repeated trips that would be necessary to carry loads up the climb. All of the recorded ascents of the Early Bird Buttress have involved an alpine style push. This has been followed by an alpine style ascent of the remainder of Hummingbird Ridge. The east ridge has become the favorite descent route.

An alpine ascent of the Early Bird Buttress and the remainder of the Hummingbird Ridge route is a good way to minimize the object hazards found on the Early Bird Buttress. However, this style of climbing leaves very little margin for error. Therefore, the team should be well acclimatized and should be technically competent in order to successfully engage such a challenging undertaking. Ref. *AAJ* 1995, p. 172. *CAJ* 1986, p. 59.

Thunderbird Variation

Another variation has been developed that allows climbers to gain access to the main ridge crest of Hummingbird Ridge. This mixed rock and ice couloir is known as the Thunderbird Variation. The Thunderbird route acquired its name from the first ascent team because as described in their own words, "likely thundering results should an avalanche sweep onto the exposed route."

The Thunderbird Variation is a 6,000 foot (1,829 m) ascent in a narrow couloir with overhanging cornices followed by an ascent on the upper face which is mostly ascended by climbing sixty degree ice which overlies the loose rock beneath it. The route starts on the west, left side of Hummingbird Ridge just above the second icefall. *See CD photo (Chapter 4) CD-V49.*

The route starts up a broken ice cliff and then moves into narrow gullies filled with soft snow. Occasionally steep rock must be surmounted. The route leads to a point near the top of the gullies just below where the route empties onto the upper ice face. The route is blocked by two deep bergschrunds. Snow bridges are the only way to cross them. The route past the bergschrunds leads onto the upper ice face, which is ascended by climbing a continuously steep thin layer of ice overlaying the rock beneath. This section of ice climbing continues unabated until the Thunderbird Variation intersects with the main crest of Hummingbird Ridge at 14,000 feet (4,267 m).

The Thunderbird Variation is a difficult climb with objective hazards. The main advantage to climbing this route is that it will bypass the horizontal traverse on the main crest of Hummingbird Ridge. The Thunderbird Variation should only be done in an alpine style push as an expedition style climb would be subject to too much avalanche danger.

The Thunderbird Variation is an excellent climb for a small, well acclimatized and technically competent team of climbers. The east ridge route is the preferred descent route after completing the remainder of Hummingbird Ridge. Ref. *AAJ* 1991, pp.96-103.

South Southwest Buttress

Immediately to the west of Hummingbird Ridge is a large blocky stair step ridge called the South Southwest Ridge. This is a technically challenging ridge, which is continually steep. The route involves some steep ice and some interesting rock climbing. Un-

Photo 21V   Photo by Richard Holmes

like the other routes on the south face of Mt. Logan, the South Southwest Ridge does not have a long horizontal snow traverse. However, the South Southwest Ridge has just about everything else. See photo 21V.

The approach to climb the South Southwest Ridge of Mt. Logan enters the cirque with Hummingbird Ridge on the right and South Southwest Ridge on the left. The base of South Southwest Ridge is unmistakable because there is a large subsidiary peak at the foot of South Southwest Ridge know as Mt. Teddy.

The approach into the cirque to climb the South Southwest Ridge is under constant threat of large avalanches from the hanging ice cornices breaking off the ice cliffs overhead. Consequently, the best site to place a base camp is in the small col at the foot of Mt. Teddy. *See CD photo (Chapter 4) CD-V50.*

The route then moves around the right side of the ridge and climbs a 2,500 foot (762 m) couloir to gain access to the ridge crest.

See CD photo (Chapter 4) CD-V51. A good spot can be chopped out of the ice at the top of the couloir sufficient to create Camp I.

A small rock band rises immediately above Camp I. The rock band is not very long but it does have a few interesting rock moves in it up to 5.8 in difficulty. The route continues past the rock band on a thin ridge crest. The ridge crest is adorned with soft snow and honeycombed ice. The narrow ridge gives way to a broad snow face above. Camp II can be established at the top of the narrow ridge below the ice face at 13,000 feet (3,962 m). *See CD photo (Chapter 4) CD-V52.*

The route past Camp II follows the broad snow and ice face. The face is climbed to the base of a large rock band. Ascending it is the crux of the climb. A good spot can be found at the base of the rock band to create Camp III. The rock band is steep but does not remain so continually over its entire length. It will require a few rock moves up to 5.8+ and some ice may be present on the rock to add to the challenge. The ridge broadens out above the rock band to create a large snow face. The top of the rock band marks the end of the technical difficulties. A good spot can be found at the top of the rock band at 16,000 feet (4,877 m) to create Camp IV.

The route past Camp IV follows the easy snow slopes onto the summit plateau. The true summit is 1,000 yards (914 m) to the right of the top of the South Southwest Ridge. The King Trench Route is the best descent route for this climb. *See CD photo (Chapter 4) CD-V53.*

The climb will require some fixed rope and the usual assortment of snow and ice protection. Pitons or camming devices are useful to fix rope on the rock band. The route is challenging but the climbing is never severe. The South Southwest Ridge has the aesthetic value of not having the usual south face horizontal snow traverse. Ref. *AAJ* 1980, pp.557-559. *CAJ* 1978, pp. 92-94.

Mt. Teddy
12,989 feet (3,960 m)

At the foot of South Southwest Ridge is a very prominent pyramidal shaped subsidiary peak known as Mt. Teddy. This peak would generally just be bypassed on the way to climb the South Southwest Ridge of Mt. Logan. However, some teams have seen fit to consider Mt. Teddy a climbing attraction in itself.

The first ascent of Mt. Teddy ascended the obvious snow couloir on the east face. The route climbed this 3,000 foot (914 m) face following the snow couloir to the summit ridge of Mt. Teddy. The summit ridge can be used to reach the summit of Mt. Teddy. Climbers can ascend Mt. Teddy even while ascending the South Southwest Ridge of Mt. Logan. The standard approach to beginning the South Southwest Ridge of Mt. Logan is to gain the ridge crest by climbing the large 2,500 foot (762 m) ice col that sits between the main Logan Massif and Mt. Teddy. A camp can be placed at the top of the col. If energy and time predominate, then the summit of Mt. Teddy can be climbed by ascending the ridge which connects the col camp with the summit of Mt. Teddy. *See CD photo (Chapter 4) CD-V54.* Ref. *AAJ* 2001, pp. 228-229. *CAJ* 1978, pp. 92-94.

West Buttress

On the extreme western corner of the south face of Mt. Logan stands a spectacular ice covered ridge known as the West Buttress. This buttress is guarded on all sides by massive overhanging ice cliffs. Consequently, one of the major challenges of climbing this route is to find a safe way onto the ridge so that the climb can begin in a safe manner.

Despite the magnificence and the grandeur of the West Buttress this spectacular ridge has no recorded ascents as of this writing. This is one of the last great potential first ascents that still exist on Mt. Logan. In addition to the fact that this ridge has not yet been climbed it is one of the ridges of the great south face that is yet unclimbed. The ridge crest is very narrow in places and there is a long thin corniced ridge crest which ascends a massive hanging glacier at 13,000 feet (3,962 m). The presence of the climbing difficulties on this ridge coupled with the formidable appearance of the ridge itself have probably contributed to the fact that this ridge has not been climbed. See photo 22V.

The first and one of the most challenging aspects of this climb is to gain the main ridge crest. Despite the fact that overhanging ice cliffs predominate in the surrounding cirque there is one potential chink in the armor of the west ridge. Near the base of the ridge on its east side there is a 2,000 foot (610 m) long snow couloir that rises to meet the main ridge crest. *See CD photo (Chapter 4)*

Photo 22V *Photo by Richard Holmes*

CD-V55. The climbing in this couloir is a straight line from the bottom to about 200 feet (61 m) from its top. At this point a rock band blocks the exit onto the main ridge crest. But it should be possible to bypass it by climbing to the right on a steep snow ramp. This snow ramp will bring the climber to the main ridge crest at about 12,000 feet (3,658 m). A good spot can be found to dig in a platform for tents below a snow dome to create Camp I.

The route past Camp I ascends the snow dome above Camp I. The route dips down into a deep col. A good spot can be found at the bottom of the col at 11,500 feet (3,505 m) to place Camp II. The crux of the route is directly above Camp II. The route above Camp II climbs a small rock buttress. Then the ridge becomes much steeper and narrower as it rises to the hanging glacier above. The ridge is now very narrow and the thin ridge crest is climbed past a hanging cornice to the base of an ice wall. A good spot at 13,000 feet (3,962 m) can be found at the base of the ice wall to establish Camp III. *See CD photo (Chapter 4) CD-V56.*

The route ascends the ice wall above Camp III. The ridge then broadens out a little as it rises to a massive plateau above a hanging glacier. A broken ice field can be climbed to reach a second plateau. The climbing at this point is on easy snow slopes and the greatest difficulty is route finding through the crevasses of the ice fields. On the second plateau a good spot can be found to establish Camp IV at 16,000 feet (4,877 m).

The route past Camp IV climbs easy snow slopes to reach the summit plateau. The climb across the plateau traverses the two miles (3.2 km) necessary to reach the main central summit. The King Trench route is the easiest descent from this climb. See Photo 57V. This is a spectacular ridge, which has not been climbed as of this writing. A full assortment of ice screws, pickets and flukes will be needed to fix rope on this challenging route. A few pitons or camming devices will

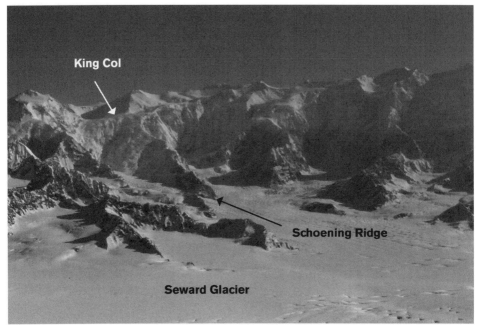

Photo 23V *Photo by Richard Holmes*

be needed in the approach couloir. This is an excellent opportunity for a first ascent on a technically demanding route. *See CD photo (Chapter 4) CD-V59.*

Schoening Ridge

Rising out of the Seward Glacier between the West Buttress and King Peak is the charming little route known as Schoening Ridge. This is a very short and rapid way to gain access to the King Col of Mt. Logan. This route is entirely snow and ice and is an interesting route on moderately easy slopes. This route is not climbed very often and therefore provides the opportunity to avoid all the climbing activity of the lower section of the King Trench route.

The route begins on a side glacier off Seward Glacier. The ridge can be approached quite easily on foot from Seward Glacier. The route begins on the left or southwest side of the ridge. See photo 23V. The route ascends an indistinct snow ridge to gain the main ridge crest of Schoening Ridge. The ridge is quite broad at this point and a good platform can be created to establish Camp I. *See CD photo (Chapter 4) CD-V58.* The route past Camp I follows the generally broad ridge on its left side. The ridge is corniced but quite broad and it is easily possible to climb far below the cornice line. A second spot can be found just below a large rounded snow dome to place Camp II at 13,000 feet (3,962 m). *See CD photo (Chapter 4) CD-V59.*

The route past Camp II follows the very broad ridge over a large rounded snow dome to reach the head of the King Trench route in King Col at 13,800 feet (4,206 m). A good camp can be placed in the King Col at 13,800 feet (4,206 m). The Schoening Ridge ends where it intersects the King Col. The remainder of the climb to the summit follows the King Trench route, which can be used as the descent route.

There is a need to secure a small amount of fixed rope lower on the side on the face leading to the main ridge crest. Snow flukes and pickets are the only climbing protection needed to secure rope on this route. This is a fun route and is not climbed very often. It is a good alternate start to the King Trench route and is a little more interesting than the King Trench route. Ref. *CAJ* 1972, pp. 22-25.

Circumski

Mt. Logan is not only the tallest mountain in Canada but it is one of the most massive mountains in all of North America. Mt. Logan has a circumference of over 100 miles (161 km). Consequently, it has become popular to ski on the myriad number of glaciers that surround Mt. Logan all the way around the entire circumference of this great mountain. This is a spectacular ski trip as it involves traveling over the vast expanse of some of the largest glaciers in North America. See Fig. 1. Additionally, the scenery is unparalleled as the views experienced while skiing include the spectacular vistas of Mt. Logan and the other great St. Elias monoliths that are present in this region. A great deal of this trip will be on glaciers with nothing in sight but the magnificent mountains and the glaciers in an unspoiled wilderness.

A circumski trip around Mt. Logan generally begins on the hydrologic divide that stands just north of Mt. Queen Mary. This innocuous little snow dome is the divide for the Donjek, Hubbard, Logan and Kaskawulsh Glaciers. This point can be reached by skiing up the Kaskawulsh from the Slims River Valley or by a drop off from a plane or helicopter.

The trip then proceeds by dropping down onto the massive Hubbard Glacier and skiing to a point just north and west of Mt. Queen Mary in full view of Mt. McArthur. The trip then turns north and

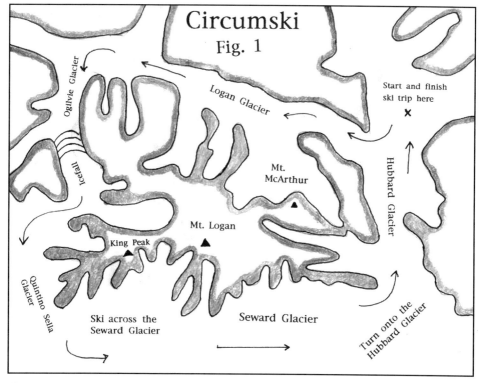

Figure 1

west and continues on the Logan Glacier. Logan Glacier is followed for about thirty miles (48.3 km) until it intersects with Ogilvie Glacier. Ogilvie is the smallest glacier that will be used to complete the circumski. Ogilvie is followed for about five miles (8 km) to a point where there is a fork in the glacier. The left-hand fork is followed and the route travels due south towards the entrance to the King Trench of Mt. Logan.

There is a small icefall on the Ogilvie at the base of the King Trench on Mt. Logan. The icefall is best done on foot with the skis carefully tied onto the pack. The route gains 1,000 feet (305 m) as it ascends this small icefall. The route rises from 7,500 feet (2,286 m) to 8,500 feet (2,591 m) where the route empties onto Quintino Sella Glacier. This broad glacier derived its name from the original ascent of the adjacent Mt. St. Elias, completed by the strong team of Italian climbers led by the Duke of Abruzzi. The duke not only succeeded in climbing Mt. St. Elias but he also left a little Italian culture behind when he departed. The Quintino Sella Glacier is followed around the western end of Mt. King where the route drops down onto Columbus Glacier.

The route then turns due east where the Columbus Glacier is followed as it rises slightly in elevation. At the highest point on Columbus Glacier, directly between King Peak and Mt. Newton, the route begins to descend slightly. The point where the glacier begins to descend is the entrance onto the massive Seward Glacier. The mighty Seward is 35 miles (56 km) long at its longest point and fifteen miles (24 km) wide at its widest point. The route follows the broad expanse of the Seward Glacier as the skier soaks in the unparalleled views of the adjacent Mt. Logan and Mt. St. Elias. This is one of the deepest valleys in North America. The Seward Glacier basin rises from an average elevation of 6,000 feet (1,829 m) to 18,008 feet (5,489 m) on its south side to reach the summit of Mt. St. Elias. The valley rises to 19,545 feet (5,957 m) on its north to the summit of Canada's tallest peak, Mt. Logan. The scenery from Seward Glacier is almost unmatched in magnificence and grandeur.

The Seward Glacier is followed to a group of very low-lying rocky hills. On the north end of these hills just below the southeast ridge of Mt. Logan is Water Pass. This small pass is ascended on easy snow slopes and the route drops down onto Hubbard Glacier. The Hubbard, North America's largest tidewater glacier, is then followed due north. The route passes the pyramidal shaped Mt. King George. The route passes within full view of the impressive south face of Mt. McArthur and continues back up Hubbard Glacier to its intersection with the snow dome where the trip began.

At this point the team can decide whether they have the time and energy to ski the remaining seventy miles (113 km) down the Kaskawulsh Glacier and ultimately the Slims River Valley to the Alcan Highway. The team might prefer to arrange for a pickup by a plane and fly out. In either case, a circumski of Mt. Logan is a physically challenging and mentally rewarding experience coupled with some of the most magnificent scenery that exists anywhere on the North American continent. For a detailed view of the suggested route to circumski Mt. Logan see the accompanying circumski map.

It will be useful in the planning as well as on the ski trip itself to use the maps for this area. The best maps to help with the circumski are the United States maps USGS Mt. St. Elias Alaska-Canada, scale 1:250,000 and USGS Bering Glacier Alaska-Canada, scale 1:250,000. Ref. *CAJ* 1986, p.59.

King Peak
16,971 feet (5,173 m)

Rising out of the southern flank of Mt. Logan is the pyramidal shaped form of King Peak. King Peak is a large and challenging climbing objective in its own right. The north face of King Peak comprises the southern edge of the King Trench. The southern escarpment of King Peak is an enormous 7,000 foot (2,134 m) steep rocky face with spectacular ice-covered couloirs. King Peak is flanked on its east and west sides by long sinuous ridges of ice and rock.

It is noticeably smaller than its neighbor Mt. Logan, but there are numerous challenging mountaineering routes on King Peak. The long ridges leading to the narrow summit are challenging and enjoyable. There is a highly technical route on the south face of King Peak which rates as one of the most difficult climbs existing anywhere in the entire St. Elias Range. King Peak has a climb of every type and difficulty to suit all levels of skill and commitment. King Peak is easy to reach from Seward Glacier and can be climbed as the main objective or in conjunction with a continuation of the climb of Mt. Logan. See photo 1W.

The United States map for this peak is USGS Mt. St. Elias Alaska-Canada, scale 1:250,000. The Canadian map for this peak is King Peak 115 C/10. scale 1:50,000.

North Face

The pyramidal shaped King Peak presents numerous climbing challenges. The earliest climbers who attempted it were faced with the difficulty of determining which route would be the most feasible to climb. The team that eventually made the first ascent approached King Peak via the King Trench. Their evaluation of the numerous ridges and faces led to the conclusion that the north face offered a feasible climbing route. The north face subsequently became the route used for the first successful ascent of King Peak.

The first ascent team climbed the King Trench route of Mt. Logan to an altitude of 13,000 feet (3,962 m) where they placed Camp I, located directly below the north face of King Peak. The team then climbed the obvious snow ramp that diagonals across the north face of King Peak until it intersected with the crest of the west ridge. The diagonal traverse across the north face crosses unstable snow slopes. Additionally, this section of the climb is menaced by overhanging cornices which sit precariously higher on the north face of King Peak. Consequently, the diagonal traverse across the face should be done in the cold early morning hours to ensure that the snow slopes are frozen into place. See photo 2W. There is a good spot on the rounded shoulder of the west ridge to place Camp II at 14,400 feet (4,389 m).

The route above Camp II follows the easy snow ridge over a large snow dome. The route then levels out again and climbs the narrow ridge crest over a horizontal traverse. The horizontal section is narrow but short and fortunately not plagued by cornices. A good spot can be found at the base of the final summit pyramid to place Camp III at 15,200 feet (4,633 m). It is possible to make a summit push from Camp II. However, the final summit pyramid is moderately difficult. The climbing is slow and requires skill and caution, as does the descent. Consequently, it is easier and safer to have a high camp at the base of the summit pyramid. This will enable the team to have a good chance for a successful summit day and have plenty of time to return to camp safely.

The route on the final summit pyramid is steep. The narrow sections of ridge on the summit pyramid can be climbed directly or on the north facing slopes below the cornices. There are numerous rock towers on the final summit pyramid. Some of them

Photo 1W

Photo by Richard Holmes

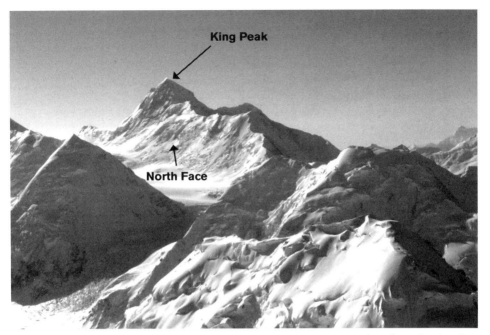

Photo 2W *Photo by Richard Holmes*

can be bypassed on snow slopes on the north side. Some of the towers must be climbed directly.

The rock on these towers is massively fractured due to the freeze-thaw action of ice at this altitude. Despite the fact that these towers are steep there are ample holds for climbing. The freeze-thaw action has nearly split some of these towers in two, creating a snow gully ascending the middle of the tower.

The upper section of ridge as well as the rock towers can be secured with fixed rope. However, the distance from the high camp, Camp III, to the summit is not very far. Therefore, using belays on the steep sections will be all that is needed to make a successful summit attempt. *See CD photo (Chapter 4) CD-W01.*

The climb will require snow and ice protection. Some rock protection is needed for the rock towers on the final summit pyramid. Large camming devices would be the ideal tools to use on the rock towers. The ascent route can be used as the descent route. This is a moderately technical climb and is a very enjoyable ascent. Ref. *AAJ* 1953, pp. 410-415.

West Ridge

Descending from the western edge of King Peak is the long and sinuous west ridge. This route has been used to ascend King Peak and finally continue on to Mt. Logan. However, the approach of using the west ridge to climb King Peak and Mt. Logan includes an excessive amount of unnecessary climbing. This effort would best be used to climb the King Trench to the west side of Mt. Logan. The west ridge of King Peak is, however, a very interesting climb to ascend King Peak by itself.

It is possible to begin the climb of the west ridge of King Peak near the base of the ridge. The main ridge can be gained by climbing easy snow slopes to the crest of the ridge. The route then climbs the narrow rocky ridge over a small subsidiary peak. The route drops down from the subsidiary peak onto the narrow ridge crest which follows mixed rock and ice. The route continues on the main ridge which is now mostly snow with only small sections of exposed rock. The ridge ascends until a wide spot is found on the wide ridge crest immediately below a subsidiary peak. A good spot can be found at the base of the subsidiary peak at 14,000 feet (4,268 m) to create Camp I. *See CD photo (Chapter 4) CD-W02.*

The west ridge is an extremely long route. Consequently, if the team would like to shorten the route by a significant amount there are several possible alternative starts to the west ridge. Just above the entrance to the King Trench route of Mt. Logan there are two broad snow faces that rise out of the King Trench to meet the west ridge. These are similar to the approach used by the first ascent team that diagonals across the north face. The main difference with these approaches, which are lower down the ridge, is that they are much safer from avalanche hazards. *See CD photo (Chapter 4) CD-W03.*

Another more interesting and shorter approach to gaining the west ridge of King Peak is to ascend a couloir on the south side of the west ridge. There is a couloir that can be climbed directly to reach the site of Camp I. The main problem with this approach is this couloir has a small but active icefall in its lower section. Consequently, the avalanche danger in the lower section of the couloir is relatively high.

An alternative to climbing this couloir is to tackle a rock buttress, which is also on the south side of the west ridge and is immediately to the right of the couloir. The main advantage to climbing the rock buttress is that it is much safer than climbing through the icefall in the adjacent snow couloir. The disadvantage to climbing the rock buttress is that it involves a fair amount of difficult rock climbing. The supplies for the remainder of the climb must also be hauled up this route if it is used. The rock buttress intersects the west ridge above Camp I near the top of the subsidiary peak at 15,000 feet (4,572 m). The rock buttress would make an excellent alternate start to the west ridge of King Peak, particularly if the entire route is done in an alpine style climb.

The west ridge is a very long route and as such there are many alternative starts to this climb. The best alternative will depend upon the skills of the team and the conditions of the snow at the time of the ascent. The snow faces found lower on the north side of the west ridge might provide the best combination of a direct and safe approach to gaining the ridge crest. *See CD photo (Chapter 4) CD-W04.*

The route past Camp I follows the corniced ridge crest to the top of the subsidiary peak. The route then drops down onto a horizontal section of ridge which is traversed for about a mile and a half (2.4 km). This section of ridge is narrow but generally not heavily corniced. Fixed rope may still be of some help on this section.

The horizontal ridge is followed to the base of a small snow dome. The route goes over the snow dome to the base of the summit pyramid. There is ample room on the broad snow slopes to place Camp I at 15,500 feet (4,724 m) at the base of the final summit pyramid. *See CD photo (Chapter 4) CD-W05.*

The route up the final summit pyramid is the same as that for the original north face route. The west ridge of King Peak is a fairly long route although it is only of moderate technical difficulty. Snow and rock protection will be needed to secure fixed rope. The elevation gain is not severe so climbing this route as an alpine style ascent would be an interesting approach for a strong team of climbers. The ascent route can be used as the descent route. Ref. *AAJ* 1967, 258-264.

Southwest Face

The southwest face of King Peak has one of the most magnificent escarpments in the St. Elias Mountains. This 7,500 foot (2,286 m) face towers like a magnificently carved Greek statue overlooking Seward Glacier. There is one route on this enormous face that follows the only natural line that ascends it. The route climbs the obvious couloir system up the remote southwest face to reach the west ridge of King Peak and the route has been aptly named "Call of the Wild." *See CD photo (Chapter 4) CD-W06.*

The base of this climb can be reached easily with skis from the Seward Glacier. The route ascends the enormous snow and ice face up and to the left for 4,000 feet (1,219m) over 55 degree ice. Near the top of the ice face the route moves right into a shallow but obvious couloir. *See CD photo (Chapter 4) CD-W07.*

The initial 500 feet (152 m) of this couloir contains the crux climbing pitches on this route. The crux pitch involves some rock climbing on loose rock. However, the predominate difficulties in this section are portions of thin ice covering the rock beneath. Some of the pitches involve climbing freestanding ice stalagmites. The climbing is difficult and sustained. The protection on these pitches is thin at best with a few rock placements and some tied off ice screws in the thin ice. *See CD photo (Chapter 4) CD-W08.*

The remaining 3,000 feet (914 m) to the summit follows the obvious left leaning couloir, a continuous 55 degree ice couloir with some solid rock and ice belays. The route intersects the west ridge just below the true summit of King Peak. The remainder of the climb to the summit follows the summit pyramid as described for the north face route. *See CD photo (Chapter 4) CD-W09.*

The southwest face is a very long and difficult climb. It is subject to rock fall from above so this route can only really be done in an alpine style ascent. Due to the length of the climb it is impractical to belay all but the hardest pitches. It is fastest and safest to climb the route while placing protection and climbing simultaneously. The route will require some small pitons including knife blades as well as an assortment of ice screws. Because this is an alpine style route it is best to keep the gear carried to a minimum.

This is a long and difficult route. The first ascent team rated the climb grade VI, WI6. Due to the length and difficulty of this route the climb should only be attempted by a highly competent and well acclimatized team of climbers. Although King Peak is considerably shorter than its nearest neighbor, Mt. Logan, the southwest face of King Peak may someday become a classic in alpine ascents. Ref. *AAJ* 1999, pp. 50-59.

South Ridge

Near the right-hand side of the southwest face of King Peak is the long and curving south ridge. This long and sinuous ridge rises out of Seward Glacier over a long narrow corniced ridge crest to reach the south summit of King Peak at 15,400 feet (4,694 m). At the top of the south summit of King Peak the south ridge and the east ridges intersect. Both ridges then climb to the true summit of King Peak.

The south ridge of King Peak is a long route as it gains nearly 7,500 feet (2,286 m) where it rises out of the Seward Glacier. The climbing is difficult in places as the route ascends occasional sixty degree black ice. This route is very seldom climbed so there will be virtually no climbing congestion on this route. The south ridge of King Peak is an excellent and moderately technical climbing objective. *See CD photo (Chapter 4) CD-W10.*

The route begins off Seward Glacier directly below the southwest face of King Peak. The route climbs a long thin snow ridge. The ridge is narrow but it is not very steep and begins to broaden out onto a broad shoulder. A good spot can be found on the broad shoulder at 9,000 feet (2,743 m) to place Camp I. See CD photo (Chapter 4) CD-W11.

The route above Camp I follows a very narrow section of ridge which is corniced on its left side. This section of ridge should be secured with fixed rope. The narrow section of ridge curves up and to the left until it merges with a broad snow face. The route stays well to the right of the corniced ridge edge. Simultaneously, the route must stay to the left of the large snow face, which is comprised of unstable snow slopes. The snow face ends at the base of the south summit of King Peak. A good spot can be found at the base of the south summit at 14,400 feet (4,389 m) to place Camp II. See CD photo (Chapter 4) CD-W12.

The route then descends down the snow face from Camp II and to the right-hand side of the large snow face to reach a long couloir. The route ascends this long snow couloir on relatively easy snow and ice slopes. The couloir ultimately narrows to just 35 feet (11 m) wide and becomes much steeper. This narrow couloir is filled with sixty degree black ice. Several pitches of steep ice in this narrow couloir are climbed before the couloir widens again and empties out onto the top of the south summit of King Peak at 15,400 feet (4,694 m). The east and south ridges intersect at the top of the south summit. A good spot can be found on the north side of the south summit to place Camp III. See CD photo (Chapter 4) CD-W13.

The route past Camp III follows a very narrow ice and rock ridge. This narrow section of ridge is corniced and should be secured with fixed rope. The ridge drops down into a small col. The route climbs out of the col and up a ridge of mixed rock and ice. The route then proceeds until it merges with a broad snow field about 900 feet (274 m) below the summit of King Peak. See CD photo (Chapter 4) CD-W14. The route climbs up the right-hand side of the broad snow field to the base of the true summit of King Peak. The northeast corner of the summit pyramid is climbed over mixed rock and ice to reach the true summit of King Peak.

The ascent route can be used as the descent route. The south ridge route involves a lot of climbing on narrow ridges. Consequently, it will require a lot of fixed rope to secure these sections. A good assortment of large angle pitons and large camming devices will be needed to secure the fixed ropes. A good mix of snow and ice protection will be needed for the snow ridges as well. This route is not climbed very often so it will prove an outstanding technical climb on a remote and isolated alpine ridge. Ref. *CAJ* 1970, p. 79.

East Ridge

Anchoring the east end of King Peak is the large blocky east ridge. This is a challenging ridge containing some good rock and ice climbing. The climbing is never severe on this route but it can still be considered moderately technical. This route is seldom climbed and would make for an excellent ascent on a remote ridge.

The east ridge descends from the large eastern escarpment of King Peak. The approach to the base of this ridge can be made easily on skis from Seward Glacier. The direct east ridge is generally not done because it is quite steep and narrow. The first ascent team chose to climb the little south spur which ascends from the head of the cirque on the south side of the east ridge. The crest of the south spur can be climbed on a short rocky face from the head of the cirque. A good spot can be fashioned on the crest of the south spur of the east ridge to create Camp I at 10,500 feet (3,200 m). See photo 3W.

The route above Camp I climbs the

Photo 3W Photo by Richard Holmes

large blocky south spur to within 500 feet (152 m) of the crest of the main east ridge. At this point the rock merges with a snow face. This open snow face is climbed to reach the crest of the east ridge of King Peak at 12,000 feet (3,658 m). The ridge is narrow here but tent platforms can be dug into the side of the snow covered ridge to create Camp II. *See CD photo (Chapter 4) CD- W15.*

The route beyond Camp I follows the narrow corniced snow ridge. The cornices can be bypassed on the right-hand side of the ridge. The narrow section of ridge eventually merges with the broad snow fields below the south summit of King Peak. The snow field is ascended to the base of the south summit where a spot can be found below and to the right of the south summit at 14,400 feet (4,389 m) to create Camp III. *See CD photo (Chapter 4) CD-W16.*

The route past Camp III climbs the same narrow couloir with steep ice that was climbed on the south ridge route. This couloir empties onto the top of the south summit of King Peak. A good spot can be selected at 15,400 feet (4,694 m) on the south summit to create Camp IV. The route past Camp IV traverses the narrow corniced snow ridge to the summit snow fields. The summit snow field is climbed up and to the right to gain the final summit pyramid. The final summit pyramid is ascended on its right-hand side to reach the true summit. *See CD photo (Chapter 4) CD-W17.*

The ascent route can also be used as the descent route. Some pitons and camming devices will be needed to fix rope on the south spur portion of the climb. Snow and ice protection will be needed to protect the narrow corniced snow ridges. This is a challenging climb that is seldom attempted. The isolation of the ridge will provide a great mountaineering opportunity on a remote peak. Ref. *AAJ* 1953, pp. 416-423.

Mt. McArthur
14,400 feet (4,389 m)

Rising from the eastern side of the Logan Massif is the beautiful and challenging peak of Mt. McArthur. This peak is an offshoot of Cantenary Ridge on the northeast corner of Mt. Logan. This humble little summit is a mere shadow of its giant neighbor, Mt. Logan, yet Mt. McArthur is a prominent peak in its own right. There are a surprising number of magnificent climbing routes on this fine peak. Some of the routes are good expedition style climbs, but most on this peak are excellent alpine style ascents. Mt. McArthur is a worthwhile climbing object and has a mountaineering challenge of every degree of difficulty that will satisfy any climbing team interested in attempting this peak. The United States map for this peak is USGS Mt. St. Elias Alaska-Canada, scale 1:250,000. The Canadian map for this peak is McArthur Peak 115 C/9, scale 1:50,000.

West Ridge

On the western edge of Mt. McArthur adjoining the Cantenary Ridge of Mt. Logan is the west ridge of Mt. McArthur. This is a large buttress which is predominately a snow and ice climb. The ridge is ascended to the summit pyramid and ends directly at the western summit of Mt. McArthur. See photo 1X.

The beginning of the west ridge route is the same as that of the Cantenary Ridge on Mt. Logan. The route ascends the Cantenary McArthur Col through a broken icefall and reaches a deep col on a broad snow slope. A good spot can be found in the upper right-hand corner to place tents to create Camp I. *See CD photo (Chapter 4) CD-X01.*

The route then traverses the col over a corniced ridge and surmounts a small snow dome. The route ascends the snow dome and reaches the base of the true west ridge

Photo 1X

Photo by Richard Holmes

that begins on a rock ridge crest. There are several gendarmes that must be climbed or circumvented as the route ascends the ridge. The route above the rock becomes steeper and merges onto a snow and ice ridge. The ice ridge rises to meet the base of the summit pyramid. The southeast corner of the summit pyramid can be climbed to reach the true western summit of Mt. McArthur. *See CD photo (Chapter 4) CD-X02.*

The ascent route can also be used as the descent route. There is really only the need for one camp on this route and it can be located in the McArthur Cantenary Col. The remaining 3,000 feet (914 m) to the summit can be climbed in an alpine style ascent. The snow slopes of the upper face are unstable and are prone to avalanches. Therefore, it is best to stay below the cornice line on any corniced section of the ridge. Some camming devices can be used for rock protection. However, the route will generally require mostly snow and ice protection. Ref. *CAJ* 1992, p. 3.

North Ridge

The dominant feature on the north face of Mt. McArthur and the route used to make the first ascent is the north ridge. It is an elegant snow covered ridge that curves up and slightly left to reach the summit plateau just below the summit pyramid. The route can be completed by ascending the summit pyramid to reach the true summit of Mt. McArthur.

The views of the east side of Mt. Logan and the views of the interior of Kluane Park are spectacular from the summit of Mt. McArthur. The north ridge route is fun but is predominately a relatively easy snow climb. There is, however, one exciting steep but short ice pitch just below the summit plateau. The north ridge of Mt McArthur is a beautiful and enjoyable route. See photo 2X.

The north ridge begins off Hubbard Glacier at the base of the ridge. A good snow ramp is ascended to reach the broad lower section of the north ridge which in turn is ascended to the base of a triangular snow face where the ridge becomes steeper. At the base of the snow face at 10,800 feet (3,292 m) a good spot can be found to create Camp I. *See CD photo (Chapter 4) CD-X03.*

The route past Camp I climbs the snow face onto a narrow ridge crest. The narrow ridge is rock with snow cornices on the right-hand side. The cornices can be easily bypassed on the left side by climbing at the snow and rock interface. The narrow ridge gives way to a broad snow face above which is climbed until it reaches the base of a steep snow face. A good spot can be found here on the broad slopes to create Camp II at 11,800 feet (3,597 m). *See CD photo (Chapter 4) CD-X04.*

The route past Camp II climbs the steep snow face until it again merges with a narrow ridge. The narrow ridge is climbed on the left side to avoid the cornices. The narrow ridge ends at the base of a rock step. The rock step is the crux of the climb and is small but steep. The rock step rises only 100 feet (30 m) but must be surmounted to reach the upper plateau.

The solution to ascending the rock step is to climb the couloir that splits the step. The couloir climbs about fifty feet (15 m) of nearly vertical snow and ice. The snow gives way to a rock ledge that is passed and a small boulder is climbed. The route past the boulder leads to the top of the couloir, which empties onto the upper plateau. An absolutely beautiful spot is found at the top of the couloir to establish Camp III at 13,000 feet (3,962 m). It is a good idea to leave a fixed rope in the couloir to facilitate the descent. *See CD photo (Chapter 4) CD-X05.*

The route past Camp III climbs the easy summit plateau to the base of the summit pyramid that can be ascended on its southeast corner to reach the true summit of

Photo 3W

Photo by Richard Holmes

Mt. McArthur. The ascent route can also be used as the descent route.

The north ridge of Mt. McArthur is a truly beautiful climb. The route involves some easy snow climbing and one truly adventurous snow and ice pitch in the crux rock step. Some alternate starts have been made on the sides of the base of the north ridge. These alternate starts involve a little bit more rock climbing which makes the route more challenging. The north ridge of Mt. McArthur is one of the true classics of the St. Elias Mountains. Ref. *AAJ* 1962, pp.43-48. AAJ 2003, pp. 244-245.

East Ridge

Rising out of the Hubbard Glacier is the long serpentine east ridge of Mt. McArthur. The east ridge of Mt. McArthur is a long but fairly easy climb comprised mostly of easy snow slopes. This route follows the eastern side of the wedge shaped Mt. McArthur over the eastern summit and ultimately on to the true western summit. See photo 3X.

The route begins on the north side of the east ridge. *See CD photo (Chapter 4) CD-X06*. The main crest of the east ridge can be accessed through an easy snow chute that is climbed to the crest of the east ridge. The ridge crest is followed along an easy and fairly broad snow shoulder to a wide spot on the ridge. This wide spot is level and sits just below a point where the ridge becomes steeper. A good spot can be found on the horizontal ridge crest at 10,000 feet (3,048 m) to establish Camp I.

The route past Camp I follows an easy but slightly corniced ridge crest. The ridge leads directly to the eastern summit of Mt. McArthur. *See CD photo (Chapter 4) CD-X07*. The route descends from the eastern summit onto the flat expanse of the summit plateau, then crosses the plateau to the base of the true summit pyramid. The route ascends the southeast corner of the summit pyramid to reach the true summit of Mt. McArthur. *See CD photo (Chapter 4) CD-X08*.

The ascent route can also be used as the

Photo 3X *Photo by Richard Holmes*

descent route. This climb is fairly straightforward and can be climbed in one long day. Alternatively, a camp can be placed at 10,000 feet (3,048 m) which will make the summit day much shorter and easier. The east ridge is used as the descent route for most of the routes which are done on the south face of Mt. McArthur.

South Face

The south face of Mt. McArthur is almost a mountain in itself. This enormous 6,000 foot (1,829 m) escarpment is split by several massive rock buttresses and large flowing icefalls. Some of the best climbs on Mt. McArthur reside on this great southern escarpment. The elevation gain from the glacier to the summit is large but the actual height of the summit of Mt. McArthur is not very high. Consequently, most of the climbs on the south face of Mt. McArthur are perfectly suited for alpine style ascents. See photo 4X.

These climbs provide excellent climbing coupled with the great challenge of accomplishing the climb within the limited time and weather window imposed by an alpine style ascent. The routes are probably best done in an alpine style ascent as there are very few good level spots on the face where tent platforms can be placed which would hold more than one tent. There are, however, ample places for a short bivouac. The routes are all moderately steep and will require an occasional belay.

A small but well selected rack of camming devices should be prepared for the rock climbing sections. The snow and ice sections will require the occasional ice screw or snow fluke. Since the climbs are alpine it is best to take only what you really need so your pack does not get too heavy. The south face of Mt. McArthur is very tall and the 6,000 foot (1,829 m) routes will take some time to ascend. Therefore, the lighter your pack the faster you can travel.

Photo 4X *Photo by Richard Holmes*

West Buttress

Near the left-hand margin of the south face of Mt. McArthur is a small rocky buttress. The buttress rises out of the side glacier that sits below the east ridge of Mt. Logan. This buttress rises at a moderate angle to meet the west ridge of Mt. McArthur at 10,000 feet (3,048 m). A good bivouac site can be found at the intersection with the west ridge.

The remainder of the route to the summit follows the west ridge route of Mt. McArthur. The ascent route can be used as the descent route. This route is one of the easier and shorter routes on the south face of McArthur. *See CD photo (Chapter 4) CD-X09.*

Fred Said Buttress

In the center of the south face of Mt. McArthur below the true western summit of Mt. McArthur is one of the longest routes on the south face. There is an excellent route on this buttress known as the Fred Said Buttress. This route is named after the ubiquitous North American alpinist Fred Beckey. *See CD photo (Chapter 4) CD-X10.*

The route begins off the side glacier from the Hubbard Glacier below the east ridge of Mt. Logan. The route follows easy snow ramps to the right of the main buttress to avoid the loose rock at the base of the buttress. The route finally intersects the main buttress at mid-height on the face. *See CD photo (Chapter 4) CD-X11.*

The route then climbs excellent granite rock outcrops which are interspersed with snow and ice couloirs to the top of the south face. The route ends directly at the true western summit of Mt. McArthur. The east ridge or the west buttress can be used as the descent routes. Ref. *Climbing Magazine* 1998, p. 27.

South Central Buttress

Immediately to the right of the Fred Said Buttress is another beautiful south face route. The South Central Buttress is somewhat less distinct than the Fred Said Buttress but it is still a magnificent route. *See*

CD photo (Chapter 4) CD-X12. The route begins by ascending the snow face to the right of the buttress. The route goes through the rock band above the snow face utilizing snow and ice couloirs whenever possible to avoid the steep rock. The route emerges above the rock band onto the large upper snow face. The upper snow face is climbed up and to the right side of the face. The rock band at the top of the upper snow face can be surmounted through an obvious snow couloir. The couloir leads to the summit plateau just below the summit pyramid of Mt. McArthur.

The first ascent team placed bivouac sites at 9,500 feet, 11,500 feet and 12,800 feet (2,896, 3,505 and 3,901 m). The ascent team descended the north ridge route. This is a very easy descent but the east ridge is also a fairly easy descent route. In addition, if you descend the north ridge you are faced with a ten mile (16 km) walk back to base camp around the east side of the mountain. The South Central Buttress has some steep rock and the ice climbing pitches range up to sixty degrees in angle at the steepest points. Ref. *AAJ* 1994, p. 154.

East Central

Just to the right of the eastern summit of Mt. McArthur is a long rock buttress. A fine route has been established on this buttress. *See CD photo (Chapter 4) CD-X13.* The route begins by climbing the long snow couloir to the right-hand side of the buttress. The route reaches an arete at the top of the couloir where it intersects with the rock buttress. The rock buttress is then climbed to the intersection with the main crest of the east ridge. The final ice pitch leading onto the east ridge is the climbing crux of the route.

This route will require at least one bivouac. The summit of Mt. McArthur can be breached by following the east ridge route which is also the easiest descent off the mountain. Ref. *AAJ* 1995, p. 173.

Southeast Central Buttress

The next buttress to the right of the south face of Mt. McArthur is the southeast central buttress. This is another beautiful 6,000 foot (1,829 m) long buttress providing a challenging climb on the great south face of Mt. McArthur. This route is comprised of fairly good granite and is interspersed with the typical snow and ice chutes. This 6,000 foot (1,829 m) climb will require at least one bivouac. The route intersects the main crest of the east ridge below the eastern summit. The summit can be reached by the east ridge route which will also be the best descent route. *See CD photo (Chapter 4) CD-X14.* Ref. *AAJ* 1990, p. 178.

Huge In Europe

One of the last major buttresses to be climbed on the south face of Mt. McArthur rises out of the Hubbard Glacier just to the right of the Southeast Central Buttress. The route begins in easy snow and ice gullies. The route reaches a rock face at about 10,500 feet (3,200 m). The rock band is ascended and 500 feet (152 m) above it is the technical crux of the route. A short but steep snow traverse on the east side of the buttress leads to a tight chimney in a large rock. After the chimney is climbed a steep traverse leads back onto the main buttress. A short section of rock climbing on a small rock wall leads upwards and has rock moves of about 5.5 in technical difficulty. A short rock slab higher on involves a short section of rock moves up to 5.6 in difficulty.

There are numerous steep gendarmes above the rock slab. These gendarmes can be avoided by rappelling into the gully on the east side of the ridge where a snow face can be climbed to reach a prominent col. A small rock step must be climbed above the col and one final steep ice pitch is climbed to intersect the main crest of the east ridge.

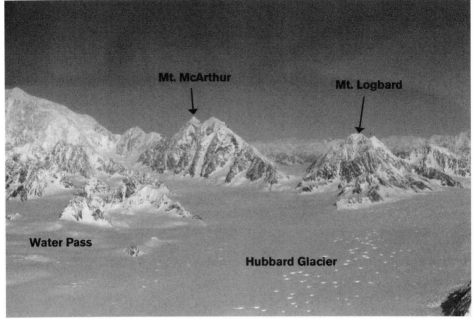

Photo 5X *Photo by Richard Holmes*

The east ridge can be followed to the summit of Mt. McArthur. The east ridge route can be used as the descent route. *See CD photo (Chapter 4) CD-X15.* Ref. *AAJ* 2003, pp. 244-245.

Astro Floyd Couloir

Near the right-hand side of the south face of Mt. McArthur is a fun little route in beautiful snow couloirs. The route ascends obvious snow and ice couloirs to the base of a rock face that is climbed through an obvious but steep snow chute.

The route intersects the main crest of the east ridge below the eastern summit. The east ridge route can be used to ascend the true summit of Mt. McArthur. The first ascent team descended the mountain by down-climbing the easy and obvious snow gullies located just to the right of the ascent route. *See CD photo (Chapter 4) CD-X16.* Ref. *AAJ* 1993, p. 158.

East Buttress

Near the right-hand margin of the south face of Mt. McArthur is the East Buttress, a small but beautiful rock buttress and the last one large enough to warrant a climbing route. As of this writing there has not been a recorded ascent of the East Buttress of the south face of Mt. McArthur.

The route ascends the obvious rock buttress starting at its base. The crux of the climbing is at its base where the buttress is steepest. The buttress reclines to a lower angle as it rises and ultimately intersects with the main crest of the east ridge, which can be climbed the final distance to the summit of Mt. McArthur. The east ridge route can be used as the descent route. *See CD photo (Chapter 4) CD-X17.*

Mt. Logbard
11,837 feet (3,608 m)

Rising out of the Hubbard Glacier virtually as an extension of Mt. McArthur is the quaint little peak of Mt. Logbard. This peak sits between the Logan Massif and Hubbard Glacier. Consequently, Mt. Logbard derives its name from the contraction of the names Mt. Logan and Hubbard Glacier. Mt. Logbard is not a tall mountain by St. Elias standards but it does provide some interesting climbing. This peak can be a good warm-up climb for Mt. Logan or Mt. McArthur. See photo 5X.

The east ridge provides an enjoyable mixed climb on rock and ice. The lower section of the east ridge is rocky and narrow. The lower section gives way to a large snow face which rises to the summit of Mt. Logbard. The ascent route can be used as the descent route. This climb can be done in one long day. As of this writing the east ridge is the only route that has been done on this peak. Ref. *AAJ* 1994, p. 152.

The southwest ridge of Mt. Logbard is a long rocky ridge. The ridge crest can be accessed through a long snow chute on its south side. The southwest ridge is a long rocky ridge which remains narrow over its entire length and rises to intersect the east ridge just below the summit. The east ridge is probably easier to descend than the southwest ridge. As of this writing there are no recorded ascents of this route, which can be done in one long day or two days with a bivouac in between.

The west ridge of Mt. Logbard is unclimbed as of this writing and can be accessed at its base on a rock buttress. The rock buttress is fairly steep but is quite broken and is easy to climb. It gives way to a snow ridge halfway up the climb that is followed to the summit. The ascent route can also be used as the descent route.

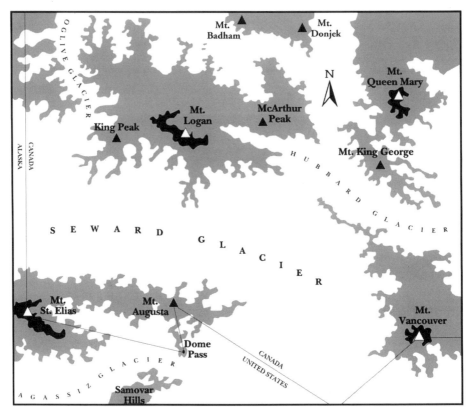

The Hubbard Group

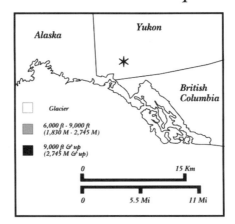

CHAPTER 5
THE HUBBARD GROUP

Introduction

Rising majestically out of the middle of the Hubbard Glacier, in nearly the geographic center of the St. Elias Mountains, are a series of small but interesting peaks worthy of a mountaineering challenge. These peaks sit directly in the middle of the massive Hubbard Glacier facing the confluence of the Seward, Logan, Donjek, Kaskawulsh and Lowell Glaciers. These peaks, known as the Hubbard Group are Mt. King George, Mt. Queen Mary and The Gnurdelhorn. Each of these peaks has its own unique features and all provide an interesting challenge in their own right.

Mt. King George is the steepest of the trio. It has several difficult climbs as well as some ridges that have never been ascended. Consequently, there are still several first ascent possibilities on this mountain. Mt. King George is not very tall compared to its neighbors Mt. Logan or Mt. Vancouver. However, Mt. King George is a steep mountain with superb climbing on steep narrow ridges and does possess the lure of possible first ascents.

Immediately north of Mt. King George is Mt. Queen Mary, taller than Mt. King George but not as steep. This peak is a beautiful mountain with rounded flowing snow covered ridges. Mt. Queen Mary is an interesting and fun climb in its own right. The rounded snow covered buttresses of Mt. Queen Mary make for enjoyable and straightforward glacier climbs. In fact, due to the nature of the climbs on Mt. Queen Mary several different routes could be done in one expedition. This peak is also a good warm-up climb for some of its better known neighbors.

The Gnurdelhorn is a whimsical little mountain with some fun but easy climbs. The peak is not tall or difficult. However, the easy nature of the climbs on the Gnurdelhorn make it an interesting climbing challenge and a good warm-up for the larger peaks in the area.

Although not directly on the Hubbard Glacier, Donjek Peak and Mt. Badham rise at the head of the Donjek Glacier, which is just across the hydrological bump from Hubbard Glacier. Due to the geographic proximity of Mt. Donjek and Mt. Badham to the other Hubbard Glacier peaks, these two peaks will be discussed within this group. They can be reached with an easy walk up Donjek Glacier. Although these are not tall mountains there are still several enjoyable ridge climbs on Donjek Peak and Mt. Badham.

The peaks of the Hubbard Glacier group

can be approached on foot from all sides of the St. Elias Range. A trek up Donjek Glacier will bring one to the peaks after a short walk. Alternatively, a long slog of nearly 75 miles (121 km) up the Kaskawulsh, out of the Slims River Valley, will eventually bring one up to the Hubbard Glacier peaks. However, since these peaks sit in the middle of the flat expanse of massive glaciers, a drop off by plane or helicopter is probably the easiest way to approach these fun and interesting mountains.

Mt. King George
12,250 feet (3,734 m)

Rising out of the middle of the Hubbard Glacier is Mt. King George, which is greatly overshadowed by its nearest neighbor, Mt. Logan, but possesses a unique character in its own right. Mt. King George is a very steep mountain with many severely inclined and narrow corniced ridges. The steep nature of the mountain gives it a majestic presence all its own. Many of the ridges on Mt. King George have never been climbed or perhaps have been climbed only once. Nonetheless, it offers a very exciting and challenging mountaineering challenge with the possibility of several first ascents. The United States map for Mt. King George is USGS Mt. St. Elias Alaska-Canada, scale 1:250,000. The Canadian Map is Mt. Queen Mary 115 B/12, scale 1:50,000.

Northeast Ridge

Rising from a cirque on the north side of Mt. King George is the elegant and slender northeast ridge. This ridge rises in a gentle arc curving up and left to reach the summit. See photo 1Y. The ridge is fairly broad over most of its length although it is corniced in places. There are good places along the ridge to place camps and the ridge makes an enjoyable and challenging climb.

The route begins in the small glacial basin that separates Mt. King George from Mt. Queen Mary. *See CD photo (Chapter 5) CD-Y01*. The route ascends the small curved ridge at the base of the mountain. The route curves up and sharply to the left over mixed ice and rock.

The narrow section of ridge gives way to a broader ridge which passes whip cream rolls of corniced snow to reach the base of a broad snow shoulder. The low angle snow shoulder is easily ascended passing the heavily crevassed area near its top on the far left side. At the top of the snow shoulder at 8,500 feet (2,591 m) is a broad level platform where Camp I can be established. *See CD photo (Chapter 5) CD-Y02*.

The route then ascends a narrow but slightly corniced section of ridge. This is followed to the base of a small ice face. The route follows the crest of the ridge through the ice face to reach a broad snow plateau below the north summit. *See CD photo (Chapter 5) CD-Y03*. A good spot can be found on the broad ice slopes below the north summit at 11,500 feet (3,505 m) to place Camp II. Placing Camp II on the summit plateau will make the traverse to the summit a much shorter climb.

The traverse from Camp II to the north summit follows the north side of this summit ridge. The summit ridge is narrow and corniced but there is ample space on the north facing slope to make the traverse. This traverse of half a mile (0.8 km) reaches the true south summit of Mt. King George, which is some 300 feet (91 m) higher than the north summit.

The ascent route can also be used as the descent route and the climb can be done in five days. There is not much need for fixed rope along the ridge as the climb is only of moderate technical difficulty. Ref. *AAJ* 1997, pp. 197-198.

Photo 1Y *Photo by Richard Holmes*

East Ridge

The only major feature along the entire eastern side of Mt. King George is the east ridge. The east ridge is typical of Mt. King George in that it is a long and slender ridge, steep near its top and narrow and corniced in places along its lower stretches.

This beautiful ridge rises out of Hubbard Glacier to end directly at the true southern summit of Mt. King George. See photo 2Y. This ridge has been attempted but has not recorded any successful ascents. It is narrow and corniced in places but certainly does not present a uniquely formidable challenge. Consequently, the east ridge of Mt. King George presents a potential first ascent as of this writing on a beautiful alpine ridge.

The route begins off Hubbard Glacier on a small side glacier. The ridge can be accessed on its north side by climbing a short low angle snow ramp. *See CD photo (Chapter 5) CD-Y04.* The route then ascends the rounded snow ridge on the large snow dome immediately ahead on the ridge. *See CD photo (Chapter 5) CD-Y05.* A good spot can be found on the south side of the rounded snow dome to place Camp I.

The route from the snow dome descends slightly and crosses a narrow and heavily corniced ridge. It is safer to stay to the left side of the ridge to avoid the cornices that overhang the right side. The route ascends the ridge until it begins to rise at a steeper angle. At the base of the steep section there is space to secure a good campsite. Camp II can be placed on a large snow platform on the north side of the ridge. It is best to dig this camp in directly below the crest of the ridge. *See CD photo (Chapter 5) CD-Y06.*

The distance from Camp II along the ridge to the summit can now easily be completed in a day. The route past Camp II ascends a narrow and slightly corniced section of ridge that rises at a moderate angle. The ridge then broadens at the base of the summit pyramid.

Photo 2Y   Photo by Richard Holmes

The route ascends the broad snow slopes of the pyramid. The bergschrund on the summit pyramid can be passed on the left side. The remainder of the easy snow slopes are followed to the true southern summit of Mt. King George. The ascent route can also be used as the descent route. Some fixed rope along the narrow corniced section of the lower ridge might be useful. Although this ridge has been attempted it has not recorded a successful ascent as of this writing. The climb is challenging but is only of moderate difficulty. The east ridge presents the opportunity for an enjoyable first ascent on a beautiful alpine ridge.

South Ridge

The south side of Mt. King George is characterized by a steep rocky face, which is occasionally split by narrow rock ridges rising to the summit. At the far right-hand corner of the south face is one of these ridges, in particular the south ridge. *See CD photo (Chapter 5) CD-Y07.*

The south ridge has several large projecting buttresses that descend out onto Hubbard Glacier. However, the best approach to climbing the south ridge is to approach it from a basin on a small side glacier off Hubbard Glacier. *See CD photo (Chapter 5) CD-Y08.* The basin leads to a small saddle at the foot of the ridge.

The climb begins in this small saddle directly above the entrance basin. The route follows the narrow south ridge along its crest until it reaches the broad south face. The large snow field on the south face is an excellent place to secure Camp I.

The route from Camp I follows the snow face until it reaches the true south summit of King George. The ascent route can be used as the descent route. There is no need for fixed rope along the south ridge as it is neither narrow enough nor steep enough to require it. The south ridge can be used as the descent route for other climbs on Mt. King George due to its low angle. As of this writing there are no recorded ascents of the south ridge of Mt. King George.

Southwest Ridge (Lauchlan Ridge)

The most spectacular and difficult ridge on the south face is the southwest ridge. This is a beautiful narrow ridge rising elegantly in a continuous steep curving arc to reach the summit ridge of Mt. King George. This route is probably the most technically demanding climb on Mt. King George.

The southwest ridge is not a long climb but it is very steep near its top. The route encompasses steep ice climbing as well as serious rock climbing. *See CD photo (Chapter 5) CD-Y09.* The first ascent team climbed the route in an alpine style fashion and descended the adjacent south ridge. Alternatively, fixed rope can be used in an expedition style climb, which would facilitate a descent down the ascent route. An alpine style climb of the southwest ridge would be more aesthetically pleasing and rewarding. The first ascent team made the ascent of Mt. King George with the financial assistance of the John Lauchlan Award. Consequently, they named the ridge the Lauchlan Ridge.

The route begins at the foot of the ridge off Hubbard Glacier. *See CD photo (Chapter 5) CD-Y10.* The route ascends the narrow and rocky ridge until it reaches the top of a small sub-peak. The top of the sub-peak can be a good place to bivouac or to place Camp I.

The route beyond Camp I follows the main crest of the ridge. The ridge along this section is very narrow but is not very steep. The narrow section of ridge eventually ends at a small indistinct snow bump. There is a shallow notch on the ridge just beyond the snow bump. This notch can be used as a bivouac site or as a place to secure Camp II.

The real climbing begins just past Camp II. Above Camp II the ridge becomes much steeper and involves serious rock climbing on exposed rock on the ridge crest. Several pitches are pieced together by climbing steep ice faces to the side of the ridge crest, thus avoiding some areas of loose rock. Several pitches of this steep climbing lead to the summit ridge. A short traverse along the south side of the summit ridge leads to the true south summit of Mt. King George.

The first ascent team climbed the southwest ridge and descended the south ridge. If fixed rope is used on the ascent then the same route can be used for the descent. However, the steep and convoluted nature of the climb would make a descent down the south ridge much easier. The upper section of Lauchlan Ridge involves the most serious climbing. The first ascent team rated this 6,000 foot (1,829 m) climb 5.9, WI3. This is a challenging climb on a beautiful ridge ascending the spectacular south face of Mt. King George. This route is one of the more visually beautiful and aesthetically pleasing lines in the St. Elias Range. Ref. *AAJ* 1999, p. 267-268.

West Buttress

The west side of Mt. King George offers the shortest and most direct approach to the summit. The west buttress rises in a multi-pronged web of ridges and buttresses out of Hubbard Glacier and was, in fact, the first ascent route of Mt. King George. The blocky nature of the buttress and the staircase series of ledges provide relatively easy access to the summit ridge.

The first ascent team began their climb in early spring. This was a fortuitous choice as the approach from Hubbard Glacier to the base of the west buttress follows gentle snow slopes, which are low angle but heavily crevassed. Consequently, the snow bridges are more likely to be intact early in the season and the route finding will be easier. *See CD photo (Chapter 5) CD-Y11.*

The route begins on a large rounded snow buttress at the base of the west buttress.

The snow buttress provides easy snow climbing but has some objective danger from slab avalanches. Consequently, this area should be done in the cold early morning hours when the snow is firm. There is ample room at the top of the snow buttress to place Camp I at 9,000 feet (2,743 m).

The route past Camp I follows a narrow and slightly corniced ridge crest that is nearly horizontal and is followed to the base of the main west buttress which rises menacingly above the ridge. *See CD photo (Chapter 5) CD-Y12.*

The main technical obstacles are found on the large protruding portion of the west buttress. The buttress has a short rock step, which must be climbed before reaching the easier slopes of the summit plateau above. The climb follows the crest of the ridge on the center of the buttress.

Some fixed rope may be useful here to facilitate carrying loads or in making the descent a little easier. *See CD photo (Chapter 5) CD-Y13.* The climbing is not as formidable as it appears as the steepest part of the rock step is just 45 degrees in angle and the steepest section is just a couple of rope pitches in length. The rock on the buttress is heavily broken from frost fracturing, thus providing ample holds for climbing.

The rock buttress yields to the snow slopes above it and ultimately leads to a short section of ridge, which is narrow and somewhat corniced. The route leads past the narrow section to the large snow platform at the very top of the buttress. The large snow platform at the top of the buttress provides a good spot to place Camp II at 11,000 feet (3,353 m).

The route past Camp II follows the corniced but horizontal summit ridge leading to the true south summit. The ascent route can also be used as the descent route. The first ascent team placed camps and fixed ropes along the route. This route would be a good challenge as an alpine style ascent for a small and competent team of climbers. Ref. *AAJ* 1996, p. 148.

Mt. Queen Mary
12,887 feet (3,928 m)

Mt. Queen Mary is the more gentle northern neighbor of Mt. King George and is a very rounded easy peak compared to the steep and more menacing ridges of Mt. King George. There are, however, a few narrow and steep ridges on Mt. Queen Mary that provide ample climbing challenges. Mt. Queen Mary generally provides fun climbs on rounded snow covered ridges located in the middle of the vast expanse of the spectacular Hubbard Glacier. Since Mt. Queen Mary has not seen much climbing activity, as of this writing it still possesses unclimbed ridges which are awaiting their first successful ascent. The United States map for Mt. Queen Mary is USGS Mt. St. Elias Alaska-Canada, scale 1:250,000. The Canadian map is Mt. Queen Mary 115 B/12, scale 1:50,000.

North Ridge

Mt. Queen Mary is characterized by rounded snow covered ridges. The north ridge is no exception to this pattern. See photo 1Z. The route begins on Hubbard Glacier where an easy snow ramp is followed through a small ice field. The easy low angle snow ramp is followed to the base of the summit pyramid of Mt. Queen Mary.

The route ascends the rounded snow covered north ridge over several false summits. The true summit is eventually reached from this ridge crest. This is an easy glacier type route. There is some route finding challenge in the ice field at the base of the north ridge. The first ascent team placed one camp at the base of the summit pyramid. The ascent route can also be used as the descent route and there is no need for fixed rope on this climb. Ref. *AAJ* 1962, pp. 231-232. *CAJ* 1962, pp. 69-73.

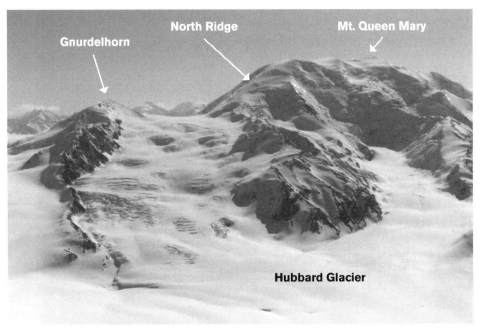

Photo 1Z   *Photo by Richard Holmes*

Northeast Ridge

The northeast ridge of Mt. Queen Mary is an interesting pursuit in mountaineering. However, this route requires the expenditure of a fair amount of energy to gain very little. The top of the ridge blends into the north ridge route so that most of the climbing on the northeast ridge can be easily avoided if desired. Nonetheless, this unclimbed ridge is a legitimate mountaineering objective and as of this writing awaits its first ascent.

The route can be gained on the northeast side of the mountain from the head of the Kaskawulsh Glacier. *See CD photo (Chapter 5) CD-Z01.* The ridge can be ascended on easy snow slopes to the top of a rounded snow dome where Camp I can be placed.

The route follows the nearly horizontal crest of the northeast ridge. The ridge is slightly corniced on its north side, so staying towards the southern lip of the ridge will allow safe passage past the snow cornices. The route eventually merges with the north ridge route. The junction between the northeast ridge and the north ridge provides a good spot to place Camp II.

The route past Camp II follows the north ridge route up gentle snow slopes to reach the true summit of Mt. Queen Mary. The north ridge route is the easiest descent from the climb. There is no need to place fixed rope along this route. As of this writing there are no recorded ascents of the northeast ridge of Mt. Queen Mary.

South Ridge

A slightly more challenging climb than the northeast ridge is the south ridge of Mt. Queen Mary. This route can be ascended from the head of Kaskawulsh Glacier. Low angle easy snow slopes can be ascended to gain the ridge. A low saddle in the ridge presents a good place to establish Camp I. *See CD photo (Chapter 5) CD-Z02.*

The route ascends the crest of the south ridge which rises at a moderate angle. The ridge is fairly broad and not corniced along its length. The route eventually reaches the base of a false summit. A level spot can be found at the base of the false summit to establish Camp II.

The route above Camp II ascends the easy snow slopes to reach the top of the false summit. The easy summit ridge is followed to gain the true summit of Mt. Queen Mary. There is no need to place fixed rope on this climb. The ascent route can be used as the descent route. As of this writing there are no recorded ascents of the south ridge of Mt. Queen Mary.

South Rib

Located in the middle of the south face of Mt. Queen Mary is the south rib. The south rib is a contrast to the other routes on Mt. Queen Mary in that it is narrow and provides slightly more exhilarating climbing than the typical snow covered ridges found elsewhere on this mountain. *See CD photo (Chapter 5) CD-Z03.*

The route begins from Hubbard Glacier on the left side of the ridge near its base. The ridge can be climbed by easy snow slopes to gain the crest of the ridge at a low saddle. A good place can be found in the saddle to establish Camp I. *See CD photo (Chapter 5) CD-Z04.*

The route past Camp I follows the narrow crest of the south rib. The climbing along this section is challenging and enjoyable but is never very difficult. Although the ridge is narrow there is no need to place fixed rope along this section of the climb. The narrow section of ridge ultimately blends into the top of the southwest buttress. At the intersection of the south rib and the south buttress is a large flat snow platform that is a good place to establish Camp II.

The route past Camp II follows the crest of the southwest buttress which is narrow at first but then becomes wider as it reaches a false summit, the top of which is the intersection with the south ridge. The route then follows easy snow slopes to the true summit.

The south rib can be used as the direct route although the north ridge is a much easier descent. There is no need to place fixed rope on this climb. The route can be done in an expedition style climb; however, a talented and fast climbing team might find the south rib an enjoyable challenge for an alpine style ascent. As of this writing there are no recorded ascents of the south rib of Mt. Queen Mary.

Southwest Buttress

The major feature on the south and west sides of Mt. Queen Mary is the southwest buttress. This is a large blocky multi-pronged buttress descending from the summit ridge to Hubbard Glacier. *See CD photo (Chapter 5) CD-Z05.* Despite the many possible ways to ascend the southwest buttress the easiest is probably from the north. The southwest buttress can be reached from a side branch off the Hubbard Glacier. This small side branch allows the buttress to be accessed at a low saddle, providing the opportunity to establish Camp I. *See CD photo (Chapter 5) CD-Z06.*

The route past Camp I climbs easy snow slopes on a large rounded snow dome, then follows a horizontal snow field to a point where the southwest buttress intersects the top of the south rib. A good spot can be found here to establish Camp II. *See CD photo (Chapter 5) CD-Z07.*

The route past Camp II follows the ridge over a false summit and eventually reaches the true summit and is fairly easy as it follows low angle snow slopes most of the way. There is no need for fixed ropes on this climb and the ascent route can be used as the descent route. As of this writing there are no recorded ascents of the southwest buttress of Mt. Queen Mary.

West Ridge

Located in the hidden col created by the southwest buttress of Mt. Queen Mary on the western escarpment is the west ridge. This hidden ridge is easy to approach and is actually quite a fun, fairly short climb as it ends directly at the summit, thus avoiding the need for endless snow slogging at high altitude.

The ridge can be approached from a side branch off Hubbard Glacier. The approach is the same as that used for the southwest buttress of Mt. Queen Mary. *See CD photo (Chapter 5) CD-Z08.* The route begins in a snow couloir at the base of the left-hand side of the ridge. *See CD photo (Chapter 5) CD-Z09.* The couloir leads to a snow face which is ultimately climbed to reach a small sub-peak. The route follows a narrow but low angle section of ridge leading to a small rounded snow dome. There is a small snow col directly behind the snow dome where a good campsite can be placed. *See CD photo (Chapter 5) CD-Z10.*

The route above the campsite climbs a steep but short ice face. It might be necessary to fix some rope on this face to facilitate the descent. The route above the ice face follows the low angle snow slopes to the summit. The first ascent team descended the ascent route. Ref. *AAJ* 1979, p. 204. *CAJ* 1979, p. 76.

Northwest Ridge

Descending from the northwest corner of Mt. Queen Mary is the beautiful mixed rock and ice crest of the northwest ridge. This is not a long route but it does provide some interesting mixed climbing on rock and steep ice.

The route can be reached on its north side directly off Hubbard Glacier. *See CD photo (Chapter 5) CD-Z11.* The ridge can be gained by following easy snow slopes off the glacier on the left side of the ridge up onto the main crest of the northwest ridge. The route continues up easy snow slopes to a small forepeak.

The route past the forepeak follows a narrow but horizontal ridge. Above the horizontal ridge crest the crux of the climb is encountered. The route follows the crest of the ridge over mixed ice and rock. It continues up a steep section of ridge crest where a small rock step must be surmounted before reaching the top of a snow dome below an ice bowl. See CD (Chapter 5) photo Z12.

At the top of the snow dome below the ice bowl a good campsite can be established. The route ascends the left side of the ice bowl and climbs the face directly above the bowl on its left side. When the bowl has been ascended the route follows easy snow slopes to the true summit.

If fixed ropes are used to secure the crux section of the route then the ascent route can be descended. If the route is done in an alpine style ascent then the north ridge is the easiest descent route off the mountain. Ref. *AAJ* 1997, p. 198.

Gnurdelhorn
10,750 feet (3,377 m)

Directly to the north of Mt. Queen Mary is a small rounded snow covered peak whimsically named the Gnurdelhorn. This small peak is barely more than a small protrusion from the glacier but due to its proximity to Mt. Queen Mary it has actually been named and climbed on several occasions. See CD photo (Chapter 5) CD-AA01. For the exact location of this peak refer to the map at the beginning of the chapter.

All the routes on the peak are equally easy. The most direct approach to climbing the peak is from the col that separates Mt. Queen Mary from the Gnurdelhorn. This is a low angle snow and rock ridge. It can be ascended and descended within three hours. This ascent might be an interesting warm-up before attempting Mt. Queen Mary. Ref.

AAJ 1967, p. 363. *CAJ* 1962, pp. 69-74.

Donjek Peak
11,742 feet (3,579 m)

Rising on the Donjek Glacier side of the Hubbard and Donjek Glacier divide is Mt. Donjek. See CD photo (Chapter 5) CD-BB01. This interesting peak can be reached from Hubbard Glacier or a hike can be made up the Donjek River Valley. However, the hike up Spring Creek and further onto Donjek Glacier is a particularly arduous one. There are numerous ascents to be made on this remote but exciting peak and the standard route on this peak is the southwest ridge. This follows a rock ridge off the glacier directly to the summit. The United States map to this peak is USGS Mt. St. Elias Alaska-Canada, scale 1:250,000. The Canadian map to this peak is Mt. Badham 115 B/13, scale 1:50,000. Ref. *AAJ* 1966, pp. 151-152, *AAJ* 1993, pp. 158-162.

Mt. Badham
12,038 feet (3,669 m)

Directly across the head of the Donjek Glacier from Mt. Donjek is Mt. Badham. This neighbor of Mt. Donjek is slightly taller than Mt. Donjek and has received some climbing attention. There are short but challenging climbs that have been done on Mt. Badham. Most notably the east face provides an interesting mountaineering challenge. This peak is a great warm-up climb before attempting the larger peaks downstream on Hubbard Glacier. The United States map to this peak is the USGS Mt. St. Elias Alaska-Canada, scale 1:250,000. The Canadian map to this peak is Mt. Badham 115 B/13, scale 1:50,000. Ref. *AAJ* 1973, p. 434, *AAJ* 1995, pp. 173-174. *CAJ* 1973, p. 92.

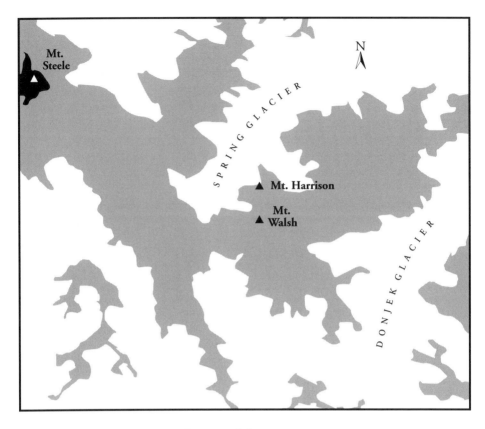

The Walsh Group

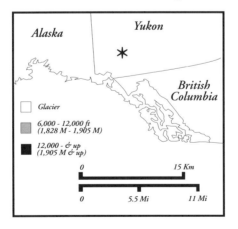

CHAPTER 6
THE WALSH GROUP

Introduction

Along the northern edge of the St. Elias Mountains bounded by the Donjek and the Wolf Creek glaciers are two beautiful peaks. These two peaks are Mt. Walsh and Mt. Harrison. These peaks are not tall by St. Elias standards but they are nonetheless challenging peaks with interesting climbs. These peaks are not climbed as much as their close and larger neighbors, Mt. Lucania and Mt. Steele. Consequently, the routes are open and not crowded. There are also numerous first ascent possibilities on these two peaks.

Mt. Walsh and Mt. Harrison are easy to access by plane or helicopter. They can be accessed on foot from the Wolf Creek Glacier, which requires a lot of "bush whacking" along its lower tributary in the Wolf Creek Canyon. Alternatively, these two peaks can be approached from the Slims River and the Kaskawulsh Glacier system. This is a much longer approach but the approach can be done on the broad expanse of the massive Kaskawulsh glacier. In either case, Mt. Walsh and Mt. Harrison provide very enjoyable climbing in a remote part of the Kluane Park. The routes are unspoiled by large numbers of expeditions and many of the climbs can be done in alpine style ascents. These peaks are a rich source of good climbing routes and potential first ascents.

Mt. Walsh
14,787 feet (4,507 m)

Mt. Walsh is a beautiful sprawling complex of a mountain. It is not tall compared to other peaks in the St. Elias Mountains but there are numerous climbing routes available. Mt. Walsh is spread out over a fairly large area and has numerous long rock ridges as well as many small glacial cirques spilling from its expansive summit plateau. It is one of the prime sources of potential first ascents on a large mountain that still remains in the St. Elias Mountains. The United States maps for this area are Kluane Lake, scale 1:250,000 and Mt. St. Elias Alaska-Canada, scale 1:250,000. The Canadian maps for this area are Mt. Steele 115 F/1, scale 1:50,000, Donjek Glacier 115 G/4, scale 1:50,000, Dennis Glacier 115 C/16, scale 1:50,000 and Mt. Badham 115 B/13, scale 1:50,000.

North Ridge

Rising out of the confluence of the Spring and the Wolf Creek Glaciers is one of the more enjoyable routes on Mt. Walsh, namely the north ridge. See photo 1CC. The

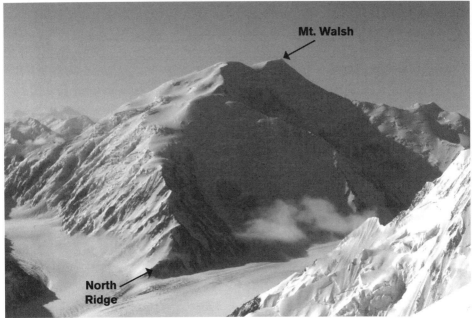

Photo 1CC   *Photo by Richard Holmes*

route involves a little bit of climbing along a narrow ridge crest, but the north ridge is generally comprised of climbing over broad gentle snow slopes. The route starts off Spring Glacier and climbs a narrow rocky ridge. A short blocky rock step is surmounted on broken rock. The route above the rock step climbs the narrow snow ridge until the ridge broadens out onto a broad shoulder at 11,000 feet (3,353 m). Where there is ample space to place Camp I. *See CD photo (Chapter 6) CD-CC01.*

The route above Camp I follows the broad north ridge which becomes a large rounded snow shoulder the higher it rises. The true summit is ultimately reached by following the easy snow slopes. The ascent route can be used as the descent route. The climb can be done in just a few days with one camp on the ridge. Placing a camp at 11,000 feet (3,353 m) makes the summit day a short and easy one. Ref. *CAJ* pp. 121-124.

Northwest Buttress

An interesting alternative to the gentle slopes of the north ridge is the steep and narrow northwest buttress. This narrow buttress rises out of Wolf Creek Glacier as an imposing narrow ridge rising to meet the north ridge at 13,120 feet (3,999 m). This is a beautiful buttress and the steep but enjoyable climbing provides an excellent alternative to the standard north ridge route. *See CD photo (Chapter 6) CD-CC02.*

The route begins on the left side of the buttress and climbs easy snow slopes left of the main ridge crest to the top of the rock buttress. Alternatively, the center face of the buttress can be climbed. This is 800 feet (244 m) of steep blue ice, which would provide magnificent ice climbing on this spectacular face. *See CD photo (Chapter 6) CD-CC03.*

The route above the rock section of the buttress follows the very narrow and corniced snow ridge. The ridge is narrow along this section but it is not very steep and blends into the main north face of Mt. Walsh at the

Photo 2CC *Photo by Richard Holmes*

base of a large rounded snow dome. *See CD photo (Chapter 6) CD-CC04*.

The northwest buttress meets the north ridge at 13,120 feet (3,999 m). This is a good spot to place Camp I. The route to the summit follows the easy snow slopes of the north ridge, which can be used as the descent route. Ref. *AAJ* 1998, pp. 231-232.

West Ridge

At the head of Wolf Creek Glacier, rising above a small icefall, is the west basin and the west ridge of Mt. Walsh. This gentle sloping portion of the mountain rises over a very short vertical rise of 4,000 feet (1,219 m) to reach the summit. This line of least resistance was, in fact, the first ascent route of the mountain and has been the route used for almost all the subsequent ascents of Mt. Walsh. See photo 2CC and *CD photo (Chapter 6) CD-CC05*.

The narrow ridge meets the upper west face of Mt. Walsh. The easy slopes of the upper west face are followed to the true summit of Mt. Walsh. *See CD photo (Chapter 6) CD-CC06*. The route can be done in one long day. Alternatively, an advanced camp can be placed in the upper basin if desired. The ascent route can also be used as the descent route. Ref. *AAJ* 1942, pp. 348-354. *AAJ* 1967, pp. 362-363.

Southwest Spur

Falling directly from the true summit of Mt. Walsh on the southwest side of the mountain is the steep and spectacular southwest spur. See photo 3CC. The route can be approached from a side glacier which sits near the head of the Wolf Creek Glacier. *See CD photo (Chapter 6) CD-CC07*. The southwest spur can be accessed at its base on a steep rocky ridge. This narrow rocky ridge is climbed to the top of a subsidiary peak. The route then traverses along a narrow corniced horizontal snow ridge.

The route above the horizontal ridge climbs a large rock buttress that can be ascended by climbing the rocky ridge crest.

Photo 3CC   Photo by Richard Holmes

The rock buttress reaches a large rounded dome. A good spot can be found on this snow dome at 11,500 feet (3,505 m) to place Camp I.

Above Camp I the route ascends a rounded snow shoulder and the top of the snow shoulder is blocked by a rock band. This can be ascended by climbing an obvious snow couloir in the middle of the rock band. The top of the snow couloir empties onto the summit slopes. The summit of Mt. Walsh can be reached by climbing the remainder of the distance to the top on the easy summit snow slopes. *See CD photo (Chapter 6) CD-CC08.*

The southwest spur is a very direct line with a lot of challenging and enjoyable climbing. The elevation gain is not significant and the access to the climb is good. The west ridge is probably the best descent route from the mountain. Some rock and snow protection will be needed for belays. As of this writing there are no recorded ascents of the southwest spur of Mt. Walsh. The southwest spur can be done very easily in an alpine style climb. This route would make an excellent first ascent climb.

Southwest Ridge

The dominant feature on the south side of Mt. Walsh is the southwest ridge. This is a long route on a big ridge with mixed rock and ice climbing. It is also a potential first ascent because there are no recorded ascents as of this writing.

This route can be ascended off a side glacier near the head of Wolf Creek Glacier. The route ascends a low angle ridge that is rock at first and then becomes a snow covered ridge. It becomes a little steeper when it reaches a large snow shoulder at the base of a large pyramidal rock buttress. A good spot can be found at 11,000 feet (3,353 m) to create Camp I. *See CD photo (Chapter 6) CD-CC09.*

The route above Camp I climbs the narrow rocky ridge crest on the pyramidal rock buttress of the subsidiary peak. The route goes over the top of the 13,000 foot (3,962 m) subsidiary peak and drops down onto the broad summit plateau. The summit plateau is crossed to reach the narrow ridge crest of a snow spur that descends from the eastern edge of the true summit of Mt. Walsh. The eastern ridge crest is followed to the true summit of Mt. Walsh. See CD photo (Chapter 6) CD-CC10.

The west ridge is probably the easiest descent off the mountain. The southwest ridge is a fairly long route and it involves some excellent and enjoyable climbing. Snow and rock protection will be needed for the occasional belayed pitch. A good camp can be placed on the mountain, although the route can be done in an alpine style ascent. As of this writing there are no recorded ascents of the southwest ridge of Mt. Walsh.

South Glacier

The broad and convoluted south face of Mt. Walsh is split by the long and circuitous south glacier. This hanging glacier spills off the summit plateau to the glacier below. It is not a technically difficult route but it is an interesting challenge in route finding. As of this writing the south glacier route on Mt. Walsh has no recorded ascents.

The south glacier of Mt. Walsh can be accessed from the large snow plateau that forms the hydrologic divide in the middle of the St. Elias Mountains. This large platform is a very interesting geologic and hydrologic plateau and is the divide from which the Logan, Wolf Creek, Donjek, Kluane, Kaskawulsh and Hubbard Glaciers emanate. This is indeed a truly unique hydrologic feature.

The route proceeds up the broad valley leading to the south glacier and ascends the broken icefall at its base. There will be some challenging route finding here as the bottom of the glacier is heavily crevassed. The largest crevasses can generally be passed on the far right-hand side. The route past the icefall leads to a snow basin. The route above follows easy snow slopes on the right-hand side of the rounded snow dome. These snow slopes lead to the upper snow basin where a camp can be placed at 12,500 feet (3,810 m). The route from the upper snow basin follows the easy snow slopes to the summit of Mt. Walsh. See CD photo (Chapter 6) CD-CC11.

The climb can be done in one long day or an intermediate camp can be placed in the upper snow basin. The ascent route can be used as the descent route. There is no need for fixed rope on this climb. It may be useful to place wands along the route to facilitate the descent if the weather turns bad. As of this writing there are no recorded ascents of the south glacier route on Mt. Walsh.

South Ridge

Adjacent to the south glacier route on the south side of Mt. Walsh is the south ridge. This is a low angle rock and snow ridge which ascends the south side of Mt. Walsh. The route begins from the large snow plateau on the south side of Mt. Walsh and leads onto easy snow slopes on a low angle ridge. This low angle ridge is climbed to the top of a subsidiary peak at 11,000 feet (3,353 m). The route descends from the subsidiary peak into the same snow basin as that of the south glacier route. The south ridge route ascends the snow dome above the basin and reaches the upper snow basin. The easy snow slopes are followed out of the upper snow basin to reach the summit of Mt. Walsh. See CD photo (Chapter 6) CD-CC12.

The ascent route can also be used as the descent route. There is no need for fixed rope on this climb although a large collection of wands might be useful to mark the route. As of this writing there are no recorded ascents of the south ridge route on Mt. Walsh.

Southeast Ridge

The southeast ridge of Mt. Walsh is a

Photo 4CC *Photo by Richard Holmes*

long and convoluted rock ridge descending from the summit plateau of Mt. Walsh at the exact southeast corner of the mountain. This is a long ridge with very little elevation gain accumulated along the lower section of the climb. Consequently, to avoid the endless traversing along the lower section of ridge crest it would be expedient to gain the main ridge crest about halfway along its length.

The southeast ridge of Mt. Walsh can be accessed through a long snow couloir that rises in the middle of a rock buttress. The snow couloir ends on the very narrow ridge crest of the southeast ridge. The route then ascends a large blocky buttress above the narrow ridge crest. The buttress is climbed on an indistinct rib at the interface of the rock and the snow. The route above the rocky buttress leads to the upper snow basin where the south glacier and the south ridge routes intersect. Easy snow slopes are followed to the true summit of Mt. Walsh.

There are no recorded ascents of the southeast ridge of Mt. Walsh. This route would make an excellent alpine style ascent. In fact, this route would probably be more enjoyable as an alpine style ascent as compared to the more cumbersome expedition style climb. The south glacier route is probably the easiest descent off the mountain. *See CD photo (Chapter 6) CD-CC13.*

East Spur

Immediately adjacent to the southeast ridge is a long serpentine rock ridge known as the East Spur. This is an interesting alternative starting point from which to begin the southeast ridge route beginning near the head of Donjek Glacier. A large snow face is climbed to reach the crest of the East Spur, which is climbed along its ridge crest at this point. The lower sections are rocky and narrow and plagued with numerous rock gendarmes which must be climbed or bypassed.

The rocky lower section of the spur finally ascends a small subsidiary peak. The route descends from this peak onto steep and unstable snow slopes which must be climbed to reach the main crest of the southeast ridge. The east spur intersects the southeast ridge just below the upper snow basin. The route to the summit is the same as that for the southeast ridge route. *See CD photo (Chapter 6) CD-CC14.*

The best descent after ascending the east spur is the south glacier route. Some fixed rope might be needed to secure the route past the rock gendarmes on the lower section of the ridge. A camp can be placed at the point where the East Spur and the southeast ridge routes intersect. As of this writing there are no recorded ascents of the East Spur of Mt. Walsh.

Northeast Ridge

On the northeast corner of Mt. Walsh is the beautiful snow crested northeast ridge. This ridge rises out of Donjek Glacier in a straight and unswerving line to reach the summit plateau of Mt. Walsh. This is a route with some interesting climbing in a beautiful and remote setting. As of this writing there are no recorded ascents of the northeast ridge of Mt. Walsh. See photo 4CC.

The route begins off Donjek Glacier on the north side of the ridge. The route ascends easy snow slopes to reach the ridge crest of the northeast ridge. The route follows the narrow crest of the northeast ridge which is exposed rock in some places and corniced snow slopes in other places. The route drops down into a saddle before reaching the main massif of the north side of Mt. Walsh. A good camp can be found in the saddle at 12,000 feet (3,658 m) to place Camp I.

The route above Camp I initially climbs a narrow corniced ridge crest. The ridge crest then merges with the north face of Mt. Walsh. The unstable and crevassed snow slopes of the north face are climbed until the route emerges onto the summit plateau which the route crosses to reach the true summit of Mt. Walsh. *See CD photo (Chapter 6) CD-CC15.*

The west ridge route is probably the easiest descent off the mountain. The ascent route can be descended if fixed rope is left in place. Some snow protection including pickets and flukes will be needed to secure fixed rope over the corniced sections of ridge. As of this writing there are no recorded ascents of this beautiful and challenging route.

Mt. Harrison
12,894 feet (3,930 m)

The adjacent and smaller neighbor of Mt. Walsh is Mt. Harrison, a beautiful compact little peak with sparkling ice-encrusted faces. Mt. Harrison is not tall by St. Elias standards and is not particularly steep; nonetheless, this mountain does provide some fun and interesting mountaineering challenges in its own right. The climbs of Mt. Harrison present a good opportunity to acclimatize before climbs on taller peaks and they can be done before embarking for its larger neighbor, Mt. Walsh. See photo 1DD. The United States maps for this area are Kluane Lake, scale 1:250,000 and Mt. St. Elias Alaska-Canada, scale 1:250,000. The Canadian maps for this area are Mt. Steele 115 F/1, scale 1:50,000 and Donjek Glacier 115 G/4, scale 1:50,000.

East Face

The east face of Mt. Harrison is a relatively easy and enjoyable glacier climb that ascends directly to the summit of Mt. Harrison and can be done in one long day. Additionally, this is a good route for a first ascent as there are no recorded ascents of the east face of Mt. Harrison as of this writing. *See CD photo (Chapter 6) CD-DD01.*

The east face route can be accessed from a side glacier off Donjek Glacier on the northeast side of the mountain. The

Photo 1DD *Photo by Richard Holmes*

route ascends the easy snow slopes of the east face. The route climbs up and to the left to reach the summit of Mt. Harrison. The route can be climbed and descended easily in one day. There is no need for fixed rope on this climb. As of this writing there are no recorded ascents of the east face route of Mt. Harrison.

North Ridge

The north side of Mt. Harrison provides a good opportunity for an enjoyable ridge climb. The north ridge of Mt. Harrison is a beautiful low angle snow ridge. As of this writing there are no recorded ascents of the north ridge of Mt. Harrison. It may be accessed from a side glacier off Wolf Creek Glacier. The low angle north ridge is ascended to reach the summit of Mt. Harrison. This route can be climbed and descended in one day. There is no need for fixed rope on this climb. *See CD photo (Chapter 6) CD-DD02.*

Northwest Ridge

The most enjoyable and challenging climb on Mt. Harrison is the long and serrated northwest ridge. This ridge does provide some challenging climbing on a serrated and corniced ridge crest but it is not a difficult climb. *See CD photo (Chapter 6) CD-DD03.* The route begins at the base of the ridge off Spring Glacier and ascends easy snow slopes just to the left of a big rock buttress. The route continues up moderately steep and unstable snow slopes until the long horizontal section of the northwest ridge is reached.

The long horizontal northwest ridge is traversed over its entire length to the true summit of Mt. Harrison. The horizontal section of ridge is mostly snow and ice. The ridge is narrow and corniced in places but there is no need for fixed rope. Some of the more corniced sections may require belays, however. This route can be climbed in one long day from the glacier. The north ridge is probably the easiest descent off the mountain. Ref. *AAJ* 1973, p.435. *CAJ* 1973, p. 92.

Harrison Walsh Traverse

One of the most unique climbs on either Mt. Harrison or Mt. Walsh would be to make a complete traverse over both mountains. A good base camp can be set up on Spring Glacier. Mt. Harrison can be climbed by either the easy north ridge route or the more challenging northwest ridge route. Once the summit of Mt. Harrison has been reached the route then traverses over to Mt. Walsh. Mt. Harrison and Mt. Walsh are connected by a thin corniced ridge crest which provides plenty of challenging climbing. The route from the summit of Mt. Harrison descends the south facing snow slopes onto the narrow corniced traversing ridge. *See CD photo (Chapter 6) CD-DD04.*

The traversing ridge is climbed along its ridge crest. It is heavily corniced in some places and some of the pitches might require a belay. The route then ascends the easy snow slopes of the north face of Mt. Harrison. *See CD photo (Chapter 6) CD-DD05.* The west ridge route of Mt. Walsh is probably the easiest descent off the mountain. The traverse can be completed with an easy walk down Wolf Creek Glacier to reach the base camp on Spring Glacier. As of this writing there has never been a traverse of Mt. Harrison to Mt. Walsh. There are no recorded ascents of the traversing ridge that connects Mt. Harrison to Mt. Walsh.

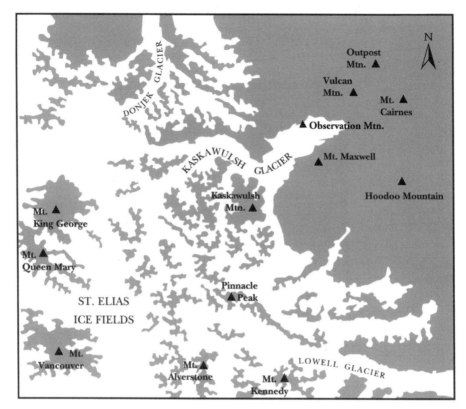

The Kaskawulsh Group

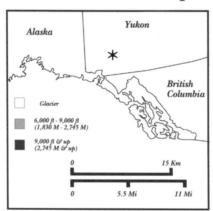

CHAPTER 7

THE KASKAWULSH GROUP

Introduction

Located at the northeastern corner of the St. Elias Mountains in the center of the Kaskawulsh glacial basin are a series of small but interesting peaks. These peaks are not tall by St. Elias Mountain standards; nonetheless, they have received some attention from climbers and have some interesting ascents.

The peaks in the Kaskawulsh area can be approached on foot up the Slims River Valley from the southern end of Kluane Lake where the Alcan Highway crosses the Slims River. The Slims River Valley is a beautiful fifteen mile (24 km) long glacially carved valley with the braided course of the Slims River flowing the length of the valley. The Slims River is formed from meltwater from the mighty Kaskawulsh Glacier.

The Slims River Valley is a beautiful glacially carved valley with a dazzling display of wildflowers in early summer. The hills overlooking the valley are home to one of the largest concentrations of Dall sheep in the world. In fact, on the northeast corner of the Slims River where the river meets Kluane Lake, is Sheep Mountain. This mountain is a refuge for Dall sheep and is the summer and fall gathering area for these sheep.

The Slims River Valley and the adjacent Alsek River Valley are home to nearly half of all the grizzly bears found in the Yukon. The bears are attracted to the salmon in the Alsek River drainage area and the sheep found in the Slims River Valley. Consequently, it is always wise to travel cautiously and alert for the occasional bear.

The walk up the Slims River Valley is an enjoyable passage through a beautiful valley with a spectacular entrance into the St. Elias Mountains. The gear that must be carried on these trips can sometimes seem overwhelming, but it is best to be prepared. *See CD photo (Chapter 7) CD-EE01.*

The Slims River is a braided river channel with many twists and turns. The east side of the river provides the easiest passage. The mud on the banks of the river are softer than they appear; consequently, it is best to remain on solid ground if possible. *See CD photo (Chapter 7) CD-EE02.*

The valley finally gives way to the Kaskawulsh Glacier. However, the last thirty yards (27 m) require a little river wading to get onto the glacier on the opposite side. *See CD photo (Chapter 7) CD-EE03.* The passage then proceeds up onto the Kaskawulsh Glacier where the hiker begins to encounter the magnificent views of the St. Elias Mountain Range. *See CD photo (Chapter 7) CD-04EE.* The march to the climbing objective then begins on the vast expanse of the Kaskawulsh Glacier. *See CD* photos (Chapter 7) CD-EE05, CD-EE06. Once on the glacier there is ample room to place campsites. *See CD photos (Chapter 7) CD-EE07, CD-EE08.*

Once the glacier has been reached the views of the St. Elias Mountains are magnificent. This setting provides the perfect backdrop for an entrance into one of the wildest and most beautiful mountain ranges in the world.

Kaskawulsh Peak
10,824 feet (3,399 m)

The view of Kaskawulsh Peak from the air is one of the most spectacular of all mountain vistas. This humble peak rises at the confluence of the Kaskawulsh Glacier and the South Arm of the Kaskawulsh Glacier. Consequently, this snowcapped and fluted peak is silhouetted perfectly by these two massive glaciers. In fact, this view is portrayed on postcards that are used to represent the whole of the St. Elias Mountains. See photo 1EE.

Kaskawulsh is truly a mighty glacier by any standards, including Alaskan standards. This spectacular fifty mile (80 km) long glacier is a true river of ice. The long glacial trail is heavily striated by the rock debris it slowly and incessantly carves from the base of the mountains through which it traverses. Kaskawulsh Glacier is more than just a beautiful river of ice; it also provides the easiest avenue of approach to reach the mountains in the Kaskawulsh Group. Kaskawulsh Glacier is easily reached on foot from the Slims River Valley in a two day walk from Kluane Lake. The glacier becomes heavily crevassed late in the season, so early season ascents in this area will benefit from the snow cover found on the glacier in April, May and early June.

Additionally, the snow covering the glacier becomes quite soft during the day, so walking during the early morning hours when the temperature is at its lowest point and the snow still has a hard crust on its surface will facilitate glacier travel considerably. The use of small plastic sleds to haul gear will help distribute the weight of the gear which is to be carried. This will in turn reduce the amount of sinking into the soft snow that will be encountered by the hikers. The United States map for Kaskawulsh Peak is USGS Mt. St. Elias Alaska-Canada, scale 1:250,000. The Canadian map to this peak is Mt. Leacock 115 B/10, scale 1:50,000.

North Arete

The north arete can be approached on foot via Kaskawulsh Glacier. *See CD photo (Chapter 7) CD-EE09.* The route begins directly off Kaskawulsh Glacier. The ridge begins on easy snow slopes on the crest of the ridge. The route then ascends a small rock band comprised of very rotten rock. It can be bypassed to a large extent by remaining on the very crest of the icy ridge. *See CD photo (Chapter 7) CD-EE10.*

The route ascends the rock band and then follows the crest of the ridge which is quite narrow for some distance. In some places the ice is just a narrow covering over the underlying rock. The ridge becomes broader the higher it ascends. The north arete ends at the northern summit, 10,332 feet (3,149 m) which is 492 feet (150 m) lower than the true southern summit.

The true southern summit can be reached from the northern summit by traversing a narrow ridge crest which connects the two summits. The ascent route can also be used as the descent route. The first ascent team chose to descend the easier but steeper snow slopes of the north face. There is no need to use fixed ropes on this route although some of the pitches will have to be secured with a belay. This is particularly true along the narrow icy section of the lower ridge. Ref. *AAJ* 1974, p. 157. *CAJ* 1974, pp. 69-70.

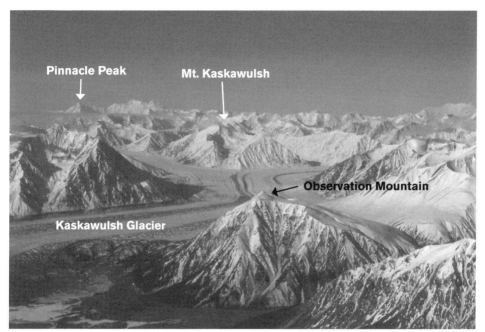

Photo 1EE   Photo by Richard Holmes

Northwest Arete

Located in a small recessed valley directly off Kaskawulsh Glacier is the narrow icy crest of the northwest arete. The route can be approached over the rocky glacial moraine leading to the base of the arete. The route ascends the narrow icy crest of the ridge for several rope lengths. The narrow arete reaches the top of a false summit. A good spot can be found on the south side of the false summit to bivouac or place a campsite. *See CD photo (Chapter 7) CD-EE11.*

The route past the false summit goes directly to the left along a horizontal corniced ridge crest ending at the base of the summit pyramid. The true south summit can be reached by ascending the easy snow slopes leading to the top of the mountain. The ascent route can also be used as the descent route. As of this writing there are no recorded ascents of the northwest arete.

East Arete

Rising out of Kaskawulsh Glacier on the northern side of Kaskawulsh Peak is the east arete. This challenging arete is quite narrow in places and rises directly to reach the southern summit of Kaskawulsh Peak. *See CD photo (Chapter 7) CD-EE12.*

The route begins on easy snow slopes directly off Kaskawulsh Glacier. The arete eventually narrows to a thin corniced ridge crest. This section of the arete is comprised of mixed ice and rock climbing and eventually broadens out to a wide expanse of snow at the base of the summit pyramid, just below the north summit. The easy snow slopes of the summit pyramid are ascended to reach the north summit. The traverse to the true southern summit can be made if desired. The north col route is probably the easiest descent off the mountain on the north and east sides. As of this writing there are no recorded ascents of the east arete of Kaskawulsh Peak.

North Col

There is a basin that separates the true

southern summit from the slightly lower northern summit. This basin is filled by a small glacier. There is a fun route which can be pursued on the little glacier in this basin, and this is the north col route.

The north col can be accessed directly off Kaskawulsh Glacier at the precise point where it and the South Arm of the Kaskawulsh Glacier meet. The col can be reached via the easy snow slopes that lead into the glacial basin. The route ascends the low angle snow slopes of the basin to reach the ridge that connects the north and the south summits. The route is fairly straightforward except for occasional route finding around the crevasse fields in the basin. *See CD photo (Chapter 7) CD-EE13.*

The route eventually reaches the ridge which traverses between the two summits of Kaskawulsh Peak. This ridge can be followed to gain the true south summit. The ascent route can also be used as the descent route. As of this writing there are no recorded ascents of the north col route of Kaskawulsh Peak.

Northeast Ridge

The northeast ridge is a large, well-defined snow crested ridge which rises out of the South Arm of Kaskawulsh Glacier to reach the true southern summit to Kaskawulsh Peak. *See CD photo (Chapter 7) CD-EE14.* The northeast ridge can be accessed off the South Arm of the Kaskawulsh Glacier via any of the fluted ridges found at the base of the northeast ridge. The center ridge is probably best as it rises to meet the main crest of the northeast ridge. *See CD photo (Chapter 7) CD-EE15.*

The route ascends the narrow crest of the fluted ridge in the middle of the face of the lower northeast ridge. The crux of the climb is about halfway up this ridge crest where the ridge is very narrow and ascends a small rock step. It eventually broadens out and reaches a rounded snow dome, which is a good place to secure a spot for Camp I.

The route past Camp I follows the low angle crest of the northeast ridge. The ridge is corniced in places but there is ample room on the south facing slopes to traverse the route without any difficulty. The ridge eventually merges with the base of the summit pyramid, and its easy snow slopes are followed to reach the true southern summit.

The ascent route can also be used as the descent route. There is no need to secure fixed rope along this ridge as it is never very steep. This is one of the more challenging and enjoyable ridges on Kaskawulsh Peak. As of this writing there are no recorded ascents of the northeast ridge of Kaskawulsh Peak.

South Ridge

Another substantial and interesting ridge on Kaskawulsh Peak is the south ridge. It rises directly out of the South Arm of Kaskawulsh Glacier to reach the true southern summit of Kaskawulsh Peak. The route begins directly off the South Arm of Kaskawulsh Glacier and follows the rounded crest of the direct south ridge. *See CD photo (Chapter 7) CD-EE16.* The route follows the rounded crest of the south ridge to reach a false summit. The snow slopes on the false summit are an excellent place to establish Camp I.

The route past Camp I follows the main crest of the south ridge which is somewhat narrower than the lower portions of the south ridge; however, the upper sections of ridge are not very steep. The upper sections of the south ridge ultimately end directly at the true summit of Kaskawulsh Peak.

The south ridge can be used as the descent route. There is no need to use fixed rope on this climb, as it is not steep enough to require it. As of this writing there are no recorded ascents of the south ridge of Kaskawulsh Peak.

Mt. Maxwell
10,168 feet (3,099 m)

Rising on the east side from the confluence of the South Arm of the Kaskawulsh and the main branch of the Kaskawulsh Glaciers is Mt. Maxwell, one of the very first mountains encountered when entering the St. Elias Mountains from the northeast side. Mt. Maxwell is not a tall or a steep mountain but it has received some attention from climbers and does have some established climbing routes. Mt. Maxwell can be an interesting destination by itself or it can be a warm-up for other climbs deeper into the St. Elias Range. In either case it provides for some fun and interesting climbing. The United States map to this peak is USGS Mt. St. Elias Alaska-Canada, scale 1:250,000. The Canadian maps to this peak are Mt. Leacock 115 B/10, scale 1:50,000 and Slims River 115B/15, scale 1:50,000.

South Ridge

The south and west sides of Mt. Maxwell are characterized by low angle snow slopes with some ice-covered rocks. The south ridge of Mt. Maxwell was, in fact, the route used for the first ascent of this peak.

The south ridge can be accessed from the South Arm of Kaskawulsh Glacier. *See CD photo (Chapter 7) CD-FF01.* The route begins on easy snow slopes and ascends the low angle snow slopes, which occasionally change to ice covered rocks. The route eventually reaches the rounded snow shoulder of the summit pyramid. The final snow slopes are climbed to the top.

The first ascent team climbed and descended the south ridge. There is no need to use fixed rope on this climb. The route can be done in one day from a base camp on the South Arm of Kaskawulsh Glacier. Ref. *CAJ* 1974, pp. 68-70.

Northeast Ridge

Facing Mt. Maxwell from the main branch of the Kaskawulsh Glacier one encounters two beautiful ridges. The left-hand ridge is the northeast ridge. The northeast ridge of Mt. Maxwell can be accessed on easy snow slopes at its base directly off Kaskawulsh Glacier. *See CD photo (Chapter 7) CD-FF02.*

The route ascends the easy snow slopes on the lower part of the ridge. The first ascent team chose to climb the small indistinct hanging glacier just left of the ridge at mid-height on the ridge. The northeast ridge can be climbed directly as well. The direct route on this ridge is probably a little more challenging as it becomes fairly narrow at mid-height.

The route past the hanging glacier reaches a broad summit plateau. *See CD photo (Chapter 7) CD-FF03.* The easy snow slopes of the summit plateau are climbed to the summit of the mountain. The first ascent team descended the ascent route. The descent down the hanging glacier provides an exhilarating 3,000 foot (914 m) glissade. The route can be done in one day from a base camp on Kaskawulsh Glacier. Ref. *AAJ* 1985, p. 214. *CAJ* 1985, p. 54.

North Ridge

Directly to the right of the large glacial basin below the north face is the north ridge of Mt. Maxwell. *See CD photo (Chapter 7) CD-FF04.* It might be the most interesting and challenging climb on the mountain and can be accessed easily off Kaskawulsh Glacier at the foot of the ridge. *See CD photo (Chapter 7) CD-FF05.*

The route ascends easy snow and rock slopes to reach a false summit at an altitude only about 500 feet (152 m) below the true summit. The ridge between the false summit and the true summit only gains 500 feet (152 m) but it is very narrow and corniced in places.

The route merges with the broad snow slopes at the base of the summit pyramid. The final easy snow slopes of the summit pyramid are ascended to the true summit. There is no need for fixed rope on this climb; however, some of the pitches on the narrow horizontal ridge crest should be secured by a belay. The ascent route can be descended although the northeast ridge is probably an easier route to descend. As of this writing there is no recorded ascent of this spectacular ridge.

Observation Mountain
7,500 feet (2,286 m)

The gateway from the head of the Slims River Valley onto Kaskawulsh Glacier and into the interior of the St. Elias Range is guarded by Observation Mountain. This mountain sits at the very head of the Slims River Valley and possesses a commanding view of the interior of the Wrangell-St. Elias Park and the hills surrounding the Slims River. As a result of this fortuitous position at the entrance to the St. Elias Range, Observation Mountain has been climbed to view the mountaineering possibilities in the interior of the Park. *See CD photo (Chapter 7) CD-1GG.*

Observation Mountain is not tall by St. Elias standards and is not steep, as it is a nice rounded mountain due to all the carving done by past glacial action. However, there are several enjoyable climbs on this peak that are not technically difficult and can be done in a single day. The United States map for this peak is USGS Mt. St. Elias Alaska-Canada, scale 1:250,000. The Canadian map to this peak is Slims River 115 B/15, scale 1:50,000.

North Face
The easiest approach to climb Observation Mountain are the very easy, low angle north snow slopes of the mountain. *See CD photo (Chapter 7) CD-GG02.* The route can be approached through a shallow canyon on the west side of the mountain. See Fig. 2.

Once at the base of the north face the easy snow slopes are climbed to the summit. Observation Mountain is an easy climb but provides spectacular views of the interior of the St. Elias Mountains. The route can be done easily in a day from Kaskawulsh Glacier. Ref. *AAJ* 1985, p. 214. *CAJ* 1985, p. 54.

South Ridge
The south ridge of Observation Mountain might be the most direct climb of this peak. It can be accessed easily off Kaskawulsh Glacier directly onto a series of low-lying hills. *See CD photo (Chapter 7) CD-3GG.* The small hills give way to the main south ridge. The easy snow and gravel slopes of the south ridge of Observation Mountain are climbed to the summit. The ascent route can be used as the descent route. The route can be climbed easily in a single day from the Kaskawulsh Glacier.

East Ridge
The east ridge is a snow and gravel ridge running directly up the east face of Observation Mountain. *See CD photo (Chapter 7) CD-4GG.* The route can be accessed by following the base of the mountain around the east side of the peak from Kaskawulsh Glacier. The route ascends the obvious but easy snow and gravel slopes of the east ridge. The north slopes might make an easier descent route than the east ridge.

Mt. Stephen Leacock
10,200 feet (3,109 m)

Directly to the east of Kaskawulsh Peak, across the South Arm of Kaskawulsh Glacier

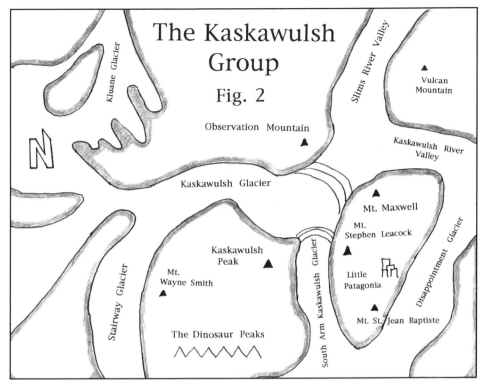

Figure 2

is the interesting peak of Mt. Stephen Leacock. The mountain was named for the renowned Canadian author, humorist and economist. The name has been officially accepted by the Canadian Permanent Committee on Geographical Names. For an exact location of this mountain see the map at the beginning of the chapter. The United States map to this peak is USGS Mt. St. Elias Alaska-Canada, scale 1:250,000. The Canadian map to this peak is Mt. Leacock 115 B/10, scale 1:50,000.

Southeast Ridge

The approach to this mountain is made along the South Arm of Kaskawulsh Glacier. At the southwest corner of Mt. Stephen Leacock a tributary glacier flows down to meet the South Arm Glacier. This tributary glacier is known as Easter Glacier. Easter Glacier is so named because the first ascent of Mt. Stephen Leacock took place over the Easter holiday. Easter Glacier winds around to the south side of Mt. Stephen Leacock. The first ascent team used Easter Glacier to reach the southeast ridge of the mountain. See Fig. 2. This rock and ice ridge was climbed along its crest to reach the summit.

The camps on the southeast ridge of Mt. Stephen Leacock were placed at 4,300 feet (1,311 m), 6,300 feet (1,920 m) and 7,800 feet (2,377 m). The ascent route was used as the descent route. There is no need for fixed rope on this climb. Refs. *AAJ* 1972, p. 138. *CAJ* 1973, p.92.

Mt. St. Jean Baptiste
9,900 feet (3,018 m)

Near the head of the South Arm of Kaskawulsh Glacier just south of Mt. Stephen Leacock is the steep summit of Mt. St. Jean Baptiste. One can only guess that this whimsical name is a result of the fact that the glacier descending from its northwest corner is the Easter Glacier. For an exact location of this mountain see the map at the beginning of this chapter as well as Fig. 2.

West Face
The first ascent team approached the mountain from the South Arm of Kaskawulsh Glacier and ascended the west side of the mountain. The route is mixed rock and ice on gentle slopes. There is no need for fixed rope on this climb. The ascent route can also be used as the descent route. The climb can be done in one long day. Ref. *CAJ* 1973, p. 92.

Mt. Wayne Smith
10,100 feet (3,078 m)

Immediately west of Kaskawulsh Peak is the steep and icy peak of Mt. Wayne Smith. For the exact location of this peak see the map at the beginning of the chapter. Mt. Wayne Smith was named after a climber who succeeded at making the first ascent of Mt. Alberta in the Centennial group of peaks in the St. Elias Mountains and was ultimately killed in an avalanche on Mt. Edith Cavell in the Canadian Rockies. The United States map to this region is USGS Mt. St. Elias Alaska-Canada, scale 1:250,000. The Canadian map is the Mt. Leacock 115 B/10, scale 1:50,000.

North Face
Mt. Wayne Smith is bound by the Stairway Glacier on its west side and Mt. Kaskawulsh on its east side. The first ascent team approached the mountain from a small feeder glacier that descends from the north side of the mountain. See Fig. 2. The route leads up this glacier onto an arete on the north side. Several small ice faces must be ascended to reach the plateau near the top and ultimately the summit.

The descent is down the ascent route. There is no need for fixed rope on this climb although some of the pitches should be secured by a belay. The route can be done in one long day from Stairway Glacier. Ref. *AAJ* 1973, pp. 434-435. *CAJ* 1973, p. 92.

Little Patagonia

An interesting diversion from the peaks of the Kaskawulsh Group is an area known as Little Patagonia. This small area just southeast of Mt. Maxwell contains numerous rock towers. It is puzzling why climbers would be interested in these towers as the rock is not very solid and the towers are not very tall. However, the small but steep rock towers in this area have received some attention. The exact location of this area can be seen on the map at the beginning of the chapter as well as Fig. 2.

Little Patagonia is found at the head of a small side valley off the South Arm of Kaskawulsh Glacier. This valley is just south and east of the south ridge of Mt. Maxwell. The view looking up the valley affords an opportunity to see the small rock towers that line the ridge crest. There are three obvious rock towers that stand above the rest. The tallest of these towers has been climbed.

The south side of this tower has the route that was originally climbed. The north side of this tower has more cracks in it than other sides but it is covered with a thin layer of blue ice. The route that was climbed ascends the southeast ridge of the tower until it becomes very steep. It moves left onto the face of the tower and then into an obvious crack system that becomes wider as it ascends higher up the face. The route is only one rope length long. Some camming devices are useful for protecting this route. The descent from the top will require a rappel. Ref. *AAJ* 1991, pp. 180-181.

The Dinosaur Peaks
10,000 feet (3,048 m)

There is one other area in the Kaskawulsh group of peaks that has received some climbing attention. This area is south of Kaskawulsh Peak near the head of the South Arm of Kaskawulsh Glacier. See Fig. 2. These peaks are all roughly 10,000 feet (3,048 m) in height. The peaks are snow ridges on rock gendarmes comprised of loose rock but solid snow. The serrated nature of the ridges gives the appearance of the back of the famous dinosaurs of eons ago. Consequently, all the peaks in this area are named after dinosaurs. The peaks are Mt. Stegosaurus, Pterodactyl Peak and Mt. Tyrannosaurus.

These peaks can be approached via the South Arm of Kaskawulsh Glacier. The peaks provide fun and interesting climbs that can be done in one day from the glacier. For an exact location of these peaks see the map at the beginning of the chapter. Ref. *CAJ* 1974, p. 70, *CAJ* 1977, p. 67.

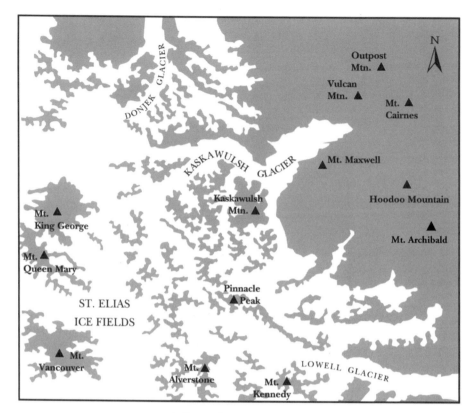

The Kluane Range

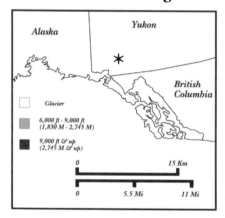

CHAPTER 8

THE KLUANE GROUP

Introduction

Located at the extreme eastern edge of the St. Elias Mountains are a few interesting peaks. These mountains are not tall by St. Elias standards. Nonetheless, several peaks in this area have received some climbing attention.

Running along a ridge in a northwest to southeast direction are the two main peaks that comprise the Kluane Range. The two peaks are Vulcan Mountain and Mt. Cairnes. Both are just over 9,000 feet (2,743 m) but there are still interesting climbs. In addition there are spectacular views available from the summits. The third peak in the Kluane group is Mt. Archibald, located near the south end of Kluane Lake just outside the city of Haines Junction, Canada. This beautiful peak is clearly visible from the city's airport. There are some very enjoyable climbs available on Mt. Archibald.

The two main peaks in this area are adjacent to the great north-south Alcan Highway; consequently, the approach to these peaks is quite short. The Kluane Range is bounded by the Alcan Highway on its north and west, the Slims River on its east side and the Kaskawulsh on its south side. Mt. Archibald is just west of the city of Haines Junction, accessible from the Alcan Highway and a short hike on the Alsek Trail.

Most of the climbs on these peaks can be done in just a couple of days from the base. The approach is generally short and straightforward and the climbs, although interesting, are generally not technically serious. For an exact location of these peaks see the map at the beginning of the chapter.

Vulcan Mountain
9,300 feet (2,835 m)

The northernmost peak of the Kluane Range is Vulcan Mountain, comprised of an abrupt scarp which forms the western side of the Shakwak Valley and Kluane Lake. The first ascent team approached the peak on its northeast corner just south of the point where the Alaska Highway crosses the Slims River. For an exact location of this peak see the map at the beginning of the chapter as well as Fig. 3. The Canadian map for Vulcan Mountain is Jarvis River 115B/16, scale 1:50,000.

The first ascent team hiked up Vulcan Creek onto the alluvial fan at the base of the mountain. The team set up its camp at 6,000 feet (1,829 m) on the moraine beside the glacier that descends from the northwest

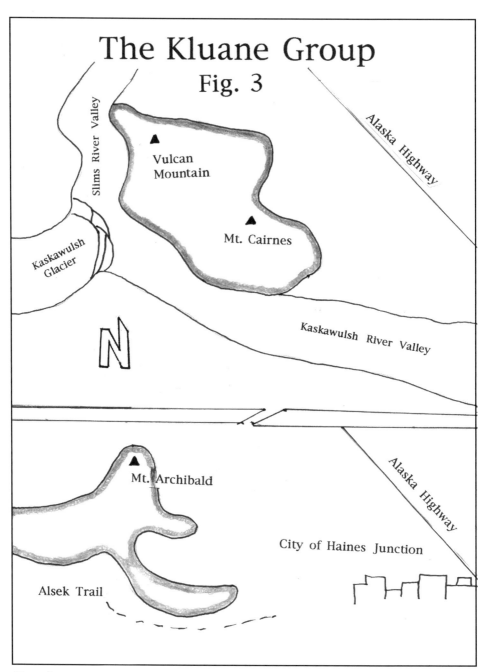

Figure 3

corner of the mountain. The following day the team climbed the northwest ridge to reach the true summit. Ref. *AAJ* 1964, p. 197.

Mt. Cairnes
9,150 feet (2,789 m)

The southernmost of the two peaks of the Kluane Range is Mt. Cairnes. This peak has seen some climbing activity. It is not only a beautiful mountain but also the summer home to a large herd of Dall sheep. The sheep graze on the slopes and seek the refuge of the higher elevations to avoid contact with grizzly bears which frequent the Slims River in the summer months. For an exact location of this peak see the map at the beginning of the chapter as well as Fig. 3. The Canadian map for Mt. Cairnes is Jarvis River 115B/16, scale 1:50,000.

North Face
This climb can be approached south of Vulcan Mountain on the northwest corner of Mt. Cairnes. The route then moves left off the northwest ridge onto the north face. The rock follows a magnificent line leading directly to the top.

The route ascends the 2,000 foot (610 m) north face on an ice face. The ice on the north face of this peak is very solid. The route climbs to the right-hand side of the face to avoid a buttress of rotten rock in the middle of the face. The ice gives way to snow on the summit plateau which is followed to the true summit. The ascent route can also be used as the descent route. Some ice screws are useful for protection on this climb. Ref. *AAJ* 1975, pp. 146-147.

Northeast Face
On the left side of the north face is the spectacular northeast ridge. This route is predominantly snow and ice climbing with some of the pitches approaching 55 degrees in angle. The route moves left onto some steep ice at the halfway point of the climb to avoid a buttress of rotten rock. The ascent route can also be used as the descent route. There is no need for fixed rope but some ice screws are useful for protection on the ice pitches. Ref. *CAJ* 1977, p. 70.

Mt. Archibald
8,491 feet (2,588 m)

Located just south of the southern end of Kluane Lake and a little west of the city of Haines Junction, Canada is Mt. Archibald. This peak is clearly visible from the Haines Junction airport. *See CD photo (Chapter 8) CD-HH01*. It is easy to access from the Alcan Highway and has beautiful snow and ice-covered ridges, which present enjoyable climbing objectives. This peak can be climbed if the main St. Elias Range is covered in clouds or it can be climbed as a prelude to climbing the larger peaks in the interior of the range.

The approach to Mt. Archibald is made by following the Alcan Highway north out of Haines Junction towards Fairbanks. Follow the Alcan Highway 6.5 miles (10.5 km) until you see a little brown road sign with the drawing of a beaver on it. *See CD photo (Chapter 8) CD-HH02*. At this sign turn left and follow the sign towards the Alsek Trailhead. The approach on the trail winds up onto the moraine at the base of the east side of the mountain. The climbs on the east side of Mt. Archibald can be accessed from a camp placed on this moraine. See Fig. 3. *See CD photo (Chapter 8) CD-HH03*. The Canadian map for Mt. Archibald is Kloo Lake 115 A/13, scale 1:50,000.

Southeast Ridge
The most obvious route on Mt. Archibald from the camp on glacial moraine is the

southeast ridge. The base of the southwest ridge can be accessed from the moraine camp on easy snow and gravel slopes. *See CD photo (Chapter 8) CD-HH04.*

The route ascends a narrow but low angle ridge on snow and ice. It follows the narrow ridge to reach a false summit about one-third of the way up the ridge. *See CD photo (Chapter 8) CD-HH05.* The route continues up the narrow ridge until it broadens onto a summit plateau just below the summit. *See CD photo (Chapter 8) CD-HH06.* The route proceeds up the final summit pyramid to the true summit of Mt. Archibald. *See CD photo (Chapter 8) CD-HH07.*

This is a beautiful route that can be done easily in a few days from the city of Haines Junction, Canada. Although there is no recorded account of an ascent of the southeast ridge of Mt. Archibald, this was undoubtedly the route of the first ascent of this peak.

Northeast Face

The other route which can be accessed from the moraine camp at the base of the east side of Mt. Archibald is the northeast face route. *See CD photo (Chapter 8) CD-HH08.* To reach the northeast face the east ridge must first be climbed.

The east ridge is a shoulder of rock and gravel and leads to a false summit which is very broad and rounded. A good camp can be placed here. The route then descends into a col and then onto the icy slopes of the northeast face. There is good solid ice on the northeast face. The ice pitches on the northeast face reach sixty degrees in angle. The northeast face is climbed to the true summit.

There is no need for fixed rope on this climb but ice screws will be needed for protection. The southwest ridge is probably the easiest descent for the east side of the mountain. This is a very interesting and fun climb without too strenuous an approach to reach the mountain. Ref. *CAJ* 1977, p. 70.

Northwest Ridge

This route can be approached from the north side of Mt. Archibald off the Alcan Highway. It is a four mile (6.4 km) hike to reach the northwest side of Mt. Archibald. A good camp can be placed at the base of the mountain at 6,000 feet (1,829 m).

The route follows an obvious couloir on the northwest side of the mountain. The couloir gives way to the northwest ridge which is followed to the summit of Mt. Archibald. The ascent route can also be used as the descent route. There is no need for fixed rope on this climb. Ref. *CAJ* 1973, p. 92.

Conclusion

The Wrangell-St. Elias Mountains provide a challenging arena for rock and ice climbing in a superb alpine setting. These are very big mountains and provide a Himalayan-style adventure on a backyard budget. The elevation gain needed to reach the summit of these peaks is often between 8,000 to 10,000 feet (2,438 m to 3,048 m). The escarpment on the south side of Mt. St. Elias rises nearly 16,000 feet (4,877 m), which is one of the largest vertical rises on any mountain anywhere in the world. Therefore, the undertaking of these climbs should not be underestimated.

Nonetheless, these climbs will be done in one of the most magnificent alpine settings found anywhere in the world. Additionally, with careful planning and preparation the climbs can be done quickly and safely.

Due to the immense area encompassed by these mountains and the sheer number of mountains present in the park, there are many unclimbed routes still available. Consequently, this is not only a spectacular place to go climbing but it also provides a rich source for potential first ascents.

Appendices

Appendix A: Expedition Organization

The time will come when you want to put together your expedition to climb in the St. Elias Mountains. There are several things to consider when preparing for such an undertaking.

The team that you compile should be as strong a one as you can possibly put together. The team should include at least four climbers and probably no more than eight, as logistics will get too difficult if you have too many people. It used to be a requirement that a team consist of at least four people to enter the Kluane National Park.

A competent team of two can do great climbs in these mountains; however, a team of four people will provide the best possibility of self rescue in an emergency. People tend to underestimate the remote nature of these climbs. Your best chance of rescue in case of an accident is a team which can rescue itself. Be sure you have enough manpower, have a good and complete first aid kit and be fully prepared for the unexpected.

The members of the team should be competent climbers. The St. Elias Mountains are huge mountains in a very remote setting with the ever present threat of inclement weather. So the team should be experienced in technical climbing, rope handling, knot tying, crevasse rescue and be able to deal with life in a small tent high on a mountain for three weeks.

Training for an expedition should include not only the technical aspects of climbing but the physical ones as well. Try to be in shape for the climb before you go. It will help tremendously to do some warm-up climbs in the months preceding the climb as well as adhering to a good exercise program. The better shape you are in when you arrive, the greater are your chances of success.

Most of the mountains in the Wrangell-St. Elias complex are not extremely tall. Most of the peaks are 16,000 feet (4,877m) or smaller, so just about the time you are getting high on the peak and feeling the effects of elevation you are on top and can descend. Whenever you are feeling poorly due to the effects of elevation, the best solution is to go downhill and regroup. If everybody recovers, go up more slowly and try again.

There are two ways to deal with medical problems associated with elevation. The first is to be acclimatized before you go. If you do long-distance running this will help. If you can get on some tall peaks to climb in the thin air this will be the biggest help of all. You don't need extreme elevation but if you can get to 8,000 to 10,000 feet (2,438 m to 3,048 m) this will help your training considerably.

The second approach to dealing with altitude is the basic tactic of the climbing that you will do on the peak. Unless you are fully acclimatized before you arrive, then ascending the mountain by a rapid alpine style ascent is very risky. It is best to take your time when ascending. Carry your gear to higher camps and deposit the supplies you need at the high camp. Then descend and sleep in a lower camp and gradually work your way up the mountain. This technique is generally referred to as carry high and sleep low. It really works.

Once you have assembled your team and everybody has made a commitment to go and train then you can begin the paperwork. If you thought you could escape the paper chase in the wild of the Yukon Territory you might be surprised.

In order to enter the St. Elias Mountains to climb, it is first necessary to notify the ranger station closest to the point of entry of your arrival. It would be best to notify the ranger two or three months in advance of your entry to let them know that you will be arriving.

The team will have to fill out forms in advance of its arrival regarding your intended destination, party size, and you will need a medical release form. These forms can be obtained by mail or by the internet. The addresses for obtaining these forms are provided in the appendix discussing ranger stations.

Upon arrival at the park headquarters it is necessary to check in with the ranger. Entry into the park from the United States side in Alaska is usually a simple formality. Entry into the park from the Canadian side, in the Yukon Territory, is a little more rigorous. In either case, just check in with the ranger and provide him with your forms and inform the ranger station of your intended plans.

Your expeditionary organization will also involve compiling the food and equipment that you will need for the ascent. Be sure you have all the climbing gear and repair equipment that you will need as there are no hardware stores on the Hubbard Glacier. Take enough food and bring along a little extra for emergencies. You will burn a lot of calories at high altitude and in case of bad weather your flight out might be delayed. Be sure you have enough food to sit out a weeklong storm. A complete list of equipment that you might need and a suggested food list is described in detail in the appendix regarding equipment.

Once you have a team, supplies and all your forms, then the last thing on your to do list is to decide how to reach your objective. The St. Elias Mountains are in a very remote corner of North America, but there are numerous ways to get to these mountains including air travel, driving a car or even arriving by boat. Each of these methods is discussed in the appendix regarding transportation.

The last leg of your journey once you reach the park is the trip into the interior. If the objective is close enough you can walk in. Remember, this will be glacier travel so you will have to be roped up and carrying all your own gear. Alternatively, you can fly to your objective. This will entail getting a ride with one of the local pilots. Transportation into the interior of the park is discussed in the appendix detail regarding pilots.

So be prepared, have a fun, safe and successful climb and be ready to enjoy one of the greatest wilderness experiences of your life.

Appendix B: Ranger Stations

Upon arrival at the Kluane National Park it is important and mandatory to check in at park headquarters prior to the initiation of your climb. The park headquarters where you check in will depend upon the mountain you choose to climb.

Prior to entering the park you should contact the main headquarters in Haines Junction, Canada to inform them of your intended plans. You must complete the required registration and medical forms. These forms and the policies of the park can be downloaded off the internet at the address following.

You should enter the park near the ranger station which is closest to your objective. You must check in and describe your plans. It is best also to place a call to the main headquarters in Haines Junction to let them know that you have arrived, in the event you do your check-in at another ranger station.

General information about the park as well as the registration forms can be found at the following internet site: http://www.parkscanada.gc.ca/kluane.

This is a marvelous website as it not only provides all the necessary information on how to get started for the planning of your expedition but also lists many useful tidbits about the park, the weather and the park animals. It also has useful information on park hiking trails which is generally hard to come by.

The main headquarters for the park is located in Haines Junction, Canada at:

Mountaineering Warden
Kluane National Park and Reserve
Box 5495
Haines Junction
Yukon Territory
Canada YOB 1LO
Phone: (867) 634-7279
Fax: (867) 634-7277

The Yakutat Ranger Station in Yakutat, Alaska is located at:

Yakutat Ranger Station
P.O. Box 137
Yakutat, AK 99689
Phone: (907) 784-3295

The Wrangell Park Headquarters is located at:

National Park Service
P.O. Box 439
Copper Center, AK 99573
Phone: (907) 822-5234
Website: http://www.nps.gov/wrst

Appendix C: Transportation to Kluane Park

Once you have decided that you would like to go to the St. Elias Mountains to participate in an expedition and you have organized your team and filled out the registration forms, then you must decide how to get there. The Kluane National Park is in a very remote part of the world, but there are several options to get there.

You can fly to a major city near the park. You can drive to Haines Junction, Canada or Glennallen, Alaska. From there you can begin your expedition. You can even take a boat. The Alaska Marine Highway offers ferry rides up the inland passage between Bellingham, Washington and coastal cities to the north. The option that you choose to get to your destination is of course dependent upon the time and financial resources available to your team.

Air Transport

The fastest and easiest way to go north is by air. Several commercial airlines travel to the northern cities. Air Canada and Alaska Air are the two most common carriers. Alaska Air will arrive in either Yakutat or Anchorage. Air Canada can be used to reach Whitehorse in the Yukon.

Air travel may be the most expensive but it is also the fastest. If you include all the meals and time involved with slower methods of travel then air travel may actually be a bargain. You can carry your luggage and an extra bag with gear onto your flight. Remember, you cannot carry flammable liquids like stove fuel on the plane. The fuel that you will need can be purchased when you reach your destination. Be sure to check with the airlines before you depart to determine the weight limitations of the bag. Once you reach the city of choice you can rent a car or use the Alaska Direct Bus route to take you the remainder of the distance to your jumping off point.

Road Travel

A logical way to get to the north is by car. The distances are far so you should be prepared to have plenty of time if you are planning to drive from the lower forty-eight states. The advantage of driving is that you have complete control over your travel schedule and you will have transport once you get to your destination.

The annual, *The Milepost,* is absolutely essential for planning a driving trip to the north. This book covers all the possible details that you could possibly need. *The Milepost* is available in most bookstores or by calling toll free (800) 726-4707. They can be reached on the internet at books@themilepost.com where they advertise their literature.

The Alcan Highway is the road which provides access to the Yukon Territory and it is thoroughly discussed in *The Milepost.* The road is almost completely paved and there are services all along its length. Be sure to leave plenty of time for your trip as it is a long way. Make sure your car is in good working order and bring extra spare tires and repair equipment. Some parts of the road are still fairly remote.

Ferry Service

It has been said that the only true way to get to the big mountains is by boat. The Alaska Marine Ferry Service provides ferry service between Bellingham, Washington in the United States and cities to the north through the inland passage. The inland passage is the route that twists through the myriad number of islands that dot the Pacific Coast of North America. This is one of the most beautiful places in the world. These islands are quite literally giant rocks studded with Sitka spruce and hemlock trees which extend all the way to the water's edge. You will likely see bald eagles soaring overhead and the occasional pod of killer whales.

There are different types of accommodations available on the ferry. These range from a private berth to bunks to the one which is the most fun and the most famous, the walk-on section. This section is a place on top at the back of the boat which is covered with Plexiglas® to protect it from the elements. It is supplied with space heaters and is quite warm and pleasant with the best views available. The best part of the walk-on section is that it is cheap. You will certainly meet an eclectic mix of people here.

The ferry will accommodate cars so that you can journey to the city of your choice and still have a car available when you get there. The boats are now getting quite fancy. Some of the newer ones are catamarans which can travel about 35 miles per hour (30 knots/hr.; 56.3 km per hour) which is quite a good speed on water. Depending on the service and your destination the journey could last three days or quite a bit less.

It is a good idea to make your reservations for a ferry ride several months in advance to be sure that you have a place secured. To make reservations and find out about costs and other details contact the Alaska Marine Highway head office in Juneau, Alaska.

Alaska Marine Highway
6858 Glacier Highway
Juneau, AK 99801-7909
Phone: Toll free (800) 642-0066
Fax: (907) 277-4829
Website: htp://www.alaska.gov/ferry

Bus Service

If you are unable to arrange for a rental car there is bus service available. Although the largest bus service, Greyhound, does go as far as Whitehorse, it does not go all the way to Haines Junction. However, a smaller carrier, Alaska Direct Bus Line, does make the journey to Haines Junction. They can be contacted at the following address:

Alaska Direct Bus Line
P.O. Box 501
Anchorage, AK 99510
Phone: (867) 668-4833 in Whitehorse, Canada; (800) 770-6652 in Anchorage, Alaska
Email: pecombs@alaska.net

Appendix D: Northern Cities

You may enter the park from any one of a number of places. Depending upon where you enter you will be in a different city and will require the services provided there. The following descriptions provide some insight into what you can find at different locations on your trip north. For overall information that you may require about Canada contact the Yukon Department of Tourism.

Yukon Department of Tourism
Government of Yukon
Box 2703
Whitehorse
Yukon Territory
Canada Y1A 2C6
Website: http://www.btc.gov.yk.ca/index.html

In addition to the Department of Tourism, one of the most valuable sources of information to the entire Yukon and Alaskan area is a book known as *The Milepost*. The book not only lists all motels and restaurants in the Yukon's big cities, it lists what is available in cities you have never heard of. The book gives a very detailed account of the Alcan Highway and the ferry service provided by the Alaska Marine Highway.

This wonderful book can be purchased at most large book stores or by calling toll free (800) 726-4704, or (867) 667-5036.

Whitehorse

Whitehorse is the capital and largest city of the Yukon Territory, and it has the main airport where you will arrive. However, you will probably go through customs in Vancouver, Canada or perhaps Toronto, depending upon your point of entry. You will catch a connecting flight to Whitehorse.

Air Canada will fly you to the major cities of Canada. All of the major car rental companies are located at the Whitehorse airport. You can arrange for a car to take your team on the remaining 98 miles (158 km) to Haines Junction where your expedition will begin.

Whitehorse's moderately large summer population is about 100,000 and somewhat smaller than that in the winter. Whitehorse was the center of the late 19th century Klondike Gold Rush. At the east end of town, anchored in a shallow dock at the edge of the mighty Yukon River is the S.S. Klondike. This is an example of one of the old paddle wheel steamers that carried miners to the gold fields. It is worth a visit. There are also numerous shops in town that display handicrafts made by the local Native American Indians. They have beautiful woven clothing and other examples of their fine craftsmanship. A visit to one of these stores may be worth the time and money in order to come away with a fine piece of Canadian craftwork.

Campsites

There are campsites on the outskirts of town if you choose to camp. Alternatively, there are fine motels where you can stay and get organized. One of the nicer, reasonably priced motels is the High Country Inn. You cannot miss this hotel as it has a twenty foot (6 m) tall brilliant red wooden statue of a Royal Canadian Mounted Policeman in front of the hotel.

High Country Inn
4051 4th Avenue
Whitehorse
Yukon Territory
Canada Y1A 1H1
Phone: (800) 554-4471
Fax: (867) 667-6457
Email: info@highcountryinn.yk.ca
Website: http://www.highcountryinn.yk.ca/

A more moderately priced yet comfortable hotel is the Stratford Motel.

Stratford Motel
401 Jarvis Street
Whitehorse
Yukon Territory
Canada Y1A 2H4
Phone: (867) 667-4243
Fax: (867) 668-7432
Toll free: (800) 661-0539

Backpacker Hostels

If you are on a true budget then you can stay very inexpensively and comfortably at the Beez Kneez Bakpakers Hostel.

Beez Kneez Bakpakers Hostel
408 Hoge Street
Whitehorse
Yukon Territory
Canada Y1A 1H1
Phone: (867) 456-2333
Website: http://www.bzkneez.com

Whitehorse is equipped with everything the traveler will need. They have many fine restaurants including the well-known fast food franchises. They have gas stations and large discount food stores should you wish to stock up on food before you depart on your trip.

Haines Junction

The main city for climbers is Haines Junction, location of the park headquarters. This is the last big city on the Alcan Highway for a great distance. It is also the connection to the Haines Road running to the city of Haines, Alaska, where you can connect with the Alaska ferry service. Haines Junction is fairly small with only about 800 full-time residents, but it has everything the traveler and climber might need.

There is camping at the Pine Lake Campground just east of the city. However, this campground is generally not open until early June. The best place to camp out is near the dirt airstrip where Icefield Ranges Expeditions is located. First of all, it is free and secondly, when the weather is good you are right there at the airstrip, ready to fly in. Windows of opportunity to fly with good weather are sometimes short so it is best to be ready to go on short notice.

There is a very nice reasonably priced motel in Haines Junction. The Alcan Motor Inn, formerly known as the Gateway Motel, has received recent renovations and is in very good condition.

Alcan Motor Inn
Box 5460
Haines Junction
Yukon Territory
Canada Y0B 1L0
Phone: (867) 634-2371
Fax: (867) 634-2833
Toll free: (888) 265-1018
Website: http://www.yukonweb.com/tourism/alcan/

Another nice and reasonably priced hotel in the middle of "downtown" Haines Junction is the Kluane Park Inn.

Kluane Park Inn
Box 5400
Haines Junction

Yukon Territory
Canada Y0B 1L0
Phone: (867) 634-2261
Fax: (867) 634-2273

Another reasonably priced hotel is The Raven.

The Raven
Box 5470
Haines Junction
Yukon Territory
Canada Y0B 1L0
Phone: (867) 634-2500
Fax: (867) 634-2517
Email: kluaneraven@yknet.yk.ca
Website: http://www.yukkonweb.com/tourism/raven/

Food Service

Immediately adjacent to the Alcan Motor Inn is the full service food store, Madleys. This grocery store has any food that you will require and is a hardware store as well. Fortuitously, it also doubles as the town post office where you can mail letters and buy stamps, and a bank where you can exchange money. So if you need it in Haines Junction it is probably located at Madleys. If they do not have it then you probably do not need it.

A conveniently located and reasonably priced restaurant is the Cozy Corner, just across the street from Madleys. They serve breakfast, lunch and dinner, all good food at a good price.

Alaska

If your trip brings you to the park through a city in Alaska then you can depend upon the services of each of these cities:

Haines

Haines, Alaska is located directly on the coast, so the only way you will pass through this city is if you take the Alaska Marine Ferry. For information regarding accommodations in Haines it is easiest to contact the Haines Visitors Bureau.

Haines Alaska Visitors Bureau
P.O. Box 530
Haines, AK 99827-0530
Phone: (800) 458-3579
Email: hcvb@haines.ak.us
Website: http://www.haines.ak.us/

Anchorage

The largest city by far in all of Alaska is Anchorage. This is where the international airport is located. This city can provide anything that you need. There are rental cars at the airport. The Alaskan Direct Bus Service can be picked up here and will help you connect with points further south towards Kluane Park. They can be reached at (800) 770-6652.

All the information that you require about Anchorage can be obtained from the Anchorage Convention and Visitors Bureau.

Anchorage Convention and Visitors Bureau
524 W. 4th Avenue
Anchorage, AK 99501
Phone: (907) 274-3531
Website: http://www.anchorage.net
Email: info@anchorage.net

Hotels

A good place to stay while in Anchorage is Duke's 8th Ave. Hotel. This is a nice, moderately priced, clean motel.

Duke's 8th Ave. Hotel
630 W. 8th Avenue
Anchorage, AK 99501
Phone: (907) 274-6213
Fax: (800) 478-4837

Another conveniently located and moderately priced hotel is the Anchorage Suite Lodge.

Anchorage Suite Lodge
441 E. 15th Avenue
Anchorage, AK 99501
Toll free: (888) 598-3114 or (866) 613-9330
Fax: (907) 278-9861

The visitors bureau will provide you with a wealth of information about Anchorage and Alaska in general. The bureau is an interesting place to visit if you get the chance as it is in a reconstructed log cabin.

Yakutat

If your expedition begins in Yakutat, Alaska there are numerous services available in this beautiful little fishing village. In fact, most of the tourists who visit Yakutat are fishermen seeking world-class salmon fishing. Climbers do number an abundant second place however.

Yakutat can be reached by the ferry service; however, you will most likely reach it by airplane. Yakutat has an unusually large runway for such a small town because it was once the regional headquarters of the U. S. Coast Guard.

Camping

This is a very remote area with lots of wide open space; camping can be done discreetly in many places just away from the airport. However, the usual camping spot is Cannon Beach, about 2 miles (3.2 km) outside of town on the coast.

Hotels

Immediately next to the airport is the Yakutat Lodge. This is a favorite with the fishermen as this lodge provides full fishing and hunting guide service. This lodge is quite convenient for climbers too with its two minute walk from the Lodge to Gulf Air Taxi to fly you to your climb. The Lodge frequently serves fresh fish caught by local fishermen.

Yakutat Lodge
P.O. Box 287
Yakutat, AK 99689
Phone: (907) 784-3232
1-800-YAKUTAT for reservations
Fax: (907) 784-3452
Website: http://www.yakutatlodge.com/

Glacier Bear Lodge
P.O. Box 303
Yakutat, AK 99689
Phone: (907) 784-3202
Toll free: (866) 425-6343
Fax: (907) 784-3663
Website: http://www.glacierbearlodge.com/

Car Rentals

Although Yakutat has only one short road running from the airport into the main town, you may find it useful to have a car anyway. Cars can be rented from Situk Leasing.

Situk Leasing
P.O. Box 289
Yakutat, AK 99689
Phone: (907) 784-3316
Fax: (907) 784-3995

Glennallen

If your plans bring you to the very northern part of Kluane Park you will enter through the town of Glennallen. You can check in at the Copper Center Ranger Station as was discussed under the section on ranger stations.

Camping

Glennallen is a remote city, so camping

outside the city can be done discreetly.

Hotels

The best and newest hotel in Glennallen is the Caribou Lodge. It is clean and reasonably priced.

The New Caribou Lodge
Phone: (800) 478-3302 or (907) 822-3302
Fax: (907) 822-3711
Website: http://www.caribouhotel.com/

Food Service

There is a nice restaurant attached to the Caribou Lodge, serving reasonably priced fine meals. Next door to the Caribou Lodge is a full service grocery store providing everything you will need.

Air Service

Just four miles (6.4 km) north of town is the Gulkana Airport. This small airstrip is where Ellis Air Service (Phone: 907/822-3368) and Copper Valley Air Service are located. They can fly you to your climbing destination.

Appendix E: Expedition Equipment

When preparing to embark on a major expedition into the St. Elias Mountains you need to carefully consider the equipment that you will take. There are no stores in the middle of the Kluane Park so you have to be self-sufficient. There are four general types of gear that you must consider taking with you.

You need your personal gear such as clothes and climbing equipment. You need the group gear such as the tents, stoves, ropes and general use climbing equipment like shovels and ice screws. You need to have a repair kit so that no matter what you break, tear or ruin you can fix it on the spot. Finally, there is the first aid kit. You need to remain healthy on this trip in order to enjoy it and be successful at it. Also, you need to be able to apply first aid to any injuries that you may sustain on the climb.

Personal Gear

An example of the personal gear you may wish to take depends upon your personal needs and how much you are willing to carry. The following list is an example of the types of things that you should consider taking along to have a complete individual gear list.

- 2 pairs of long underwear, nylon or other synthetic material
- 2 wool or polyester cotton-blend shirts
- 2 pairs of wool pants
- 1 light wool sweater
- 1 light synthetic pullover or zip up sweater
- 1 heavy nylon or Gor-Tex® wind parka
- 1 heavy synthetic or Dacron® parka
- 1 pair Gor-Tex® wind pants
- 1 completely waterproof rain jacket or cagoule
- 2 pairs of nylon mitten shells
- 2 pairs of warm Dachstein mitts
- 2 pairs of light wool gloves
- 1 pair of light silk or nylon gloves
- 2 pairs of glacier goggles or sunglasses
- 1 light wool hat
- 1 balaclava
- 3 pairs of light wool socks
- 3 pairs of heavy wool socks
- 1 pair of crampons and perhaps a backup set as well
- 1 complete repair kit with tools for the crampons
- 1 pair of high gaiters
- 1 pairs of insulated overbooties that will fit over the crampons
- 1 pair of skis or 1 pair of snowshoes with binds and poles and a repair kit for each
- 1 large expedition-style backpack

- 1 light daypack
- 1 standard ice axe
- 1 small ice tool
- 1 down or synthetic sleeping bag
- 1 sleeping bag liner
- 1 sleeping bag outer cover
- 1 foam pad at least 2 inches (5 centimeters) thick
- 1 set of eating utensils including a knife, fork and spoon. The eating kit should include a bowl and a coffee cup
- Toothpaste and toothbrush
- Toilet paper
- Personal medication
- 2 1-quart (1 liter) plastic water bottles
- 1 compass and your maps
- 1 pair of jumars or Gibbs ascenders
- 1 pulley
- 1 sit harness
- 1 space blanket
- Several extra stuff bags of different sizes
- 1 hand-held flashlight (torch) with extra batteries
- 1 headlamp large enough to fit over your wool hat also complete with extra batteries
- Suntan lotion, glacier cream or zinc oxide
- ChapStick® or other lip gloss
- A notebook and several pencils and pens
- A camera and extra film or digital memory cards
- A large handkerchief

You may wish to expand or contract from this list of gear but it is a good place to start when considering what you will bring along.

Group Gear

The group gear is something that is best discussed among the climbing team before you go. This will ensure that you do not forget anything and that everybody is satisfied with the types of equipment that will be available on the climb. The type and amount of gear will of course depend upon the difficulty of the climb undertaken.

The first consideration is a tent. Expedition-style climbing involves a lot of time in a tent and you may have to sit out long storms. Consequently, the most important aspect of a tent is making sure it is big enough. You should have a three-man tent for two people in order to accommodate all your gear and yourselves. The tent should have a vestibule as this is the best and safest way to cook. This way the stove is not outside but it is not sitting on the floor of the tent either.

You will need enough stoves to cook adequately for everyone. The stoves should be lightweight and durable. Be sure to test them at home first. I would not recommend going on a trip with a stove you have never used. You cannot carry stove fuel on airplanes; however, you can purchase plenty of stove fuel when you arrive at Kluane Park. Several stores located near the park headquarters will sell fuel. You should have a repair kit for each stove so you can fix or replace anything. You must have operational stoves.

If you plan on doing much glacier travel you should have a toy plastic sled. If you attach a little piece of aluminum about 1 inch (2.5 centimeters) high and about 2 feet (61 centimeters) long to the bottom of the sled it will act like a perfect rudder and guide it smoothly through the snow. This way you can carry some of your gear in your pack and some on the sled to help distribute the weight.

The team should have several small and large shovels. There are plenty of lightweight aluminum shovels available to choose from. The St. Elias Mountains are adjacent to the Gulf of Alaska. It can really snow here so you must be prepared to dig out tent platforms. A good alternative is to obtain a grain scoop which is just a broad flat shovel used to shovel grain. If you cut this shovel down a little and shorten the handle it makes a great little snow shoveler.

The team will need climbing rope. First

you will need your standard 11mm climbing rope which should be the water-resistant variety, then a backup 9mm rope for crevasse rescue. You may need to secure some fixed rope on the climb. This should be 9mm rope or thicker nylon-type rope which is solid and safe to jumar on. It would be wise to have about 1,000 feet (305 m) of rope available to use for fixed rope. More rope might be needed if you are doing a very difficult route and plan to fix long stretches of the climb.

The St. Elias Mountains are predominantly snow and ice with some rock sticking out here and there. Most of the climbing equipment that you will need will be snow and ice protection. Snow pickets are useful to anchor ropes. About ten to fifteen long ones will be good. One of the most useful items that you can have in the St. Elias Mountains are snow pickets that you have cut in half. These half pickets are excellent in that you can use them in snow and the mushy type of ice that you will find in these mountains.

Plenty of carabiners for attachments and rope anchors will be necessary for good rope management. D-shaped carabiners are nice but not essential. Locking carabiners are nice when used at anchor points for fixed rope.

A good selection of ice screws is necessary. The 12 inch (30 centimeter) variety are good and a selection of shorter ones will help.

It will be useful to have plenty of extra sling for carrying gear. It is also useful when anchoring ropes. It is generally useful for belays and securing items to the tents or the belay stations.

Snow flukes or deadmen and deadboys are excellent anchors. In the type of soft snow often found in the St. Elias Mountains it is necessary to have enough surface area to make a good anchor. Snow flukes make excellent anchors for ropes or belays.

You will encounter occasional exposed rock on these climbs, so you will need rock protection for belays and for fixing rope. You will find that pitons are excellent in the soft rock and the wide cracks that you will encounter. Large-angled pitons are good for the cracks found in these mountains. It is good to have a wide selection of sizes in camming devices as well. Camming devices will fit in anything and are also easier to place and remove particularly with bulky gloves.

You will be traveling on glaciers and some of the summit plateaus are so large that they are nearly glaciers in themselves. Consequently, to ensure you do not get lost on the descent you should have plenty of wands. You can make hundreds of wands very inexpensively if you like. You can use narrow diameter bamboo sticks and attach iridescent surveyors tape on the top. Be sure it is a color that will be noticed in the fog or low light conditions. Several hundred of these may be useful and they are cheap to construct and easy to carry.

It may be useful to have a GPS (global positioning device) available to the team or for each member. These will not only fix exact locations but are the only true way to get elevations. Utilizing a GPS device will help you determine your location and altitude under all types of conditions. These devices are inexpensive, durable and widely available at electronic stores like Radio Shack. GPS units are very accurate for determining elevations and were used to determine the true altitude of Mt. Logan.

It is essential to have some form of communication to contact park headquarters or arrange for your pickup by the pilot. One of the better devices is the VHF Marine Transceiver. These are line of sight radios so you will have to be on a ridgetop to get good communication. But these will help you contact everybody you need to talk to and they also pickup weather forecasts from broadcasts intended to help the fishing fleets in the Gulf of Alaska. These can be purchased at any electronic store. A satellite phone may be useful in the park as well, since it should be able to contact someone from almost anywhere.

Repair Kit

Your repair kit is your hardware store. It should be able to help you fix anything that you have on your expedition. You will need the always reliable duct tape that can fix just about anything. You will need small tools to fix your crampons and your stove. You will need some needle and thread to sew up torn parts. A good tube of fast-acting superglue wouldn't be a bad idea. You may even consider throwing in an extra pair of glacier goggles and crampons in the repair kit in case of extreme emergency. It would be wise to include extra batteries, candles, matches and butane lighters as group gear and bring it along as a supply in case of emergencies.

First Aid Kit

Finally, you will need some type of first aid kit. You should have your own personal medication that you require, but it is best to have a group first aid kit available that can be used by everyone. The following list is a suggestion of the types of items that you may consider taking on your trip:

- 2 tubes of Neosporin® antibiotic ointment
- Codeine tablets or other pain relief medicine
- Aleve® tablets for headaches
- 3 Ace® bandages
- 2 rolls of cling tape to tape ankles or wrists
- 15 square gauze pads
- Assorted butterfly bandages
- Vitamin tablets
- Antibiotic tablets like tetracycline or penicillin
- Benadryl® or other tablets for colds or sinus conjestion
- Salt tablets
- Foam for blisters
- Zinc oxide

Appendix F: Food List

Climbing on big mountains at high altitude will burn a lot of energy. Consequently, it is important to replace the calories lost and to remain hydrated. The following food list is a suggestion for the types of food and menus that you may wish to have on your trip. The food you take will of course depend on your personal needs and taste.

Breakfast

Menu 1
Hot chocolate
Oatmeal
Sugar
Applesauce bar
Powered milk
Boxed fruit drink

Menu 2
Hot chocolate
Granola
Sugar
Power fruit bar
Powered milk
Orange drink

Menu 3
Hot chocolate
Cream of Wheat®
Sugar
Packaged fruit mix
Powdered milk
Powdered Tang®

Menu 4
Hot chocolate
Wheat Hearts®
Sugar
Apple bar
Powdered milk
Orange drink

Menu 5
Hot chocolate
Ralston® meal
Sugar
Mixed fruits
Powdered milk
Tang®

Menu 6
Hot chocolate
Roman meal
Sugar
Peaches and fruit
Powdered milk
Fruit drink

Lunch

Menu 1
Roasted peanuts   Wylers® Fruit Drink
Candy bars   Salami
Triscuits®   Raisins
Brach's® creams

Menu 2
Brazil nuts   Wylers® Orange Drink
Candy bars   Salami and cheese
Logan bread   Peanut butter and honey

Menu 3
Mixed nuts   Lemon drink
Candy bars   Toffee candy
Cheddar cheese   Triscuits®
Dried apples

Menu 4
Mixed salted nuts Lime drink
Candy bars   Hard candy
Logan bread   Pilot biscuits
Dried apricots

Menu 5
Cashews   Orange drink
Hard candy   Pilot crackers and cheese
Dried apples   Honey

Menu 6
Energy bar   Lemon drink
Candy bar   Assorted jellies
Logan bread   Raisins

The meals that comprise lunch often contain a lot of sugar. This is important to replace the calories lost while climbing. After a couple of weeks the amount of sugar can sometimes get tiresome. Consequently, things like biscuits and dried bread or Logan Bread are a nice change of pace. They also provide a good source of calories.

Dinner

Menu 1
Beef stroganoff   Cup-a-Soup®
Beef bouillon   Jell-O®
Blueberry cobbler   Tea or coffee

Menu 2
Mac & cheese   Peas and carrots
Chicken soup   Jell-O®
Butterscotch pudding
Tea or coffee

Menu 3
Chicken à la King   Cup-a-Soup®
Carrots   Jell-O®
Chocolate pudding   Tea or coffee

Menu 4
Port chop dinner   Cup-a-Soup®
Peas   Jell-O®
Banana cream pudding
Tea or coffee

Menu 5
Beef steak dinner   Cup-a-Soup®
Pineapple pudding   Tea or coffee

Menu 6
Beef stroganoff   Cup-a-Soup®
Jell-O®   Tomato soup
Applesauce   Tea or coffee

The meals discussed here are of course meals which are commercially available and are freeze-dried to save weight. There is a great latitude in choice when it comes to freeze-dried meals these days. There is not only a wider choice but they also taste better. The choice of food has improved dramatically in recent years.

Condiment Bag

One person may emerge as a chef and alternatively it might be wise to exchange this duty and trade-off occasionally. In any case it would be wise to have a condiment bag as a group item to help spice up some of the meals. The following is a suggestion for a group condiment kit:

Instant rice for emergencies
Sugar or artificial sweetener
Salt and pepper
Powdered milk
Vitamins
Candles and matches

Appendix G:
St. Elias Maps

It will be important to have a good map of the area that you plan to visit. The identification of the peaks is fairly easy. If you fly in then you will be very close to your objective. Nonetheless, a map is an essential part of being in the wilderness. There are two sources of maps for the Wrangell-St. Elias complex of mountains. One is the Canadian Map Office and the other is the United States Geological Survey. These organizations make the maps for their respective countries.

The climbing descriptions in this guidebook have given map names and numbers for both Canadian and United States-made maps for every mountain. Consequently, it is just a matter of contacting the appropriate office and obtaining the map that you need.

United States Geological Survey maps may be obtained from the USGS office in Anchorage, Alaska. You can contact them at the following address:

US Geologic Survey
Earth Science Info Center
4230 University Drive
Room 101
Anchorage, AK 99508-4664
Phone: (907) 786-7011
Fax: (907) 786-7050

Website: http://mapping-ak.wr.usgs.gov/esic.html

You can obtain an index of maps for Alaska from this office. You can obtain the map that will be relevant to your climb from the index and from the references in this book.

The Canadian Map Office makes, but does not distribute, maps. You must obtain Canadian maps from a distributor. A good distributor for Canadian maps is in Vancouver, British Columbia. This company can provide you with an index for 1:250,000 maps as well as the very useful 1:50,000 maps, as well as the maps themselves.

International Travel Maps and Books
ITMB Publishing Ltd.
530 West Broadway
Vancouver
British Columbia
Canada V5Z 1E9
Phone: (604) 879-3621
Fax: (604) 879-4521
Email: order@ITMB.com
Website: http://www.itmb.com/

Appendix H:
St. Elias Pilots

Once you arrive at Kluane Park you will need to arrange a way to get to your objective inside the Park. Once you have checked in with the ranger you can secure your flight into the mountains. Assuming you do not choose to walk to your objective you have several choices regarding pilots who will fly you to where you are going. Your choice depends upon where you start from.

If you are starting from the Canadian side from the park headquarters in Haines Junction, Canada you have several choices. The most economical way to get into the mountains is by fixed wing craft, which means an airplane. The usual choice for such a trip is with the pilot, Andrew Williams, who owns and operates Icefield Ranges Expeditions. He operates at the airfield at the southern end of Kluane Lake which is about 30 miles (48 km) north of park headquarters in Haines Junction, Canada along the Alcan Highway. There will be a small sign saying Kluane Park Research Station which is a university run Arctic research station sharing space at the airport. Drive down that small dirt access road to the small dirt landing strip where Andrew Williams is located. Andrew Williams can be reached at:

Icefield Ranges Expeditions
59-13th Avenue
Whitehorse
Yukon Territory
Canada Y1A 4K6
Phone in Whitehorse: (867) 633-2018
Phone at the airstrip: (867) 841-4561
Email: icefields@yukon.net
Website: http://www.icefields.ca/Company/Home.html/

If your landing site is going to be difficult to reach or poor snow conditions make landing a plane impossible then you could consider using a helicopter to reach your destination. Although its use to reach your objective is much more expensive, a helicopter can land anywhere. There are two companies who offer helicopter flights into the interior of the park:

Heli Dynamics Ltd.
Box 4
Whitehorse
Yukon Territory
Canada Y1A 5X9
Phone: (867) 668-3536
Fax: (867) 668-5637
Website: http://helidynamicshelicopterch.supersites.ca/dor/

The other service offering helicopter flights into the interior of the park is Trans North Turbo Air.

Trans North Helicopters
Box 5311
Haines Junction
Yukon Territory
Canada Y0B 1L0
Phone: (867) 634-2242
Website: http://www.tntaheli.com/

If you enter the park from the Alaskan side and start from Yakutat, Alaska there is one flight service which handles all the flights into the park. This company is Gulf Air Taxi. They handle all the flights for the climbers. The Gulf Air Taxi service can be reached as follows:

Gulf Air Taxi
P.O. Box 367
Yakutat, AK 99686
Phone: (907) 784-3240
Fax: (907) 784-3380

If you are flying into the northern end of the park or into the Wrangell Mountains, you may wish to enter from the town of Glennallen after checking in with the Cooper Center Ranger Station. In Glennallen there are a couple of flying services who will fly you into the park.

Ellis Air Taxi
(800) 822-5312
Website: http://www.ellisair.com/

or you can fly with:

Copper Valley Air Service
(907) 822-4200
Website: http://www.majesticadventures.com/index.html

Both of these air services are located at

the Gulkana Airport, four miles (6.4 km) north of Glennallen.

Appendix I: St. Elias Weather

The weather in the St. Elias Mountains can be described as wild and unpredictable. The storms blow in from the adjacent Gulf of Alaska to unleash their power on the towering peaks of the St. Elias Range. It is important to be ready for anything. One interesting feature of the weather patterns recently is that things are getting warmer. Global warming has reached the far north.

The best time to find good stretches of clear weather is in May when the best weather of the year occurs. Additionally, the snow is still present that covers much of the rock which is generally fairly loose and unconsolidated. The snow bridges are strongest in May and pilots have the easiest time landing on the unbroken glaciers that abound in the range.

The later in the year you arrive the warmer it is, but the more chance you have of experiencing snowstorms. Although a strong storm can blow in at any time, these storms are more frequent in the summer and fall than in the early spring.

It is possible to get a weather report before you fly in from the park headquarters where you enter the park. Alternatively, there is a weather service on the Canadian side of the park that will give you updates on the weather at frequent intervals. They can be reached at phone 0-867-841-4242.

Another possibility is to contact the National Weather Service in Yakutat, Alaska. They have the most comprehensive data gathering system in the area and are located across the road from Yakutat airport. You can just walk in and ask them for a long-range forecast. Look at their weather screens and computer models to get a good idea of what kind of weather is coming in. They can also be reached at (800) 472-0391. Their website is http://www.alaska.net/-nwsar/.

When you are in the park you should have a marine-band radio with you for communications regarding weather and your final pickup. You can listen to this and get weather reports broadcast for the fishing fleet located in Yakutat. Alternatively, you can call park headquarters for updates. It may be best overall to just be prepared and use good judgement. If you watch the sky you can begin to understand the cloud patterns and you can make good judgments this way.

Appendix J: Geology and Glaciers

Geology

The St. Elias and Wrangell complex of mountains is the most heavily glaciated region in the world outside of Greenland and the polar icecaps. This is due simply to the fact that such high mountains are immediately adjacent to the Gulf of Alaska. The powerful storms that can blow in from the gulf at any time of year meet the barrier created by the St. Elias Mountains and deposit copious quantities of snow. The annual collection exceeds melting and thus the glaciers of the St. Elias are born.

Despite the abundance of snow and ice, some rock is exposed which becomes prevalent as the season progresses. Consequently, it is important to know something of the geology that comprises this area.

The major geologic feature of the area is the Kluane Lake Area. This is where the park headquarters is located and most expeditions start from here. Kluane Lake is the largest lake in the Yukon Territory. This area is bisected by the northwest trending

Denali Fault and its associated depression, the Shakwak Trench.

The Kluane Lake area has undergone extensive geologic activity in recent human memory. Kluane Lake once flowed down the Slims River Valley towards the snout of the Kaskawulsh Glacier where it picked up the added meltwater from the glacier. This flow then continued down the Alsek River to the Gulf of Alaska.

Within the last two centuries there was a rise in the landmass associated with the Slims River. Consequently, the drainage from the Kaskawulsh Glacier changed dramatically. The snout of the Kaskawulsh Glacier actually forms a watershed. Streams issuing from the ice on the south side of the Kaskawulsh Glacier reach the Pacific Ocean directly by way of the Alsek River.

But the Slims River which flows north out of the Kaskawulsh Glacier now flows into rather than out of Kluane Lake. When this transformation first took place in the mid-eighteenth century, the water began to back up and Kluane Lake rose in elevation by some 150 feet (46 m). This rise in water then caused locally extensive flooding. The area where the town of Haines Junction now sits, as well as the park headquarters, was under 150 feet (46 m) of water. Eventually, the north side of Kluane Lake broke out and the Slims River and the Kluane Lake outfall now flow north into the Yukon River and ultimately into the Bering Sea.

The bedrock in the Kluane area is comprised of a steeply southwest dipping, folded and faulted sedimentary rock. In places it is overlain with volcanic rock such as in the Wrangell Mountains, which are almost entirely a result of recent volcanic eruptions.

There is sedimentary rock such as slate, sandstone and quartzite, all of which tend to break easily. Consequently, we end up with the "rotten" rock that is prevalent throughout the St. Elias Mountains. However, there has been an intrusion of granitic rock which is very solid and provides the best rock climbing in these mountains. The granite is solid but heavily fractured due to the frost heaving in the severe winters. The granitic rock intrusion can be found on mountains such as Mt. Maxwell. The granite is found on the north and east side of Mt. Kennedy as well. The great eastern buttress of Mt. Kennedy is almost entirely granite and as such is one of the great unknown and unclimbed routes in the entire park. The granite also intrudes into portions of the south and east sides of Mt. Logan.

Another type of good solid rock present that provides a good platform for rock climbing is green stone. This is a dense, structureless, green and slightly metamorphosed volcanic rock. This rock is found in many forms on some of the higher peaks of the St. Elias Range.

Fortunately, the high snowfall in this range facilitates a lot of snow cover. Consequently, the peaks of the Wrangell-St. Elias complex are predominately snow and ice climbs with the occasional rock intrusion.

Glaciers

The Wrangell-St. Elias complex of mountains is the most heavily glaciated place in the world outside of the polar icecaps and Greenland. Moist Pacific air moves in from the Gulf of Alaska and collides with the towering peaks of the St. Elias Mountains resulting in the deposition of huge amounts of snow.

The Wrangell-St. Elias mountain complex has hundreds of glaciers that spill down the valleys from the massive icefields. These are classic valley glaciers, some exceeding 60 miles (100 km) in length. The glaciers carve and grind the mountains as they flow downhill carrying away thousands of tons of loose rock and gravel. This gravel is deposited along the perimeters of the glaciers forming the beautiful variegated stripes commensurate with glacial formation. The Kaskawulsh Glacier is a beautiful and classic example. It has a beautiful medial moraine made from the stripes of ground rock and is one of the most widely observed and photographed glaciers in the entire park.

Glaciers do not continue to grow unchecked; there are processes that counteract the accumulation of ice until the glacier reaches its equilibrium. Ablation is the process of melting or sublimation of the ice. Glaciers that end in rivers or lakes lose ice mass by calving. Ablation is affected not only by air temperature but also by the amount of the sun's radiation that is reflected from the glacier surface.

At some point the glaciers will lose as much ice as they gain in a single year and this is their equilibrium point. They will not grow or shrink in size unless there are changes in environmental factors. The glaciers of the world, including those of the St. Elias Mountains are definitely shrinking. There are many signs of global warming and glacier reduction throughout the world. It is apparent that river ice is breaking up sooner, growing seasons are longer and plants not generally associated with the arctic are impinging on the arctic tundra. Glaciers in the St. Elias Mountains have shrunk to some extent as well. This is readily apparent by examining photographs of the region taken in the early part of the twentieth century. However, there is no reason for alarm; the glaciers of the St. Elias Mountains will be intact for decades to come.

From a more pragmatic viewpoint, glaciers mean climbers must engage in glacier travel. This means wearing a rope at all times and knowing how to perform crevasse rescue. People expect crevasses to occur at the steepest spot on a glacier, which does of course happen. However, crevasses can occur at any point on a glacier where there is significant change in slope.

The massive valley glaciers of the St. Elias Mountains appear to be sterile ribbons of ice-covered wasteland. However, there are numerous little dirt hummocks known as nunataks that dot the glaciers. Nunatak is an Inuit Indian word meaning land attached. These nunataks are little oases of life. In early summer these nunataks come to life with flowers and insects and even a few burrowing rodents. They add a little color to a region otherwise expressing itself in black and white.

Glaciers may seem like colossal, impersonal ice streams that evade the limits of time. They appear to flow steadily and incessantly forward. From time to time, however, a dramatic natural event will take place that astounds scientists and general observers alike. One of these events is the phenomenon of the surging glacier.

Such an event did occur in 1965 when the Steele Glacier surged forward at an unprecedented rate. The Steele Glacier travels forward at an average rate of about 3 feet (1 m) per month. Suddenly in 1965, the glacier began advancing at 1,200 feet (366 m) per month. The event eventually ran its course and slowed to its normal crawl. However, for a brief period the strength of the forces of nature were displayed with magnificent grandeur.

Another extraordinary example of nature's power occurred in 1986 with the Hubbard Glacier. The Hubbard Glacier is the largest tidewater glacier in the world and flows into Disenchantment Bay at the mouth of the Russell Fiord. The Russell Fiord has a narrow entrance into Disenchantment Bay to begin with; the mouth is only about 800 yards (732 m) across. In 1986 the Hubbard Glacier pushed across the Russell Fiord, damming up all the water that accumulates from the rivers feeding the fiord.

The Hubbard Glacier dam lasted four months until suddenly and catastrophically one day the dam broke, releasing all the water behind it. For nearly two days the water flowed out at 3.7 million cubic feet per second. This is three times larger than the peak flow of the mighty Yukon River. The water finally emptied and Russell Fiord returned to its quiescent state.

Glaciers are not only mountain sculptors but they are also spectacular tools of nature's creation. They can build as well as destroy. They are an integral and beautiful part of the St. Elias Mountains.

Appendix K: Mountain Medicine

The maintenance of the health of the climber on a climbing expedition is of vital importance. The medical dilemmas that can be experienced on a climb are numerous. They can range from mild sunburn to frostbite. Some medical problems are mild such as developing a cold or experiencing temporary hypothermia. Some medical problems such as pulmonary or cerebral edema can be life threatening. It is important to recognize symptoms of each problem as they occur and to know how to deal effectively with them before they get out of control.

Acute Mountain Sickness

Acute mountain sickness (AMS) is a generalized term to describe a variety of ailments that can occur when the climber reaches higher altitude. High altitude sickness can happen to anyone who is careless enough to climb too high too fast. One of the major symptoms of AMS that occurs if a climber ascends too rapidly without acclimatization is high altitude pulmonary edema (HAPE). HAPE occurs in unacclimatized individuals who ascend rapidly to altitudes greater than 8,000 feet (2438 m).

The occurrence of HAPE has pronounced and easily recognizable symptoms. The symptoms include a deep cough coupled with a fluid gurgling sound from the lungs. HAPE is characterized by fatigue and the inability to breathe deeply and comfortably. The onset of these symptoms are not necessarily dangerous. It must be recognized that the symptoms have occurred and it is important to act immediately to rectify the problem before it becomes serious.

The best way to treat HAPE is to descend. The lower you get, the more oxygen is present and the easier it will be to breathe and symptoms should clear up fairly soon. If you choose to ascend again then you must do so slowly. If symptoms of HAPE appear again then descend and terminate the climb. If symptoms persist, you should fly out and acquire advanced medical treatment immediately.

Another medical malady that can occur at altitude in unacclimatized individuals is cerebral edema (CE). Cerebral edema is less common than pulmonary edema but it is more serious. CE is characterized by severe headaches, a staggering gait and hallucinations. These symptoms can result in coma and ultimately death if left unchecked.

Headaches can occur even at lower altitudes, but CE is accompanied by the other more serious side effects. It is believed that lack of oxygen causes swelling in the brain which leads to the headaches. Again, the treatment for CE is to descend rapidly. Symptoms should disappear slowly and completely.

If the climber attempts to ascend again, check continuously for signs of the symptoms. If such symptoms occur again then the climber should descend and terminate the climb. If symptoms persist then medical treatment should be sought immediately.

Acute mountain sickness can occur in anyone. The more physically fit one is before the climb, the greater the likelihood that one can avoid such problems. The best solution is to prevent the symptoms of AMS from starting by training before you begin the expedition. It is wise to run or walk long distances before a climb. Also, it is best to get up to at least 5,000 feet (1,524 m) in the mountains a few times before the expedition begins. The better prepared you are the greater your chances for success.

Aside from the physiologic problems associated with altitude there are the physical ones as well. As you ascend it gets colder and it is harder to stay warm. If you are extremely fatigued or lack adequate clothing you can experience hypothermia.

When your body begins to lose heat faster than it produces it you are experiencing exposure. This will lead to involuntary shivering. Additionally, you may wish to engage in some additional movement to stay warm. Ultimately, if the exposure continues you will use your energy reserves and become exhausted. If the loss of heat continues you will begin to lose movement in your feet and hands. The cold will affect your judgment and you will not realize you are experiencing trouble.

To avoid hypothermia it is important to stay dry. Use multiple layers of insulation. Synthetic material will dispense perspiration and condensation rapidly. Wool has a tendency to retain liquids but it is still warm when wet, although it becomes heavier.

The wind will affect your body temperature dramatically. If wind penetrates your clothing it is the same as reducing the insulation that you are wearing. The windchill effects of an air temperature of +20º F (-6.7 C) coupled with a 45 mile per hour (72.4 km per hour) wind are identical to a –40 F (-40 C) air temperature with a 2 mile per hour (3.2 km per hour) wind. The wind will make a big difference in what you feel and the effect of the cold on your skin. So protecting yourself from the wind with wind resistant garments is essential.

The best way to prevent hypothermia is to wear multiple layers of clothing. This way you can add or shed clothing as needed and you shouldn't become overheated or too cold. You will lose more heat from your head than any other part of your body, so it is important to keep your head warm and dry.

There is no need to be a hero in the mountains. If you are losing body heat then descend, put on more clothes or dig a snow cave. It is important to get out of the wind and cold and reduce the heat loss.

If hypothermia persists then your body will respond by sending less blood to the extremities and keeping more blood in the core of the body. The problem that will occur from this event is that your fingers and toes will not receive adequate blood flow to stay warm and they will begin to freeze. The freezing of the extremities results in frostbite. If the tissue damage is severe enough then the tissue around the extremities will die and this will ultimately lead to amputation of the damaged parts.

The solutions to avoiding frostbite are the same as those for hypothermia. Be sure to wear correct clothing. Make sure you can recognize the symptoms of hypothermia and frostbite. Take immediate action, such as getting into a tent or a bivy sack. Put more clothing on if possible or descend as quickly as possible. If the symptoms of frostbite continue you must terminate the climb. If darkening of the tissues occurs you will have to seek advanced medical help.

Another problem that can occur at high altitudes is snow blindness. Snow blindness is very painful and accounts for continuous discomfort to anyone who experiences it. Fortunately, snow blindness is generally temporary and the discomfort usually lasts no more than four or five days.

Snow blindness is a result of the temporary damage caused by ultraviolet light to the delicate layer of the outer eye, the cornea. Ultraviolet light is invisible to the naked eye. However, under permanent snow and ice conditions the glare from the reflection of the sun is enormous. It is painful to stand around without your sunglasses or glacier goggles. The precaution that one can take to avoid this problem is very simple. If you keep your goggles on when you are outside you will have no problems.

Finally, the direct effect of the sun or the reflection of the sun on the snow can cause serious sunburn. It is not impossible to develop a second degree burn in less than a week on glaciated mountains.

In order to avoid sunburn it is wise to use a high degree sunblock lotion. Use the lotion early and often. Apply it everywhere the skin will be exposed to the sun. This includes the back of the neck and the top of the ears; these parts burn too. The use of copious amounts of sunblock will preclude any burning problems. If you have fair skin and burn easily you may wish to use zinc oxide. This is a bit messy but it prevents all sun exposure to the parts that are covered. It will peel off as you perspire but you can simply apply more.

When you prepare for your expedition just be sure to train as much as you can. Bring the right tools and medical supplies for the job. Use your best judgment of climbing and tactics. It is fine to push yourself but leave a little room for safety. The altitude of the St. Elias Mountains is not severe, so a well prepared and well trained climber should enjoy a magnificent climbing experience under a safe and spectacular setting.

Appendix L: The Climbing Rating System

Rating the difficulty of a climb is a very subjective thing. The technical difficulty of a climb may be very different to people of varying skills and commitments. There are numerous rating systems used by different countries around the world. This short description will try to describe some of the differences of these systems and how they compare to each other.

In the St. Elias Mountains you will generally come across three major categories of climbs. These can be described by words and to some extent by the numbers presented by the main rating systems.

The first type of rating that might be encountered in the St. Elias Mountains is that of the glacier route. Generally these are straightforward climbs following easy snow slopes to reach the summit. However, these climbs might be decorated with anywhere from a few to many crevasse fields. The crevasses may be easy to cross or in some years may be next to impossible. Also, the overall height of the mountain and the weather conditions experienced at any particular time will play an influence as well.

For instance, following the snow slopes between the NE and SW summits of Mt. Foresta will bring you to the summits of either of these peaks fairly easily. There are, in fact, crevasses that must be crossed, but early in the year this is fairly easy. Conversely, the King Trench Route on Mt. Logan is also considered a glacier route. There is roughly 7,000 feet (2,134 m) difference in height between Mt. Logan and Mt. Foresta, so the difference in elevation and weather conditions experienced at these different altitudes must be considered. These are examples of the glacier type climbing route.

The second type of climb that is encountered in the St. Elias Mountains is the intermediate type route. These types of routes are not only some of the most popular but also the most abundant type of routes. A good example of the intermediate type routes would be either the East Ridge Route on Mt. Logan or the classic Southwest Ridge and the Harvard Route on Mt. St. Elias.

Both of these routes present moderate but not highly technically difficult climbing challenges. The East Ridge of Logan has some narrow sections of ridge to climb and Mt. Logan is the tallest mountain in the entire range. The Southwest Ridge route of Mt. St. Elias is very long with an extreme elevation gain but has only about two rope lengths worth of difficult climbing. Even though the objective difficulties are unique, the overall difficulty is about the same.

These routes will require roped climbing and some belaying and will perhaps involve the placement of some fixed rope. However, they present enjoyable ascents with some straightforward and beautiful climbing.

The third category of climbing route that will be encountered in the St. Elias Mountains is, of course, the severe type of climb. These types of climbs might be exemplified by most of the routes on the South Face of Mt. Logan. Another example of a severe route would be something on the North Face of Mt. Kennedy.

These types of routes are continuously steep and sometimes subjected to noticeable avalanche danger. These climbs will involve roped climbing and belaying on most of the pitches. They will involve steep rock and ice and the careful placement of protection for the climber.

The type of route that a climber chooses to climb will depend entirely upon the skills of the team and the commitment needed to succeed. The descriptions in this book should prove to be at least a valuable guide in judging the difficulty of any undertaking. In addition, the photos provided by this book and the companion CD-ROM have been provided specially to enable the climber to get a good look at the climbing objective and judge for themselves the difficulty of the undertaking to which they are about to commitment themselves.

Beyond general descriptions, a numbering system has evolved. The numbers are an attempt to describe the overall difficulty with a simple number. Different countries have slightly different systems but a couple of numbering systems have emerged as the most widely used system in the literature. These systems are described below.

The Roman numeral system, also called the engagement grade, involves Roman numerals from I to VII. The length of the climb is considered to be a factor as is the sustained nature of the climbing, the difficulty of the approach, the descent. and objective hazards which might be encountered. The Roman numeral system is one of the most frequently cited rating systems found in the climbing literature.

Roman numeral I represents a short and easy glacier type climb as described by the glacier routes listed above. These are generally easy climbs with very little approach and an easy descent. There is no great overall commitment or difficulty to these types of climbs.

Roman numeral II represents a multi-pitch type of route or a shorter route with a longer and more arduous type of approach. There are generally no sustained technical difficulties on these climbs and there is generally no type of objective hazard on these climbs. The descent from these climbs is not long or involved.

Roman numeral III represents a multi-pitch type of route at moderate elevation. These climbs might be represented by a very short route also, but one which has a long and complicated approach. These climbs might be moderate summer climbs but done in the winter. These climbs will have some objective hazards and may require a moderate commitment of effort and time to descend and retreat from the climb.

Roman numeral IV represents multi-pitch type of routes in more remote and inaccessible areas. These routes may also involve some extensive elevation gain. The approach to these routes is generally fairly involved and the climb itself will involve some objective hazards while on the route. The descent from these climbs are more complicated and arduous. The descent may involve the placement of anchors or numerous rappels or the avoidance of crevasse fields. These climbs are the start of the type of climbs that require some extensive commitment in order to succeed.

Roman numeral V represents a long climb that might require more than one day to complete. These climbs are the types of climbs that are engaged by serious and competent climbers. They generally involve some significant elevation gain and may require an involved descent.

Roman numeral VI represents a long climb and generally an alpine-type climb in a remote area. There will be some serious objective hazards that will be encountered which will require careful planning and execution to surmount. There will be technically challenging pitches involved on these climbs and the descent will be long and complicated.

Roman numeral VII represents the longest, hardest and most sustained routes. Since the pinnacle of physical and mental achievement advances with each generation, the top climbs probably have yet to be done. Still, there are plenty of serious and challenging climbs that have already been done that will qualify as a Roman numeral VII. These are long, difficult climbs with sustained sections of technical difficulty. Also, the approach and descent will be long and complicated. These are the routes generally done by the professional and serious alpinist.

The St. Elias Mountains are not very cold mountains as far as big mountains go, but there are places where ice climbing is encountered and as such a discussion of the rating system for ice climbing will be presented. Ice climbing is not only challenging but can involve very steep ice with a difficult approach and a long and involved descent. As a result, ice climbing has developed its own unique rating system which is described here.

W1 is generally just frozen water such as a flat surface found on a frozen lake in the far north in winter. Generally no technical climbs are rated WI.

W2 describes a climb which contains a short section of difficult climbing with plenty of opportunity for placing anchors and there is generally an easy descent.

W3 describes ice climbs that are more sustained. These climbs are steep but generally do not involve vertical climbing. There may be numerous sections of steep ice but the quality of the ice is generally good and there is ample opportunity to place protection.

W4 describes the first ice climbs which can be described as serious climbing. These are generally multi-pitch climbs which have numerous sections of steep ice. Generally these climbs do not have any sustained vertical ice and the protection is generally good. There may be some challenging and unique features to these climbs such as large protruding bulges or long run outs with little protection.

W5 describes very difficult ice climbs. These climbs will involve long run outs with little protection which is hard to secure. There may be long, sustained sections of vertical or near vertical ice and the quality of the ice may be questionable in places. These are serious ice climbs.

W6 represents ice climbs of a serious nature. These climbs will have long, sustained sections of vertical ice where the quality of the ice may be poor. The protection will have to be placed with the greatest care and technique and will have to be placed while standing on front points.

W7 describes the most difficult and serious climbing. There will be many pitches containing sustained vertical ice with long run outs. It will be difficult to place protection and there will be at least one extraordinarily difficult pitch that you may remember for the rest of your life. It may require great skill to maneuver around difficult sections as well as find adequate placements.

Appendix M: Objective Hazards

Crevasses

There are two main types of major objective hazards that you will encounter in the St. Elias Mountains. The first one is the hidden danger of crevasses.

The St. Elias Mountains are heavily glaciated. The valleys are filled with some of the world's longest glaciers. The large summit plateaus of the large peaks are glaciated. There are also bergschrunds at the base of all the climbs, so one must be prepared to deal with these hidden dangers.

It is imperative to be roped up at all times when traveling on glaciers. It is necessary to be roped up when traveling to your climbing objective. It might be necessary to be roped up when standing around the tent at base camp. When a camp is established on the glacier at the base of the climb or on the route, the immediate area must be secured.

It is easy to use an ice axe or a long wand to probe the snow around the area where you will be camped. If hidden crevasses are found then they can be marked and avoided. If you are not sure then it is best to be roped up.

Sometimes a climber will fall into a crevasse despite the best efforts to avoid them. When this happens it is very important to be able to rescue the climber from the crevasse before hypothermia sets in. Standard crevasse rescue techniques can be used to anchor the rope and allow the climber to jumar out.

Climbers should carry jumars or other types of ascenders at all times to facilitate crevasse rescue when needed.

Avalanches

The second major type of objective hazard that will be encountered in the St. Elias Mountains are avalanches. Since these mountains are predominantly snow and ice, avalanches are quite common.

It is important to be aware of your surroundings at all times. The site selection of a base camp must be examined thoroughly so that it is not in danger of being hit by an avalanche. You may think it is safe based on previous experience, but the avalanches in the St. Elias Mountains are huge and can travel great distances. *See CD photos (Appendix) CD-II01, CD-II02, CD-II03 and CD-II04.*

It is necessary to make sure that camps are not under ice cliffs. When approaching a route sometimes it is necessary to walk in an area that is subject to avalanches. If it cannot be avoided then you simply have to go through the area. But be sure to do this in the coldest hours of the day and travel as quickly as possible.

The ridges of these mountains are corniced in many places, so you may have to climb over or around corniced sections of a ridge. Be sure to climb as far below the cornice line as possible to minimize knocking off a cornice and falling off with it. Be sure that when you set up a camp on a narrow ridge it is not sitting on top of an unsecured cornice. If the site selection is near a cornice then be sure to anchor the tent and everyone in it to a more secure part of the ridge.

Objective hazards are an unavoidable part of climbing. However, if you exercise caution and good judgment you will be able to minimize the risks these dangers pose. If you know how to use the proper rescue techniques then you can rescue anybody who is subjected to one of the hazards discussed.

Appendix N: Climbing Magazines

Reading as many articles about your intended climb before you depart is a vital step in your planning. There are many excellent climbing journals that you can find on the rack of most climbing or sporting goods stores.

The two most valuable references for climbs in the St. Elias Mountains are *The American Alpine Journal* and *The Canadian Alpine Journal*. These two journals have been referenced wherever possible in this guidebook for the climb in question. They are published annually and articles regarding any climb can be obtained by writing to the head office of the club that publishes them.

The American Alpine Club
710 Tenth Street, Suite 100
Golden, CO 80401
Phone: (303) 384-0110
Fax: (303) 384-0111
Email: getinfo@americanalpineclub.org
Website: http://www.americanalpineclub.org

The Canadian Alpine Club of Canada
P.O. Box 8040
Canmore
Alberta
Canada T1W 2T8
Phone: (403) 678-3200 x1
Fax: (403) 678-3224
Email: info@AlpineClubofCanada.ca
Website: http://www.alpineclubofcanada.ca/index.html
and: http://www.alpineclubofcanada.ca/publications/caj.html

Volume II

Volume II will contain information about the remaining mountains not discussed in Volume I. Specifically it will include the Steele Group, the University Range, the Icefield Group, the Centennials and the Wrangells. Volume II will be completed when the photographs are gathered to support the text.

INDEX

A

Abruzzi Ridge, 105, 106, 108, 113, 121, 124
Acute Mountain Sickness, 246
Agassiz Glacier, 124, 127, 134, 135
Air Transport, 230
  Air Canada, 232
  Copper Valley Air Service, 236, 242
  Ellis Air Service, 236
  Ellis Air Taxi, 242
  Gulf Air Taxi, 242
  Heli Dynamics, 242
  Icefield Ranges Expeditions, 242
  Trans North Helicopters, 242
Alaska, 9
Alaskan Direct Bus Service, 234
Alaska Direct Bus Line, 232
Alaska Marine Ferry Service, 231, 234
Alaska Marine Highway, 230, 232
Alcan Highway, 223, 225, 226, 231, 232, 242
Alsek River, 244
Alsek River Valley, 213
Alsek Trail, 223, 225
Alverstone Glacier, 63
Amenity Ridge, 144
American Alpine Club, 252
American Alpine Journal, The, 252
Anchorage, Alaska, 230, 234
  Anchorage Convention and Visitors Bureau, 234
  Anchorage Suite Lodge, 235
  Duke's of 8th Ave., 234
Appendix A: Expedition Organization, 228–229
Appendix B: Ranger Stations, 229–230
Appendix C: Transportation to Kluane Park, 230–232
Appendix D: Northern Cities, 232–236
Appendix E: Expedition Equipment, 236–239
Appendix F: Food List, 239–241
Appendix G: St. Elias Maps, 241–242
Appendix H: St. Elias Pilots, 241–242
Appendix I: St. Elias Weather, 243–244
Appendix J: Geology and Glaciers, 243–245
Appendix K: Mountain Medicine, 246–248
Appendix L: The Climbing Rating System, 248–251
Appendix M: Objective Hazards, 251
Appendix N: Climbing Magazines, 252
Arctic Institute of North America, 64
Astro Floyd Couloir, 188
Augusta Glacier, 133
Avalanches, 251

B

Backpackers Hostels, 233
Baird-Malaspina Traverse, 129
Baker, Marcus, 43
Bellingham, Washington, 231
Bering, Vitus, 103, 104, 137
Boundary Peaks, 19
Boundary Route, The, 106, 115, 116
Bride Peak, 105
Bus Service, 231

C

Cakewalk, 145
Call of the Wild, 179
Canadian Alpine Club, 137
Canadian Alpine Club, The, 252
Canadian Alpine Journal, The, 252
Canadian Map Office, 241
Canadian Permanent Committee on Geographical Names, 219
Cannon Beach, 235
Cantenary Col, 154, 155
Cantenary McArthur Col, 182
Cantenary Peak, 154, 155
Cantenary Ridge, 139, 152, 153, 182
Carpe, Allen, 138

Cathedral Glacier, 63, 64, 65, 68, 72, 73, 76, 84, 88, 90, 92, 93
Centennial Ridge, 149
Centennial Route, 53–56
cerebral edema, 246
Chaix Hills, 104
Chitina River, 139
Circumski, 173
Clone Ridge, 51
Cocks Comb, 145
Colorado Route, 147
Columbus Glacier, 116, 174
companion CD-ROM, 249
Conclusion, 227
Cook, James, 30, 104
Copper Valley Air Service, 242
Cordova, 138
Crevasses, 251

D

Dak Peak, 154
Dall, W.H., 43
Denali Fault, 244
Disenchantment Bay, 9, 245
Dome Pass, 105
Donjek Glacier, 173, 191, 200
Donjek Peak, 191, 200
Donjek River Valley, 200
Duke of Abruzzi, 105, 106, 138, 174

E

Early Bird Buttress, 167
Easter Glacier, 219
Ellis Air Taxi, 242

F

Ferry Service, 231
First Aid Kit, 239
Fitzroy in Patagonia, 83
Foster, W.W., 137, 138
Fred Said Buttress, 186
frostbite, 247

G

Geological Survey of Canada, 137, 140
Glennallen, Alaska, 235
 Air Service, 236
 Camping, 235
 Food Service, 236
 Hotels, 236
Gnurdelhorn, 191, 200
Good Neighbor Peak, 43–59
Gulf Air Taxi, 242
Gulf of Alaska, 18, 112, 140, 238, 243

H

Haines, Alaska, 234
 Haines Alaska Visitors Bureau, 234
Haines Junction, Canada, 223, 225, 229, 233, 241, 242
 Alcan Motor Inn, 233
 Food Service, 234
 Kluane Park Inn, 233
 The Raven, 234
Haines Visitors Bureau, 234
Harrison Walsh Traverse, 211
Harvard Mountaineering Club, 113
Hayden Glacier, 18, 34, 36
Haydon Bench, 113, 114, 115
Haydon Col, 114, 115
Haydon Peak, 113, 114
Heli Dynamics, 242
high altitude pulmonary edema, 246
Hubbard, Father Bernard, 63
Hubbard Glacier, 9, 14, 16, 20, 22, 24, 26, 27, 28, 30, 43, 45, 46, 47, 48, 49, 50, 51, 52, 53, 157, 173, 183, 184, 186, 187, 189, 192, 194, 195, 196, 197, 198, 199, 200, 229, 245
Hubbard Group, 191
Hubsew Ridge, 159, 161
Huge In Europe, 187
Hummingbird Ridge, 164, 167, 168
Hump, The, 106, 115
hypothermia, 247

I

Icefield Ranges Expeditions, 233, 242
ice climbing, 250
Igloo Peak, 93–94
  East Face, 93
  North Ridge, 93
  West Ridge, 93–94
Independence Basin, 150
Independence Ridge, 150, 152
Institute Peak, 44, 45, 60, 61
International Boundary Commission, 10
International Boundary Survey of 1913, 116, 138
International Travel Maps and Books ITMB Publishing Ltd., 241
ITMB Publishing LTD., 241

J

Jefferies Glacier, 140

K

Karakorum Range, 105
Kaskawulsh Glacier, 94, 138, 173, 191, 192, 198, 213, 214, 215, 217, 218, 220, 244
  South Arm, 216, 217, 218, 220, 221
Kaskawulsh Group, 213
Kaskawulsh Peak, 214–216, 218
  East Arete, 215
  Northeast Ridge, 216
  Northwest Arete, 215
  North Arete, 214
  North Col, 215–216
  South Ridge, 216
Kennedy, John F., 76
Kennedy, Senator Robert F., 76
Kennedy Group, 63, 64, 93
Kennedy Massif, 63, 65, 76
King Col, 140, 172
King Peak, 172, 174, 175–181
  East Ridge, 180–181
  North Face, 175–177
  Southwest Face, 179
  South Ridge, 179
  West Ridge, 177–179
King Trench, 138, 139, 140, 143, 144, 145, 153, 155, 157, 159, 161, 164, 167, 171, 174, 175
Kluane Group, 223
Kluane Lake, 213, 214, 223, 242, 243, 244
Kluane Park, 183, 228, 229, 234, 237, 241

L

Lambert, H.F., 138
Lauchlan Ridge, 195
La Perouse, 104
Leacock, Stephen, 218
Libbey Glacier, 112
Little Patagonia, 220–221
Logan, William, 137
Logan Glacier, 152, 153, 173, 174, 191
Lowell Glacier, 63, 88, 89, 90, 91, 191
Lowell Peak, 98–100
  Southeast Ridge, 99
  Southwest Ridge, 99
  South Ridge, 99
  The Lowell Traverse, 100
  West Ridge, 100
Lowell Traverse, The, 100
Lucia Glacier, 18, 34, 36

M

MacCarthy, 138, 139
MacCarthy, A.H., 137, 138
MacCarthy Gap, 142
Malaspina, Alejandro, 104
Malaspina Glacier, 18, 39, 40, 104, 105
Maps
  Corwin Cliffs 115 C/1 1:50,000, 30, 129
  Corwin Cliffs 115 C/8 1:50,000, 30, 129
  International Travel Maps and Books ITMB Publishing Ltd., 241
  ITMB Publishing LTD., 241
  Jarvis River 115B/16 1:50,000, 223, 225
  King Peak 115 C/10 1:50,000, 140, 175
  Kloo Lake 115 A/13 1:50,000, 225
  McArthur Peak 115 C/9 1:50,000, 140, 182
  Mt. Alverstone 115 B/6 1:50,000, 64, 73,

76, 93, 94, 98
Mt. Badham 115 B/13 1:50,000, 200
Mt. Kennedy 115 B/7 1:50,000, 64, 73, 76, 84, 87, 94, 98
Mt. Leacock 115 B/10 1:50,000, 214, 217, 219, 220
Mt. Queen Mary 115 B/12, 1:50,000, 192, 197
Mt. Seattle 115 B/3 1:50,000, 64, 73, 76
Newton Glacier 115 C/2 1:50,000, 106, 121
Newton Glacier 115 C/7 1:50,000, 106, 121
Slims River 115 B/15 1:50,000, 217, 218
Ulu Mountain 115 B/2 1:50,000, 64, 73, 76, 88
USGS Bering Glacier Alaska-Canada 1:250,000 map, 106, 175
USGS Mt. St. Elias Alaska-Canada 1:250,000 map, 20, 30, 64, 73, 76, 84, 87, 88, 93, 94, 98, 106, 121, 129, 140, 174, 175, 182, 192, 197, 200, 214, 217, 218, 219, 220
US Geologic Survey Earth Science Info Center, 241
Marvine Glacier, 105
McArthur Cantenary Col, 183
McArthur Col, 154
Mira Face, 115, 116, 117
Mt. Alberta, 220
Mt. Alverstone, 72–76
  Cathedral Glacier, 73
  Northeast Ridge, 75
  Northwest Ridge, 74
  North Ridge, 74–75
  Point Blanchard, 75–76
    Left Pillar, 76
    Point Blanchard Central Pillar
      Pugalist at Rest, 75
      Wilford Couloir, 75–76
    Right Pillar, 76
  West Ridge, 73–74
Mt. Archibald, 223, 225–226
  Southeast Ridge, 225–226
Mt. Augusta, 103, 121, 129–135
  East Ridge, 132–133

Northeast Buttress, 131
North Rib, 130–131
North Ridge, 131–132
Southwest Rib, 135
South Buttress, 134–135
South Ridge, 133–134
West Ridge, 129–130
Mt. Badham, 191, 200–201
Mt. Baird, 127–128
  Baird-Malaspina Traverse, 129
  East Ridge, 128
    South Side, 128
  North Ridge, 128
  West Ridge, 128–129
Mt. Baird Col, 130
Mt. Bering, 125–126
  Northeast Ridge, 126
  North Ridge, 126
  Southwest Ridge, 126–127
  South Ridge, 127
  West Ridge, 126
Mt. Cairnes, 223, 225
  Northeast Face, 225
  North Face, 225
Mt. Cook, 30–43
  Central Spur, 32
  East Ridge, 31–32
  Northeast Buttress, 42
  Northwest Cook, 40–41
  North Buttress, 42
  North Ridge, 41–42
  Southeast Spur, 32
  Southwest Ridge, 39–40
    North Buttress, 40
  South Amphitheater, 34–37
    Central Pillar, 37
    Left Rib, 37
    Right Pillar, 36–37
  South Buttress, 32–33
  South Face, 18
  South Ridge, 34
  The South Face, 33–34
  Turner Glacier, 42–43
Mt. Eaton, 132, 133
Mt. Edith Cavell, 220
Mt. Foresta, 19–30

Northeast Peak, 26–30
    East Col, 30
    East Ridge, 29–30
    Northeast Ridge, 28–29
    North Face, 27
    North Ridge, 27–28
    West Ridge, 26–27
  Southwest Peak, 20–26
    East Ridge, 20–22
    Southwest Spur, 24–25
    South Ridge, 22–24
    The West Col, 25–26
    West Ridge, 24
Mt. Harrison, 209–210
  East Face, 209
  Harrison Walsh Traverse, 211
  Northwest Ridge, 210-211
  North Ridge, 210
Mt. Hubbard, 63–72
  Cathedral Glacier, 64–65
  Southwest Ridge, 68–69
  South Buttress, 67–68
  South Face, 65–67
  West Ridge
    Central Pillar, Left Side, 69–71
    Central Pillar Right Side, 71–72
    Left Pillar, 72
Mt. Huxley, 116
Mt. Jeannette, 123–125
  Central Buttress, 124–125
  East Buttress, 124
  North Col, 123
  North Rib, 123–124
  North Ridge, 123
  Southern Escarpment, 124
  South Ridge, 124
    East Peak, 125
    Middle Peak, 125
  West Ridge, 123
Mt. Kaskawulsh, 220
Mt. Kennedy, 76–84, 244
  Cathedral Glacier, 76–77
  East Ridge, 79–81
  North Face, 79
  North Ridge, 77–79
  Southeast Buttress, 81, 83

  Left Side, 83
  Right Side, 81
  South Buttress, 83–84
Mt. King, 139
Mt. King George, 174, 191, 192–197
  East Ridge, 194–195
  Northeast Ridge, 192–193
  Southwest Ridge (Lauchlan Ridge), 195–196
  South Ridge, 195
  West Buttress, 196–197
Mt. Logan, 137, 138, 140–170, 177, 183, 192, 244
  Amenity Ridge, 144–146
  Cantenary Ridge, 153–157
  Centennial Ridge, 149–150
  Circumski, 173–175
  Colorado Route, 147–149
  East Ridge, 157–159
  Hummingbird Ridge, 164–167
    Early Bird Buttress, 167–168
    Thunderbird Variation, 168
  Independence Ridge, 150–152
  Northwest Ridge, 146–147
  Orion Spur, 152–153
  Raven Ridge, 161–162
  Schoening Ridge, 172–173
  Southeast Ridge
    Hubsew Ridge, 159–161
  South Southwest Buttress, 168–169
  The King Trench, 140–142
  Warbler Ridge, 162–164
  West Buttress, 170–172
  West Ridge, 142–143
Mt. Logbard, 189
Mt. Malaspina, 103, 127–128, 129
  South Ridge, 127–128
Mt. Maxwell, 217–218, 220, 244
  Northeast Ridge, 217
  North Ridge, 217–218
  South Ridge, 217
Mt. McArthur, 139, 173, 182–188
  Astro Floyd Couloir, 188
  East Buttress, 188
  East Central, 187
  East Ridge, 184–185

 Fred Said Buttress, 186
 Huge In Europe, 187–188
 North Ridge, 183–184
 Southeast Central Buttress, 187
 South Central Buttress, 186–187
 South Face, 185
 West Buttress, 186
 West Ridge, 182–183
Mt. Newton, 121–123, 174
Mt. Poland, 87–88
 Northeast Ridge, 87
 South Ridge, 88
 South Side, 87
 West Ridge, 87–88
Mt. Queen Mary, 173, 191, 197–200
 Northeast Ridge, 198
 Northwest Ridge, 199–200
 North Ridge, 197–198
 Southwest Buttress, 199
 South Rib, 198–199
 South Ridge, 198
 West Ridge, 199
Mt. Robson, 137
Mt. Seattle, 9–19
 East Ridge, 16–17
 Northeast Ridge, 17–18
 North Ridge, 14–16
 South Face, 10–13
 West Ridge, 13–14
Mt. St. Elias, 103–121, 137, 174
 Abruzzi Ridge, 106–108
 North Spur, 121
 Southeast Ridge, 109–110
 Southwest Ridge, 113–115
 South Buttress, 115
 South Face, 112–113
 South Ridge, 110–112
 The Boundary Route, 116–118
 The East Ridge, 108–109
 The Northwest Ridge, 118–121
 West Ridge, 115
 Mt. St. Elias Satellite Peaks, 121
Mt. St. Jean Baptiste, 220
 West Face, 220
Mt. Stegosaurus, 221
Mt. Stephen Leacock, 218–219

 Southeast Ridge, 219–220
Mt. Teddy, 169, 170
Mt. Tyrannosaurus, 221
Mt. Vancouver, 43–61
 South Summit(Good Neighbor Peak), 43–61
  Centennial Route, 53–56
   Left Side, 55
   Right Side, 55–56
  East Ridge, 49–51
  Northeast Ridge, 48–49
  Northwest Ridge, 43–46
   North Rib Variation, 45–46
  North Buttress, 46–48
  Sotheast Ridge
   East Rib Variation, 53
  Southeast Ridge, 51–53
   North Rib Variation, 52–53
  Southwest Buttress, 59
  Southwest Ridge, 57–59
  South Spur, 56–57
  West Buttress, 60–61
  West Face, 59–60
 True North Summit, 43
Mt. Walsh, 203–209
 East Spur, 208–209
 Northeast Ridge, 209–210
 Northwest Buttress, 204–205
 North Ridge, 203
 Southeast Ridge, 207
 Southwest Ridge, 206–207
 Southwest Spur, 205–206
 South Glacier, 207–208
 West Ridge, 205
Mt. Wayne Smith, 220
 North Face, 220

N

National Geographic Society, 76, 105
National Weather Service, 243
Newton Glacier, 105, 106, 108, 124, 126, 127
Nice Peak, 160

O

Observation Mountain, 218
  East Ridge, 218
  North Face, 218
  South Ridge, 218
Ogilvie Glacier, 138, 174
Orion Spur, 152
Osod Couloir, 165

P

Pacific Ocean, 9
Pine Lake Campground, 233
Pinnacle Pass, 105
Pinnacle Peak, 94–98
  East Ridge, 96–97
  Northeast Face, 96
  Northwest Face, 95
  North Ridge, 95
  South Couloir, 98
  South Face, 98
  South Ridge, 97
  West Ridge, 94–95
Point Blanchard, 75, 76
Pterodactyl Peak, 221
Pugilist at Rest, 75

Q

Queen Peak, 142, 143
Quintino Sella Glacier, 140, 174

R

Raven Ridge, 161
Read, N., 138
Repair Kit, 239
Road Travel, 231
Roman numeral system, 249
Russell, Israel, 105
Russell Col, 105, 108, 124
Russell Fiord, 245

S

Savoia-Aosta, Luigi Amedeo di, 105, 106
Schoening Ridge, 172
Schwatka, Fredrick, 104
Sella, Vittorio, 105
Seward, William, 105
Seward Glacier, 18, 30, 40, 41, 42, 43, 60, 103, 105, 118, 123–133, 159, 161, 162, 163–165, 172, 174, 175, 179, 180, 191
Shakwak Trench, 244
Shakwak Valley, 223
Sheep Mountain, 213
Slims River, 244
Slims River Valley, 138, 173, 192, 213, 218
Smid, Miroslav, 117
Smith, Wayne, 220
snow blindness, 247
South Arm Glacier, 219
South Lowell Glacier, 65, 81, 83, 84
Spring Creek, 200
St. Elias Range, viii, ix, 9, 63, 64, 83, 137, 175, 179, 213, 214, 218, 223, 229, 237, 238, 243, 244
Stairway Glacier, 220
Steele Glacier, 245
sunburn, 248
Swiss Geographical Society, 104

T

Taylor, Andrew, 138
The Dinosaur Peaks, 221
The Milepost, 231
Thunderbird Variation, 168
Tinglit Indian, 104
Topham, Harold, 104
Trans North Helicopters, 242
Turner Glacier, 18, 31, 32, 33, 34, 42, 43
Tyndall Glacier, 104, 106, 113
Tyne Sound, 104

U

Ulu Mountain, 88–90
  East Ridge, 89–90
  Northwest Ridge, 90
  North Ridge, 88–89
  South Rib, 90
  West Ridge, 90

Ulu North Peak, 90–93
  East Ridge, 91–92
  Northwest Ridge, 92
  North Ridge, 92–93
  Southeast Rib, 91
  South Rib, 91
  West Ridge, 92
United States Coast and Geodetic Survey of 1874, 104
United States Geological Survey, 105, 241
USGS Mt. St. Elias Alaska-Canada, scale 1:250,000 map, 20, 30, 64, 73, 76, 84, 87, 88, 93, 94, 98, 106, 121, 129, 140, 174, 175, 182, 192, 197, 200, 214, 217, 218, 219, 220
US Geologic Survey Earth Science Info Center, 241

V

Valerie Glacier, 19, 30
Varigated Glacier, 10
Volume II, 252
Voyage of Discovery, 30
Vulcan Creek, 223
Vulcan Mountain, 223

W

Warbler Ridge, 162
Washburn, Bradford, 78
Water Pass, 174
Weisshorn Mountain, 84–87
  East Ridge
    Left Side, 86
    Right Side, 86
  Northeast Ridge, 86–87
  Southeast Ridge, 84–85
  South Ridge, 85
  West Ridge, 85
Whitehorse, Alaska, 138, 230, 232
  Beez Kneez Bakpakers Hostel, 233
  Campsites, 232
  High Country Inn, 233
  Stratford Motel, 233
Wilford Couloir, 75, 76
Williams, Andrew, 241, 242
William Logan, 137, 140
Windy Peak, 116, 117
Wood, Colonel Walter, 64, 65, 73
Wrangell-St. Elias Mountain Range, viii, ix, 63, 103, 104, 106, 139, 140, 162, 218, 227, 228, 241, 243, 244

Y

Yahtse River, 104
Yakutat, Alaska, 105, 138, 230, 235, 243
  Camping, 235
  Glacier Bear Lodge, 235
  Hotels, 235
  Situk Leasing, 235
  Yakutat Lodge, 235
Yukon Department of Tourism, 232
Yukon Territory, 138, 232